MATERIALIST ETHICS AND LIFE-VALUE

ENR 'TYPE' VIEW
P. 194

McGill-Queen's Studies in the History of Ideas
Series Editor: Philip J. Cercone

MATERIALIST ETHICS AND LIFE-VALUE

Jeff Noonan

McGill-Queen's University Press
Montreal & Kingston • London • Ithaca

© McGill-Queen's University Press 2012
ISBN 978-0-7735-3964-8 (cloth)
ISBN 978-0-7735-3965-5 (paper)

Legal deposit first quarter 2012
Bibliothèque nationale du Québec

Printed in Canada on acid-free paper that is 100% ancient forest free
(100% post-consumer recycled), processed chlorine free

McGill-Queen's University Press acknowledges the support
of the Canada Council for the Arts for our publishing program.
We also acknowledge the financial support of the Government of
Canada through the Canada Book Fund for our publishing activities.

Library and Archives Canada Cataloguing in Publication

Noonan, Jeff
Materialist ethics and life-value / Jeff Noonan.

(McGill-Queen's studies in the history of ideas; 56)
Includes bibliographical references and index.
ISBN 978-0-7735-3964-8 (bound). – ISBN 978-0-7735-3965-5 (pbk.)

1. Ethics. 2. Materialism. I. Title. II. Series: McGill-Queen's studies
in the history of ideas; 56

BJ1031.N66 2012   171'.2   C2011-907524-5

This book was typeset by Interscript in 10/12 New Baskerville.

The great idea of immortality would have vanished, and they would have to fill its place; and all the wealth of love lavished of old upon Him, who was immortal, would be turned upon the whole of nature, on the world, on men, on every blade of grass. They would inevitably grow to love the earth and life as they gradually became aware of their own transitory and finite nature.

Fyodor Dostoevsky, *A Raw Youth*

Contents

Acknowledgments

THE CORE ARGUMENT OF *Materialist Ethics and Life-Value* developed out of the position sketched in the final part of my previous book, *Democratic Society and Human Needs*. I first extended my thinking from the historical development of the needs-ground of social morality into a systematic materialist ethics in a graduate seminar that I taught in 2007. Therefore, my first thanks are to the students in that seminar: Jennifer Barnes, Amy Butchart, Lucia Costa, Ali El-Mokadem, Adefunso Haastrup, Scott Johnston, Neil Langshaw, and Jeffrey Renaud. They were able to tolerate my initially piecemeal thoughts and then helped give them organization, focus, and structure.

Thanks must also be extended to Malak Nassereddine, who served as my research assistant through most of the writing of this book. She was not only tireless in pursuit of the papers and sources that I requested but also found many others on her own initiative which I would otherwise have overlooked.

My colleagues in the Department of Philosophy at the University of Windsor continue to create a dynamic intellectual environment in which to work. The energy they collectively create fuels my drive to contribute to the department's philosophical vitality as best I can. More particularly, they contributed important criticisms when I presented early formulations of the arguments that form the substance of part one of the book in our faculty paper series.

The position continued to be developed in many papers given in a variety of conferences and lectures, and I thank all who engaged me in debate during those sessions. In particular I would like to thank David Camfield of the University of Manitoba for his invitation to give two papers there in 2009. David also read important sections of the text and challenged me to think more robustly about the emotional life-requirements of human beings.

As always, everyone at McGill-Queen's who has been involved in the project deserves enormous thanks for all their efforts at shepherding the book from writing through to publication. In particular all those involved with the editing of the book have provided most welcome insights whose incorporation into the final text has improved it considerably. The anonymous readers selected by the press also proved invaluable in identifying those areas where the initial argument needed to be reworked.

Thanks are also due to Josie, who enables my thinking more than she believes, especially now that she is engaged in the important task of extending life-value thinking into the health care field.

This book is dedicated to my nephew, Liam Noonan, and my niece, Neroli MacDougall Ladanyi, in the spirit of hope that is born with new life.

MATERIALIST ETHICS AND LIFE-VALUE

INTRODUCTION

Ethics and Materialist Philosophy

1 THE HISTORY OF MATERIALIST ETHICS: HEDONISM AND LIFE-REQUIREMENT SATISFACTION

Alain Badiou argues that it is not possible to ground ethical thinking "on the self-evidence of what is harmful to man." "Considered in terms of its mere nature alone," he contends, "the human animal must be lumped in the same category as its biological companions. This systematic killer pursues ... interests of survival and satisfaction neither more nor less estimable than those of moles or tigers or beetles."[1] Badiou reserves the terms *good* and *evil* for actions that serve commitments to higher truths of science, politics, art, and love, actions that elevate us above our animal nature.

Badiou's arguments are thematically connected to an ancient critique of materialism. This tradition assumes that materialism rests on the principle that every phenomenon is truthfully understood only when it has been explained in terms of elemental physical constituents and processes. If this ontological position is essential to materialism, then *good* and *bad*, if they refer to anything at all, must refer to physical states, and pleasure and pain seem to be the most basic physical states possible for the human organism. The belief that materialism must be reductionist leads contemporary critics like Tim Kasser to conclude that materialism can *value* only things like money and consumer commodities. He thus rejects it as a viable ethics, claiming that "materialism conflicts with valuing the characteristics of strong relationships (loyalty, helpfulness, love) and with caring about the broader community (peace, justice, equality)."[2] For this tradition, a materialist ethics must be hedonistic and egocentric – the precise opposite of a true ethical disposition and more akin to the

1 Badiou, *Ethics: An Essay on the Understanding of Evil*, 58–9.
2 Kasser, *The High Price of Materialism*, 65.

life of animals. To live according to the criterion of pleasure and pain is to live, in Plato's words, like "cattle, grazing and copulating, ever greedy for more of these delights."[3]

On first glance, egocentric hedonism does seem to typify the history of materialism, East and West. Carvaka, an early Indian materialist, counsels: "When life is yours, live joyously;/none can escape Death's searching eye:/When once this frame of ours they burn,/how shall it e'er return?"[4] Epicurus provides a Greek echo: "we say that pleasure is the starting point and goal of living blessedly. For we recognise this as our first innate good, and this is our starting point for every choice and avoidance and we come to this by judging every good by the criterion of feeling."[5] Yet, while egocentric hedonism is present, there are other values at work in the history of materialist ethics. Materialism need not be reductionist and, because it need not be reductionist, it need not affirm the values of, in Andrew Collier's felicitous phrase, "totalitarian commercialism."[6]

Alternative readings of what is ethically relevant in materialism contend that it allows for a scientific, naturalized account of ethical values that translates old and imprecise language into rigorous terms. Marxist-inspired materialism, on the other hand, claims to bring a different type of precision to vague evaluative terms by exposing the class interest behind purportedly universal values.[7] While the life-grounded materialist ethics I defend agrees that ethical values have natural foundations and that these values can be ideologically appropriated and employed, it does not agree that these values themselves can be reduced to either survival strategies or justifications of exploitative class rule. Instead, the values that materialism alone is able to uncover, I argue, are the comprehensive values made possible by the organic-social and finite nature of human life.

<hr>

3 Plato, *Republic*, in Hamilton and Cairns, *The Collected Dialogues of Plato*, 8,13.

4 Quoted in Radhakrishnan and Moore, *A Source Book in Indian Philosophy*, 228. For more on the history of materialism in Indian thought see Radhakrishnan, *Indian Philosophy*, 271–85. I am not able to pursue in any detail the links between Eastern and Western materialism but have to concede to the limits of my own philosophical education, which has for the most part been confined to Western traditions. Given the ultimate ethical conclusions of this work, however, I felt it important to note the universal scope of materialist ideas.

5 Epicurus, "Letter to Menoeceus," in Inwood and Gerson, *Hellenistic Philosophy*, 23.

6 Collier, *Being and Worth*, viii.

7 I discuss the relationship between the supposed vagueness of normative terms and the supposed rigour of naturalistic accounts of human ethical behaviour below. Regarding the class character of moral claims, see Marx and Engels, *The Communist Manifesto*, 50. For a more philosophically general account see Horkheimer, "Materialism and Morality". For a subtle and complex exploration of the relationship between historical struggle and ethical universals in Marx, see Gilbert, "Historical Theory and the Structure of Moral Argument in Marx."

Twenty-six hundred years of systematic investigation of the natural universe have undermined all *reasonable* grounds for hope in any sort of afterlife. Thus, ethical principles for the conduct of life on earth must comprehend the real limitations of human life, not only in the sense that what is good must be something of which human beings are capable but also in the sense that what is good for human beings is discerned on the basis of knowledge of the general sorts of harm to which we are liable. All ethical theories that have sought some transcendent ground of value have necessarily, even if unintentionally, tended to ignore the harms to which humans are liable as finite material beings. These harms are caused by the deprivation of basic life-requirements. If terrestrial life is not of ultimate importance, then the problems of harm and life-requirement deprivation are not essential. If, as I hold, there are no reasonable grounds for belief in a spiritual afterlife, it follows that there is no alternative but to make the understanding of our real life-requirements central to ethical thought. The life-grounded materialist ethics that I defend does not begin with the feelings of the abstract ego but with an inquiry into the shared life-requirements that link human beings to one another and to the natural world.

If one reflects on the history of materialist ethical thought in light of shared life-requirements, one discovers that the requirements are omnipresent and at the very core of the philosophies often derided as egocentric and hedonistic. Consider once again the foundational theorists of materialist ethics, Democritus and Epicurus. Democritus argues that "'poverty' and 'wealth' are words for need and sufficiency. Hence the needy man is not rich, nor is the man not in need poor."[8] Epicurus likewise argues that "natural wealth is limited and easily acquired. But wealth [as measured by] groundless opinion extends without limit."[9] Later, in the rebirth of materialist ethics in the French Enlightenment, D'Holbach argued that "La société est utile et nécessaire à la félicité de l'homme, il ne peut se rendre heureux tout seul; un être ... remplé des besoins exige à toute moment des secours qu'il ne peut se donner à lui meme."[10] Lange astutely comments in his history of materialism that D'Holbach's argument "stood at the very threshold of a materialist moral philosophy ... what is needed is the final principle that will carry us beyond egoism."[11]

---

8 Warren, *Epicurus and Democritean Ethics*, 54.

9 Inwood and Gerson, *Hellenistic Philosophy*, 27.

10 "Society is useful and necessary for the felicity of humanity, he cannot make himself happy alone; a being ... filled with needs requires at each instant assistance which he could not provide for himself." D'Holbach, Système *Sociale*, 1: 200.

11 Lange, *History of Materialism*, 2: 114.

D'Holbach's argument implies such a principle insofar as he draws attention to the connections to the natural world and to other people established by what he calls needs (*besoins*) and I call life-requirements. Yet it is true that D'Holbach never completely or coherently explicates the principle.

The same argument can be made in relation to contemporary liberal and social democratic attempts to establish needs as central to theories of social justice. Motivated to resist the ravages capitalist globalization has imposed on people in the Global South, political philosophers from social democratic, egalitarian, and cosmopolitan liberal backgrounds have increasingly converged around the central ethical importance of basic need satisfaction. Thinkers like Ian Doyal and Len Gough, David Braybrook, Lawrence Hamilton, Peter Singer, David Held, David Beetham, Martha Nussbaum, Amartya Sen, and Thomas Pogge have drawn attention to the systematic failures of life-requirement satisfaction caused by current global socio-economic and political priorities.[12] As important as these contributions have been to vindicating the ethical significance of life-requirements, none develops a systematic conception of a comprehensive range of life-requirements; all confine attention to basic physical needs. Perhaps because they focus narrowly on organic need satisfaction, they confine their conception of social justice to redistribution of wealth and resources within existing capitalist structures, without inquiring more deeply into whether the ruling money-value system of global capitalism is capable of even recognizing, let alone coherently meeting, the comprehensive needs of everyone. As I argue in chapter 6, while the best of this work comes close in spirit to the life-grounded materialist ethics I construct, it fails to provide a systematic, normative alternative to the ruling money-value system.

One might reasonably assume that the systematic understanding of the depth normative causes of need-deprivation and the systematic normative alternative are found in Marx and the Marxist tradition. The materialist ethics that I defend concurs with Marx's famous aphorism that a good society is one governed by the principle "from each according to his abilities, to each according to his needs."[13] Despite the failure to build a democratic socialism in the twentieth century, the ongoing crises of capitalism, both economic and environmental, provide grounds to support arguments in favour of systematic alternatives. Marx's aphorism continues

12 Doyal and Gough, *A Theory of Human Needs*; Braybrooke, *Meeting Human Needs*; Hamilton, *A Philosophy of Human Needs*; Singer, *One World*; Held, *Global Covenant*; Beetham, *Democracy and Human Rights*; Nussbaum, *Frontiers of Justice*; Sen, *Development as Freedom*; Pogge, *Global Justice*.
13 Marx, "Critique of the Gotha Program," 531.

to inspire those efforts. Michael Lebowitz, for example, defends Marx's original vision of socialism as society governed by the principle of comprehensive need satisfaction for the sake of "real human development."[14]

While Marxism is thus a major step in the development of life-grounded materialist ethics, I argue that it suffers from important conceptual limitations, not least of which is its failure to explicate the notion of "life-ground" that its critique of capitalism implies. Because explicit theorization of what human lives actually require to survive and develop is absent from Marx, he conflates human needs with consumer demands, thereby opening the door to ecologically unsustainable conceptions of socialism as unlocking the secret to limitless wealth. Twentieth-century thinkers looking to Marx as the foundation for a historically and politically sophisticated version of moral realism have not overcome this limitation.[15] Nor does Marx or subsequent Marxists provide a criterion by which to distinguish good forms of capacity realization from destructive forms of capacity realization. Typically, they have valorized the development of productive forces as necessarily good, with no or too little attention paid to the material implications of this development. While "ecosocialists" have attempted to break the link between socialism and unbridled, environmentally destructive productivity, they too have failed to explicate a complete, coherent, and systematic account of human life-requirements.[16] On the political front, Marxists have historically found it difficult to explain how a society structurally determined by the particular class interests of workers can at the same time ensure the flourishing of the universal human values which justify socialism against capitalism. The first and second problems leave the door open to conceptions of socialism which are as environmentally destructive of the natural life-support system as capitalism. The third has prevented Marxist conceptions of socialism from building unified social movements that unite in a coherent synthesis all oppressed and exploited social groups.

The life-ground of value and life-value, ideas derived from the pioneering work of John McMurtry, provide the conceptual basis needed to

---

14 Lebowitz, *The Socialist Alternative: Real Human Development*, 56.

15 I spell out this limitation in Marx's own work in *Democratic Society and Human Needs*, 121–30. Among twentieth-century Marxists perhaps the most systematic effort to construct a moral theory centred on need-satisfaction from Marxism is found in the work of Alan Gilbert. Gilbert's argument suffers from the same lack of a criterion by which to distinguish needs from non-necessary demands that limits Marx's original work. See Gilbert, "Moral Realism, Individuality, and Justice in War"; Gilbert, "An Ambiguity in Marx and Engel's Account of Justice and Equality"; Gilbert, "Historical Theory and the Structure of Moral Argument in Marx."

16 See, for example, Kovel, *The Enemy of Nature*, 53.

solve these ethical and practical problems. They constitute the foundations that allow materialist ethics to grow beyond egocentric hedonism, liberal and social democratic redistribution, and the ethical and practical limitations of classical Marxism.

The life-ground of value has been implied throughout the history of materialism to the extent that materialism has concerned itself in general with the conditions of survival and development. This focus on life-conditions is the transhistorical thread that marks out a distinctive history of *materialist* ethics. Lacking in this history, however, is an explicit understanding of what this focus on the general conditions of maintaining and developing terrestrial life implies: the life-ground of value. McMurtry defines the life-ground as "the connection of life to life's requirements as a felt bond of being." [17] It is the intentional connection between life and life-resources that elevates the struggle to maintain this connection, to secure and elaborate and strengthen it, from a mere fact of life into the basis of all ethical value. All value is *rooted* in that which is required to maintain and develop life and its sentient, cognitive, imaginative, and creative-practical capacities. Life is thus the ground of value as a baseline of what I will call materially rational judgments of what is and is not good. In the most basic sense, what is good is what enables life to survive and develop. Previous materialist ethics tended to become bogged down in abstractions such as the feelings of individual egos (pleasure or pain) or class interests to the exclusion of deeper consideration of what links all egos or members of all classes together as living human beings with shared needs and potentialities. By emphasizing the connection between self and natural and social worlds, the life-ground of value enables the development of a particular materialist ethics. For life-grounded materialist ethics, the good for each individual is to satisfy her life-requirements in ways that enable her to contribute back to the fields of natural life-support and social life-development from which the resources and practices that satisfy those requirements all derive.

2 MATERIALISM, NATURALISM, AND VALUE

The claim that human nature makes possible a universal form of the good which different individuals can express in their own way perhaps suggests that the life-grounded materialist ethics that I will construct and defend is a species of ethical naturalism. I would resist this identification because life-grounded materialism, as I will explain in more detail in part one, is not reductionist. Instead, it argues that value develops out of, as

17 McMurtry, *Unequal Freedoms*, 23.

opposed to being reducible to, genetically encoded survival and reproductive goals. Naturalized ethics, by contrast, attempts to reduce ethical
dispositions and values to evolutionary adaptation strategies.[18] Defenders
of this view might agree that life-requirements are relevant to ethical theory but deny that these life-requirements extend beyond the physical
conditions of organic survival and reproduction. As Michael Ruse maintains, "normative ethics has evolved to make us good cooperators because
... cooperation is a good adaptive strategy in the struggle for survival. But
there is nothing beyond this."[19] The problem of the good is arrested at
the level of one of its basic physical conditions, the survival and reproduction of life. However, this restriction of the problem of the good life to the
problem of the satisfaction of only one of its conditions ultimately fails to
say anything of ethical interest about all that human beings do and struggle to become beyond copying themselves from generation to generation. For naturalized ethics, there is just survival and reproduction; ethical
theory is really knowledge of how best to survive and reproduce.

Naturalized ethics, by linking ethical systems to human survival, has a
life-grounded materialist moment. However, by rejecting the normative
dimension of ethical theory as metaphysical, it abandons the link to comprehensive *meaning and value* across the spectrum of life-requirements
and capacities that a coherent and complete life-grounded materialist
ethics demands. Clearly, within its natural ranges of tolerance, life can be
better or worse in a range of senses many of which, while not departing
from terrestrial limits absolutely, are not explicable in evolutionary or
physicalist terms. As Anthony O'Hear rightly argues, "the development
of our reasoning powers which has been made possible through self-
consciousness has given us cognitive goals that have nothing to do with
the acquisition of adaptive beliefs or skills."[20] The cognitive ability to
experience the beauty of a painting or a song or to formulate political
plans for freedom have nothing directly to do with the survival of genetic
material (slaves were encouraged to reproduce) but are human capacities and goals which open up for socially self-conscious, creative beings
once the problem of survival has been solved. To be sure, these capacities are not immaterial. There is no aesthetic enjoyment without human
senses and objects of aesthetic contemplation, and there is no motivation for political struggles for freedom that does not grow from the root
of access to means of life and life-development.

18 See, for example, Casebeer, *Natural Ethical Facts*, 9–13.
19 Ruse, "Evolutionary Ethics in the Twentieth Century: Julian Sorell Huxley and
George Gaylord Simpson," 218.
20 O'Hear, *Beyond Evolution*, 69.

As I write, North Africa and the Middle East continue to roil with the struggles of peoples, long politically oppressed, fighting for responsible democratic government. Yet, there can be little doubt that these struggles have more mundane material roots in the growing inability of the poor majorities in these countries to pay for the food they require just to live. As Peter Popham reports, "For the poor of the Middle East, the price shocks at the start of this year were like experiencing a second killer earthquake in three years – but unlike with an earthquake, there was someone you could blame. So angry were the food price protesters in Tunisia that, after Mohamed Bouazizi set fire to himself, President Zine el-Abidine Ben Ali declared a state of emergency and promised to reduce the price of food. But it was too little, too late: by mid-January he was gone."[21] The match struck in Tunisia continues to ignite flames across the region. Yet the flame that now burns is demanding more than bread. It has sparked demands for free trade unions, for women's equality, for new constitutions, and for a more vibrant civil life generally. Life-grounded materialist ethics sees these as higher expressions of life-value that grow out of the fundamental demand for access to the physical conditions of life-support. If naturalized ethics were true, the totality of the political demands would all reduce to demands for bread and leave inexplicable women's demands to be treated as more than wombs.

Human life is not just bread and sex but the self-conscious expression and enjoyment of capacities for creation and world-building which have no real analogues in the rest of nature. To be sure, these capacities develop out of unconscious metabolic processes and biological systems. These processes and systems are the soil out of which grow human beings able to self-consciously govern their lives by collectively instituted rules and values. Our individual and collective capacities are limited by physical forces over which we have no control but within which we are able to create and transform socio-cultural life according to irreducible values like freedom and dignity. The highest humanly possible freedom is not merely the absence of external constraint (negative liberty) or the mere satisfaction of basic physical needs (freedom from want), but the purposive realization of human capacities in "more coherently inclusive ranges of thought/experience/action."[22] The organism capable of achieving this goal is the product of evolution; the goal itself is the creation of conscious thought and collective struggle.

21 Popham, "The Price of Food is at the Heart of this Wave of Revolutions," *The Independent*, 27 February 2011.
22 McMurtry, "What Is Good, What Is Bad," 72.

3 MATERIALIST ETHICS AND LIFE-VALUES

Life-grounded materialist ethics thus neither reduces the normative dimension of ethics to a mere adaptation strategy nor abandons the natural and social fields for some transcendent plane of ideal goodness. Instead, it seeks to discover values in the facts of life-requirements on which the *development* of human life-capacities depends. However, it might be objected that in seeking to find objective value in the facts of life, life-grounded materialist ethics runs the risk of committing what Moore called the "naturalistic fallacy," of confusing the good with a natural kind found ready-to-hand in nature.[23]

Others have urged formal arguments against the coherence of the naturalistic fallacy.[24] There is no need to repeat those arguments here. Instead, I am interested in responding to the substance of the argument. The substance of the argument maintains that the good cannot be identified with any natural state of affairs because "good" is an evaluative term *applied to* states of affairs and not, therefore, a state of affairs itself. Hence the meaning of "good" refers us not to objective conditions and states of affairs but to subjective states of feeling. What Moore fails to ask is why some states of affairs produce better feelings than others, a question which is crucial for life-grounded materialist ethics. Evaluations are not the products of disembodied minds. States of affairs that systematically damage our capacities – a debilitating disease, for example – are not called good in virtue of the debilitating effects they have on us. They are called bad precisely because of these measurable effects on our capacities. The proof of the badness is the intellectual and technological effort marshalled in society-wide efforts to prevent diseases or cure us of them when they occur. Materially rational evaluations of objective states of affairs that have implications for our capacity to live and act are those that are capable of a coherent distinction between what sustains and develops life and what does not. The term "good" thus does not express a mere subjective preference but an objective judgment that the object in question will satisfy a real life-requirement so as to enable higher-level expression and enjoyment of life-capacities. "Good" in life-grounded materialist ethics refers to resources, institutions, relationships, and practices that maintain life (instrumental life-values) and the expression and

---

23 Moore, *Principia Ethica*, 9–21.

24 Since my major concern is not to refute Moore, a long examination of formal criticisms of the naturalistic fallacy would constitute an unnecessary digression. For detailed formal critiques of the naturalistic fallacy see Joyce, *The Evolution of Morality*, 146–56; and Casebeer, *Natural Ethical Facts*, 23–9.

enjoyment of the capacities that the satisfaction of life-requirements enables (intrinsic life-value).[25] All human values are thus at root life-values: that in the object which satisfies a life-requirement and that in human experience and activity which is enjoyed as an expression of our human capacities to feel, sense, think, imagine, and create.

For purposes of introduction, the key point is that life-values are not the product of arbitrary individual judgments.[26] Life-value cannot be created by the choices of abstract egos if the object of choice is objectively destructive of that ego's life-capacities. If one eats a piece of fruit in the expectation that it is nutritious, but it turns out to have been poisoned, then no power of positive thinking or consumer sovereignty can convert what is objectively life-disvaluable (the poison) into life-valuable nutrition.

I employ this example only for purposes of introductory explanation of the core idea of life-value. Life-grounded materialist ethics is not primarily concerned with the mistakes or the choices that abstract egos make but with the social structures, and in particular the ruling value-systems, within which these choices are made. Like ancient ethical philosophy, life-grounded materialist ethics argues that the study of ethics is at the same time the study of the social, political, and economic conditions that make good lives possible. I argue that ethics occupies the social space between what the ruling value system of a given society *asserts* to be valuable and what the intelligent application of life-grounded reasoning reveals to be actually valuable. This application takes the form of conscious, critical comparison between what the ruling value system asserts to be good and the observable effects (generally negative) this purported good actually has on people's ability to satisfy their life-requirements and express and enjoy their life-capacities. The core ethical problem for life-grounded materialist ethics is thus the contradiction between what ruling value systems assert to be good and the deleterious effects on people's lives caused by the social dynamics justified by the ruling value system.

---

25 McMurtry, "Human Rights versus Corporate Rights," 25.

26 On the connection between materialism, scientific realism, and moral realism see Boyd, "How to Be a Moral Realist," in Moser and Trout. I will make my position on the nature of values more complete below, but the development of the argument will hold to the normative content of materialist ethics proper. The first chapter spells out what I mean by materialism and its relationship to the natural sciences, but the complex relationships between scientific realism and materialist ethics constitutes a distinct problematic which is not specifically investigated here. Philosophy is unique in the field of human scientific inquiry insofar as it must reserve a central place for second-order reflections on method and the meaning of its key terms. However, in order to be a living science, it must also be permitted to set aside these issues in order to make a positive case for a position. Otherwise it soon devolves into conference-floor debates between professionals with no real life-connection.

For example, where it is acknowledged that adequate food is a universal condition of life, but where the ruling value system determines that only those with the ability to pay have the right to eat, with the result that it is thought legitimate that one who cannot pay goes hungry, the ruling value system contradicts the requirements of human life. In such cases, because objective harm is systematically imposed upon people, not because of absolute or even relative scarcity, but because they lack an arbitrary system-requirement (money to pay for food), life-grounded materialist ethics concludes not only that the ruling value system is ethically wrong but that it requires systematic transformation.

The aim of life-grounded materialist ethics is thus not simply to advance an abstract account of the good life but to contribute in a nondogmatic way to the resolution of conflicts between ruling value systems and the life-values the normal operation of those value systems prevents people from enjoying. Ruling value systems up to now have been rooted in fundamental asymmetries of power, prestige, honour, life-chances, and degrees of well-being, and their primary function has been to justify these asymmetrical distributions, both to the winners and to the losers, within and between societies. The concrete results of the operation of these ruling value systems have therefore been to produce, reproduce, and legitimate the unequal life-value of different lives relative to the position occupied in the social structure. These inequalities in expressed and enjoyed life-value are always illegitimate from the life-grounded materialist perspective. Its aim is thus to discover and defend the social conditions in which all life-bearers may participate as fully as possible in the production and enjoyment of life-value.[27]

It remains only to sketch very briefly the structure of the argument. Part one begins with a general explanation of what I mean by materialism and derives from that account ethically relevant materialist conceptions of nature and society. Following these metaphysical preliminaries, the focus narrows to concentrate on the irreducibly organic-social nature of human beings. Part one concludes with an explication of three classes of universal human life-requirement grounded in our organic-social nature and a defence of their universality against salient objections.

27 Although the ends of life-grounded materialist ethics can be achieved only through social and political change, neither the means nor the precise institutional structures necessary to attain this end are the focus of my argument. Instead I concentrate on the ethical justification of social and political change, confining my arguments about social and political structures to proof of the general claim that existing structures are unethical from the life-grounded materialist perspective. The corresponding social, political, and economic arguments relating to the necessary direction of social change may be found in Noonan, *Democratic Society and Human Needs.*

Part two shifts the focus from the metaphysical basis of life-grounded materialist ethics to the concrete ethical problems its basic concepts expose. It will become evident that the concrete ethical problems which concern life-grounded materialist ethics are caused by conflicts between the reproductive requirements of given societies and the life-requirements of human beings. Part two begins with an examination of how particular system-requirements emerge from the general struggle of human life to survive and reproduce. It then proceeds to examine how emergent system-requirements enter into conflict with the universal requirements of human life. Two forms of the conflict are examined. The first form, exemplified by colonialism, holds between societies at different levels of productive development. The second holds between different groups within the same society. The latter is exemplified by different forms of social cleavage in which a ruling group employs structural differences and invidious ideologies of superiority and inferiority to justify the exploitation and oppression of subaltern groups. Part two concludes with a comprehensive examination of the harms that both forms of conflict generate within the contemporary world.

Part three develops the life-grounded materialist idea of the human good implied by the conception of the organic-social nature of human beings and the critique of the systematic harms examined in parts one and two respectively. It begins by distinguishing between the social aims of life-grounded materialist ethics and the egocentric traditions of ethics typical of the history of liberal philosophy. Once the social orientation of life-grounded materialist ethics has been clarified, a more precise explication of the relationship between the essential capacities of human beings and the universal form of the good life for human beings can be developed. The text concludes by explicating the general political implications that follow from the life-grounded materialist conception of the good: what forms of political struggle are legitimate, what the relationship is between the existing institutions of liberal-democratic capitalism and a more coherently life-valuable alternative, and how conflicts between individuals, and between individuals and social institutions, that derive from different demands on natural and social wealth would be resolved in that alternative society.

PART ONE

Materialism, Human Finitude, and Ethics

1

Materialism

1.1 INTRODUCTION: HISTORICAL OUTLINES OF MATERIALIST PHILOSOPHY

Although the origins of materialism extend back to the awakening of philosophical consciousness West and East, it is not easy to state the shared principles of materialist philosophy. Nothing in its history is analogous to Hegel's *Science of Logic.* Hegel's masterpiece, if not an uncontroversial canon of idealism, provides a systematic and comprehensive exposition of idealism's basic principles. In contrast, abstract ontological principles describing materialism as "an acknowledgement that physical matter pre-exists all human thought and actions and exerts its particular determinations upon the latter," taken as free-standing assertions about nature treated as if human beings themselves were not part of it, with their own powers of "particular determination," say little of concrete interest to self-conscious beings trying to make sense of their place in the universe.[1] Yet, if materialism is not a commitment to physical reality as ultimate, to what is it a commitment? In some sense *materialism* must insist on the primacy of physical nature, but just what this primacy means is not initially clear. If abstract principles are not helpful at the outset, perhaps a better place to turn is experience.

Whatever anyone's ontological commitments, all must agree in some sense that the world outside the mind constitutes a limitation, if not on what it is possible to think and hope, then at least on what it is possible to do and achieve.[2] Different materialist ontologies derive, I believe,

---

1 Soper, "Marxism, Materialism, and Biology," 70.
2 A possible exception would be the work of Alain Badiou. Badiou situates his work within the materialist tradition but argues that nature has a definite sort of mathematical structure that he explains through a particular interpretation of set theory. The ultimate

from this experience of the hardness of the world in its confrontation with human consciousness. By "hardness" I mean that the world does not always respond to the demands and decisions of human beings in the way we might hope. The structure of the natural world has its own dynamics which human beings ignore at their peril. No matter how high and wide human speculation might soar, we remain, even in the midst of a supposed all-illuminating grasp of the transcendent, tied to the life-sustaining and life-enabling (but also life-damaging and life-destroying) powers of nature. Long before the infant is capable of uttering, "I think, I am," it searches with hand and dim eyesight, like a piglet or a kitten, for its mother's life-sustaining breast. As George Novak rightly observes, "materialism derives its life, its meaning, its power, its radicality, from the inseparable connection with the habitual, inescapable, million-times repeated practices of every member of the human race."[3]

If this experience does not immediately yield materialist first principles, it does explain what the basic object of materialist philosophy is: nature in the widest sense, the universe of space, time, matter, and energy out of which human consciousness evolved and upon which it is dependent. Whatever diversity there is within the history of materialist philosophy, each epoch of its development has reaffirmed the primacy of the natural universe. Thus Lucretius begins his poetic exposition of atomism with the assertion that "all nature as it is in itself consists of two things – bodies and the vacant space in which bodies are situated."[4] More than a millennium later, D'Holbach, in his *System of Nature*, argued that the fundamental object of philosophical thought is "the Laws which Nature prescribes to the things she contains, in the different orders they occupy, under the various circumstances which they are obliged to pass."[5] Marx too reiterates the same general point: "All historical writing must set out from these natural bases [of life-support] and their modification in the course of history through the action of men."[6] In

---

conclusion of his sophisticated argument is that nature does not set limits to what human beings can accomplish because nature has no finite and fixed structure; the structure ultimately depends on how nature is determined mathematically, and that ultimate determination cannot be divorced from the power of choice. I say that Badiou is a possible exception to my argument because I am not convinced that his work is actually materialist. On the other hand, I do not want to dogmatically exclude his work from the materialist tradition. Hence, I leave it an open question. See Badiou, *Being and Event*, 123–72, 394–400; Badiou, *Logics of Worlds*, 1–40. See also the discussion in Bryant, Srnicek, and Harman, "Towards a Speculative Philosophy," 1–18.

3 Novak, *The Origins of Materialism*, 18.
4 Lucretius, *On the Nature of the Universe*, 20.
5 D'Holbach, *System of Nature*, 16.
6 Marx, *The German Ideology*, 37.

contemporary philosophy of mind, materialism rests on the claim that "we are creatures of the natural order whose mental activity is dependent on the operations of our brain."[7]

The general primacy accorded the natural universe in materialist philosophy is thus a shared commitment across its different articulations. As will become apparent, this general agreement about the ultimate object of materialist philosophy conceals fundamental methodological and ontological disagreements, disagreements whose importance for present purposes concern the possibility and content of an ethically relevant materialism.

Before examining the broad disagreements, I note one further basis of agreement. A commitment to the primacy of the natural universe is compatible with varied methodological and ontological positions, but in every permutation it is inconsistent with any explanatory role for ideal substances. By ideal substances I do not mean ideas as mental phenomena through which human beings consciously relate to the world, but ontologically distinct substances that *do not in any way* derive from the evolution of matter and energy in space and time. In this sense ideal entities include a conscious creator god or gods, divine providence as a causal power in the universe, ideal ruling principles like Empedocles' Love and Strife or Lao Tsu's *Tao*, as well as souls as immaterial causes of action.

These ideal substances were posited in order to explain the origin and order of the observed universe and human thought and freedom. Yet idealist explanations are unsatisfactory because the appeal to ideal substances is question begging. The explanation of universal origins, human intelligence, and freedom is always circular in idealist systems of thought – we are free because we have a free soul, we are intelligent because we are composed in part of a thinking substance, the universe exists because an omnipotent creator god created it. Answering empirical and historical questions with stipulative definitions, a priori principles, and deductive inferences cannot satisfy the real demand for an explanation of the power by which God created everything from nothing, or how an immaterial intelligence can cause a material body to act. Marx's critique of Bruno Bauer's understanding of history exposes the essential problem with all idealisms: "For Herr Bauer, as for Hegel, truth is an automaton that proves itself. Man must *follow* it. As in Hegel, the result of real development is nothing but the truth proven, i.e., brought to consciousness."[8] Materialism, by contrast, follows Marx's historicization of knowledge in the *Theses on Feuerbach*. The truth is not disclosed in any a priori

7 Dennett, *Freedom Evolves*, 103.
8 Marx, *The Holy Family*, 99.

speculative system. Truth is a practical problem, or better, an open-ended series of practical problems the solutions to which do not lie in self-justifying, closed metaphysical systems but in diverse forms of research that build on historically contingent successes and failures of inquiry. However, the specific problem that concerns me is not materialist episte-mology but an ethically relevant materialism. Thus, I now turn to the task of answering the related question of how a materialist understanding of nature can make room for real but irreducible ethical values.

1.2 ETHICALLY RELEVANT MATERIALISM
AND THE NATURAL UNIVERSE

Two broad tendencies characterize the history of materialist interpreta-tions of nature. The dominant tendency, stretching from Democritus through the French Materialists to contemporary physicalist naturalism, is reductionist. The goal of reductionism is the ultimate unification of human knowledge in a systematic grasp of the causal determination of all action by a consistent set of physical laws. In the reductionist tendency qualitative differences between phenomena (for example, between con-sciousness and brain states) are not denied, but they are assumed to be explicable in the final analysis by a complete knowledge of the basic laws determining the fundamental organization and behaviour of matter and energy, thereby rendering any other form of understanding and inter-pretation redundant. It would be contrary to all historical evidence from the development of the natural sciences to deny outright the validity of reductionism. At the same time, if the reductionist program is valid for all phenomena, it is difficult to see how a normative ethics could be any-thing more than an illusion. As the physicist Steven Weinberg concludes, "the more we know about the universe the more it is evident that it is pointless and meaningless."[9]

Does it follow from the pointlessness of the *origins and elements* of the natural universe that the human life which has developed out of those elements is meaningless? This conclusion would be entailed if the only true knowledge of phenomena is knowledge that reduces qualitative meaning to quantitative structure. This complete reduction has proven an elusive goal. No successful reductionist program has explained the concatenation of causes that link the conditions immediately after the Big Bang to Shakespeare writing *Hamlet*. One might dismiss this claim as a weak *reductio ad absurdum*, but reductionists themselves invite such

9 Weinberg, quoted in Pagels, *The Cosmic Code: Quantum Physics as the Language of Nature*, 307.

objections when they assert that "all tangible phenomena, from the birth of the stars to the workings of social institutions, are based on material processes that are ultimately reducible, however long and tortuous the sequence, to the laws of physics."[10] Any materialist must agree that all phenomena are *based on* material processes, but I argue that it does not follow that they are all thereby reducible in understanding to the laws of physics. The phenomena of the universe include practices such as art and ethics which can only be evaluated in terms that accept the emergent reality of their objects – beauty, goodness – which have no meaning in the science of physics. Therfore, simply holding the two basic materialist commitments – the primacy of the natural universe and a rejection of ideal substances as causal determinants in nature's development – does not entail reductionism because reductionism cannot provide consistent and complete reductions of meaningful human practices and values to the interactions of meaningless fields of energy.

The second broad tendency shares these two basic commitments but is not reductionist. It stretches from Aristotle (in the materialist elements of his work), through Giordano Bruno, to Marx's historical materialism, to contemporary critical realism and certain tendencies in modern biology. This tendency argues that life cannot be explained by the same laws as non-living energy and that, in particular, human life and its distinctive forms of action cannot be explained in abstraction from the social institutions and systems of value in which humans live as self-conscious subjects of their own activity. To stress the creative role of human subjectivity does not cut human beings loose from material constraints; it emphasizes that human beings do not live in unmediated nature but in a social world of their own creation.

What distinguishes this second tendency at the methodological level is a commitment to a complex ontology. By "complex ontology" I mean two things. First, I mean a commitment to giving equal explanatory weight to the physical elements out of which phenomena are constructed and the phenomena themselves as constructed forms with properties and powers not present in the elements. My home is made of brick, but its being a home is not reducible to the material from which it is constructed. These bricks have been organized into a coherent structure to serve a definite purpose, and I have certain emotional dispositions toward this structure that I do not have toward others. This structure, the purpose it serves, and my dispositions toward it are all irreducible elements of the bricks forming a home. The basic point about structure

10 Wilson, *Consiliance: The Unity of Knowledge*, 291. | |

and purpose is familiar from Aristotle, although materialism cannot rest content with his understanding of forms as immaterial powers.

Second, "complex ontology" means a commitment to the need for different forms of inquiry and analysis which are determined by the nature of the phenomena under investigation. As Adorno argued, "it is by passing to the object's preponderance that dialectics is rendered materialist. The object [is] the positive expression of non-identity [of thinking and being.]"[11] The same physical thing can function as more than one object relative to the interests of the inquiring subject. For example, if I want to understand the physical structure of my volume of Shakespeare's sonnets, I ought to consult my colleagues in the Physics Department. On the other hand, if I want to deepen my understanding of their meaning as poems, I ought to consult my colleagues in the English Literature Department. The objects of investigation – physical structure and meaning – are not more and less real in the complex reality "poem." While it is true that the meaning of Shakespeare's poetry would not be available to me if paper and ink did not have the physical properties they do, it is equally true that knowledge of those properties does not tell me anything about the sonnets' meaning. The *poem* is the complex whole not reducible to the structure of the atoms composing the ink with which the poems were printed. Commitment to a complex ontology is thus a commitment to the belief that the meaning of a phenomenon is as real as whatever material vehicle bears the meaning. Any ethically relevant materialism requires a complex ontology.

A complex ontology is necessary because if every true explanation were an explanation of phenomena in terms of meaningless fields of energy, then a true explanation of ideas like "good," "valuable," "worthy object of struggle," and so forth must be an explanation that would prove that whatever action they motivate is ultimately pointless. If reductionism is true, it follows that valuing life as meaningful is an illusion sustained by superstition, or ignorance, or wishful thinking. Clearly, no normative ethics is possible if it is true that the life it values is really pointless. In fact, the truth of Weinberg's claim would render all ethics, even of the naturalized sort, impossible. If the universe is meaningless then so is life, and therefore the struggle to survive and reproduce, and therefore any ethics reduced to a survival strategy.

Yet it seems impossible for human beings to struggle for life and at the same time admit that this struggle is meaningless. A complex ontology allows the materialist to claim that the very existence of beings whose life is essentially distinguished from inanimate matter and energy by *active valuation of that which supports and develops their lives* is proof of the reality

11 Adorno, *Negative Dialectics*, 192.

of value and meaning for those beings. Hence we arrive at the "life-ground of value" cited in the introduction. To recall, the life-ground of value is "the connection of life to life's requirements as a felt bond of being."[12] In this view, values exist in the universe to the extent that it is capable of supporting life and enabling the general capacities that make life worth living. Life becomes better and more free to the extent that society is organized so as to enable "more coherently inclusive ranges of thought/experience/action."[13] Reductionist explanations have proven useful in explaining the processes by which life developed, just as knowledge of the chemistry of ink can aid its production and thus its use in recording poems. The fact that a poem is written in ink whose own existence is meaningless does not entail that the poem is meaningless. So too life: the fact that it is written in a chemical code which is further analysable down to atoms, and then to quarks, and then to who knows what beyond, does not entail that life is meaningless precisely because this chemical code "creates" a form of social self-conscious being that relates to its life-conditions and its life-activity as valuable.

Ironically, the reductionist makes the same error as the religious idealist. Absent a creator god who will redeem our mortal finitude, the religious idealist concludes that life is meaningless. The reductionist assumes the same connection between immortality and meaning, i.e., that since life will one day be extinguished from the entire universe, the present activity of living subjects is pointless. The only difference is that the reductionist affirms the meaninglessness of life from which the religious idealist flees into a spiritual otherworld. Both share the assumption that finite, mortal, embodied, terrestrial life is without ultimate value. *Life-grounded* materialist ethics, by contrast, maintains that life is of ultimate value *just because* it is finite, mortal, embodied, terrestrial, of contingent origins, always fragile, and thus a necessary object of care and concern for its bearers. This is a conclusion, however, for which a complete argument has yet to be supplied. To begin, a more detailed exposition of the idea of complex ontology, centring on the idea of emergent properties essential to it, is required.

The idea of emergent properties was first proposed in the 1920s within evolutionary theory, but the problem that it tried to solve goes back at least to Aristotle.[14] That problem is the seeming impossibility of accounting for

12 McMurtry, *Unequal Freedoms*, 23.
13 McMurtry, "What is Good, What is Bad," 72.
14 For an overview of the development of emergentist theories as well as their limitations, see McDougall, *Modern Materialism and Emergent Evolution*, 130–56, 237–73; and Reid, *Biological Emergences*, 72–8.

the origin of life and consciousness out of non-living and unconscious elements. Prior to the development of consistent theories of emergent properties, the only alternative to reductionism or idealism was the doctrine of hylozoism, derived from Aristotle and central to early modern materialisms such as that of Giordano Bruno.[15] The problem from a materialist perspective with the hylozoic claim that the organization, structure, and active capacities of living things is due to the presence of an inseparable but nevertheless non-material form is that it is either question begging or idealist. If the form is simply "materialized," as in Bruno, then the essential questions of how the form itself came to be and by what power it operates are begged. What needs to be explained, the origin and power of form, are simply assumed as given in the nature of matter. On the other hand, if an account of the origin of form is attempted, it is explicated by reference to the operation of a divinity or a teleological ruling principle in the universe.[16] In the last twenty years, however, more sophisticated theories of emergent properties have been developed which avoid the problems of hylozoism and idealism while offering materialism an alternative to reductionism.

The contemporary theory of emergent properties has been pioneered by biological research. Since living things seem most resistant to complete explanation in reductionist terms, the connection between biology and a theory of emergent properties should not be surprising. Indeed, the major problems of biology cannot even be approached in strict reductionist terms because to consistently reduce living things to their basic elements is to reduce life to non-life. Hence, a reductionist biology must abstract from the very object of biological research: the living organism. The argument that Robert Reid advances against population geneticists holds generally against any strict biological reductionism: "population thinkers have transferred the essence of the organism to the population – not a population of actual creatures interacting with each other in a real environment, but a mathematical model devoid of life."[17] However, because there is no way to model the inner striving to live that distinguishes living from non-living things, life cannot be understood by abstract mathematical models alone. As John H. Holland argues, reductionism works when "the whole can be treated as the *sum* of its parts" but

15 Aristotle, *Physics*, in McKeon, *The Basic Works of Aristotle*, 240; Bruno, *Cause, Principle, Unity*, 131.

16 This problem beset the first theories of evolutionary emergence as well. For a detailed critique see Reid, *Biological Emergences*, 74.

17 Ibid., 45.

fails when "the parts interact in less simple ways."[18] The interactions of the parts of living things are clearly an example of the latter.

The most fundamental difference between living and non-living things is that living things respond to their environment in creative ways which do not violate but are not predictable from the known laws of physics and chemistry. As Nicholas Georgescu-Roegen argues, "The epistemological import [of novelty produced by combination] extends from chemical compounds to all forms of Matter: colloids, crystals, cells, and ultimately biological and social organisms. Novelty becomes more striking as we proceed along this scale. Certainly, all the qualitative aspects of the entity called elephant ... are novel with respect to the properties of the chemical elements of which an elephant's body is composed ... We can explain ... why... the biological man needs water ... but we cannot explain in the same manner why human societies have felt the need for belief in some God, for pomp, for justice."[19] The idea of emergent properties functions as a mediation between the predictable behaviour of non-living elements and forces and the unpredictable, creative action of living things. The origin of novel emergent properties can be understood causally by reference to the interactions of basic elements, but this understanding does not permit us to "predict the outcome [of their actions] even after the same combination has been observed once, twice, or even several times." This difference, he concludes, "separates by a broad line the sciences of life-bearing structures from those of inanimate matter."[20] Hence the need for a complex ontology that is capable of housing all the sciences of matter and life without artificial privilege bestowed upon the former to the prejudice of the "rationality" of the latter.

What, however, is an emergent property? Emergent properties are wholes that are greater than the sum of their parts. Michael Silverstein and John McGeever define emergent properties as "properties of a system taken as a whole that exert a causal influence on the parts of the system, consistent with, but distinct from, the causal capacities of the parts themselves."[21] Human social self-consciousness, consciousness of oneself as a unique reality in institutional fields of meaningful relations to others, is a whole greater than the sum of its neural, chemical, electrical, and atomic elements. To be socially self-conscious clearly presupposes the basic physical elements and connections between those elements out of which social self-consciousness is generated, but to *be*

---

18 Holland, *Emergence: From Chaos to Order*, 14.
19 Georgescu-Roegen, *The Entropy Law and the Economic Process*, 116.
20 Ibid., 117.
21 Silverstein and McGeever, "The Search for Ontological Emergence," 182.

socially self-conscious is not the same as being made out of these elements. Social self-consciousness is an irreducible form of meaningful life-
experience that shapes the whole but not the parts in abstraction from
the whole. As John Searle argues, "a symptom that something is radically
wrong with the [reductionist] project is that intentional notions are in-
herently normative. They set standards for truth, rationality, consistency,
etc. And there is no way that these standards can be intrinsic to a system
consisting entirely of brute, blind, nonintentional causal relations."[22]
The only way to understand the actual experience of being a socially self-
conscious person and the sorts of normative relationships that such a
person establishes with its environment is, therefore, to treat it as an
emergent reality, neither more nor less real than its constituent elements
but with a set of capacities not found in the elements. The evolutionary
and historical processes by which this, or any other, emergent whole develops is an open empirical question. What is certain is that the emergent
wholes can be understood fully only if they are understood as wholes,
material realities with capacities distinct from their constituent parts.

To say that emergent properties have capacities that are distinct from
the capacities of their constituent parts entails that emergent properties
have causal powers to initiate forms of activity that their parts considered
in isolation do not. This claim is controversial; it appears to assert that
the causal powers of emergent wholes, since they are not reducible to
the causal powers of the parts, violate, as Searle says, "even the weakest
principle of the transitivity of causation."[23] In other words, to deny that
there is a reductionist relation between the whole and its parts might be
read to mean that there is no causal relationship at all, thus lending the
causal powers of emergent properties a supernatural dimension.

However, the causal powers of the emergent wholes are not supernatural
but generated by the relationships and interactions between the parts.
As Searle says of the most important emergent property, consciousness,
"[its existence] can be explained by the causal interactions between elements of the brain at the micro level, but consciousness cannot itself be
deduced or calculated from the sheer physical structure of the neurons
without some additional account of the causal relations between them."[24]
The point of calling the causal powers of the whole *emergent* is not to
deny that they are themselves caused by complex interactions between
the parts, but to insist that what the emergent properties are capable of

22 Searle, *The Rediscovery of the Mind*, 51.
23 Ibid., 112.
24 Ibid.

doing is not fully explicable or understandable on the basis of the powers or capacities of the parts considered in abstraction from their connections and interactions.

It follows that a complete grasp of emergent causal powers is distinct from an understanding of the interactions that generate those powers in the emergent wholes. A complete causal account of the interactions between neurons at the micro level would not be a complete understanding of the normative claims that socially interrelated human beings can make precisely because a complete account of the normative claims requires an evaluation in terms (good, self-undermining, etc.) that make sense only to a social self-conscious person who cares about the quality of her life.

It does not follow that there is *no* relationship between the elemental forces that structure physical and biological reality and the higher-level capacities of living things. The relationship between parts and emergent wholes is one of constraint or framing rather than mechanical determination. Biological organisms cannot violate any laws of physics, but to understand biological organisms by reduction to the laws of physics alone is impossible. By the same argument, human action and interaction cannot violate any known biological laws, but a simple knowledge of biological laws cannot explain the normative structure of human socio-historical organization that emerges from them. There is no reductionist account of human action and interaction, in terms of either physics or genetics, that could explain why the French Revolution broke out exactly when it did, why it developed into a struggle between Girondins and Jacobins, and why the Jacobins ultimately lost. Social realities can be explicated only by reference to the actual historical interactions through which definite human beings have produced their societies. Natural pressures to survive form an irreducible foundation for history, but history itself is structured by causes that emerge from the actions and interactions of people governed not only by survival considerations but also by considerations of what is right, legitimate, just, and, in sum, good.

Emergent properties thus express a degree of freedom from direct determination by the causal forces that govern the parts. This claim means that more highly organized systems have greater latitude for different responses to the same stimuli. This characteristic of emergent properties is most important for the understanding of the freedom of living organisms. The underlying point is nicely explained by the biologist Robert W. Korn. "Life [is] not just chemistry and physics ... there [is] also information. ... Information is not only relevant to understanding thought but it resides at the very heart of life, as in the symbolic nature of DNA as well as the multiple examples of negative feedback found in microbes, plants, and animals."[25] Given the fact that organisms process information coming from the environment, their responses are determined not simply by the environment as an external reality but also by the ways in which information coming from the environment is internally processed. The more types of information and the more ways an organism is able to interpret it, the wider the space for creative action. Organismal action is not identical to mechanical response to the environment because the organism's own information-processing capacities always mediate environment and action. Thus, the wider the scope of its possibilities for action, the more creative an organism can be within its environment. The more creatively it can act, the more the organism is capable not only of adapting to environments but changing them to suit its own life-requirements. The more it is capable of changing its environment to suit its life-requirements, the more self-determining, or free, it can be.

The study of life is always a study of non-mechanical behaviour and interaction because what makes an organism alive is its capacity to process and respond creatively to environmental signals which its own activity in turn alters. As Richard Lewontin argues, "the organism is not specified by its genes, but is a unique outcome of an ontogenic process that is contingent on the sequence of environments in which it occurs."[26] The relationship between organism and environment, as Lewontin goes on to show, is not mechanical, which means that even a knowledge of the phenotype and the environment in which that phenotype will develop into a real organism will not yield precise and infallible predictions about the unique appearance and behaviour of the organism. Organic activity always involves a degree of freedom from the environment. This degree of freedom is what distinguishes living things from inanimate objects. As Reid elaborates, "there are no genes for behaviour, genes are 'for' proteins and 'for' regulating other genes. And to carry out these functions they need to be helped and prodded by the rest of the organism. It is slightly closer to the truth to say that there are proteins for behaviour, since behaviours are clearly catalyzed or coloured by proteins such as hormones or neurotransmitters. Yet again, proteins are 'for' a wide variety of functions, they are not 'for' behaviour. They too need to be stimulated by the rest of the organism and its responses to environmental influences. Their amino acid sequences do not contain the structure of behaviour, only functions that contribute to it."[27] If Reid is correct, then it follows that the action of living things is neither programmed by

25 Korn, "The Emergence Principle in Biological Hierarchies," 147.
26 Lewontin, *The Triple Helix*, 20.
27 Reid, *Biological Emergences*, 337.

genetic sequences nor determined in any strict sense by the environment, but involves a wider or narrower scope for creative organismal activity. This scope for action extends along a continuum in living things ranging from simple survival strategies to the normative governance of action by ethical principles in human beings. Reid again puts the point clearly: "once biological emergences appear, they fall into dynamically stable organismal and ecological states that resist change. Paradoxically, the higher the level of emergence, the easier it becomes to escape stasis. This is because of greater freedom of choice for the organism, and more alternatives of habit and habitat from which to choose."[28] Since we are dealing with living things struggling to survive, these choices are not arbitrarily free. That is, they are tied to the overriding goal of life-maintenance. Yet the goal of life-maintenance can be pursued in different ways even by the same organism. This capacity for creative response to the challenge of survival shows that life itself is the ground of freedom where freedom means, in its most rudimentary sense, self-activity, in contrast to the inertia of non-living things.

In human beings, freedom describes a much richer set of possibilities for self-determined life-capacity realization. Reid again puts the point well: "the last great emergences, intelligence and mind, were products of developmental, physiological, behavioural, and social evolution. Some elements may simply have appeared at critical points in the expansion of the cerebrum, the increased capacity of its neurons to form new dendritic connections, and repetitive variation of chemical messengers, that allowed the brain to distinguish between new functions ... Innovative integrations of brain areas for logic, language, memory, and vocalization, and aesthetic sensibility were part of the emergent constellation. To be meaningful they had to be connected to hand eye coordination. To be fully effective they had to be able to override older, hereditary, behavioural mechanisms ... The emergent result was greater freedom from gene determination."[29] The emergent capacities for truly productive and creative labour, for social world-building, and for symbolic interpretation of the natural field of life-support and the social field of life-development, take the study of human life beyond the study of biology to the study of socio-historical and cultural development, political struggle, and the role of value systems within those developments and struggles.

Because it provides the hinge between mechanical nature and self-determining activity, an emergentist, as opposed to a reductionist, understanding of the universe is fundamental to any ethically relevant

28 Ibid., 366.
29 Ibid., 367.

materialism. It enables materialism to leave behind the plane of the physical organization of energy as the necessary causal background for comprehending the meaning and value that life has for self-conscious human beings acting in definite social contexts. If the universe is in every respect a meaningless play of unconscious forces, then a meaningful normative ethics, since it must be part of that universe, is by definition impossible. If, by contrast, those elements and forces are understood as the bases of life, but life and, beyond that, human social self-conscious, caring life are understood as emergent properties with a material reality of their own, a reality that can be understood only through concepts that grasp their unique emergent powers, then the universe itself is meaningful. Its meaning, however, does not depend on supposing that it has a divine creator or obeys any transcendent purposes. The meaning of the universe, judged over its entire history of development, is that it is the most universal condition for the possibility of life. Understanding the structure, forces, and dynamics of that universe is thus an understanding of the most basic conditions for our being here as living entities whose hearts, as Kant said, are filled with wonder by the starry heavens above. The heavens do not cease to be wonderful if we deny that they have a divine cause; on the contrary, they become more wonderful as we see in them the non-miraculous origins of the heavy chemical elements on which our life depends. Insofar as nature describes the most fundamental conditions of life, and life, especially social self-conscious human life, is the subjective condition for the reality of values, then the natural universe, though in its origins without meaning or purpose, *becomes* meaningful as the objective basis of life-values. The existence of social self-conscious living things who care about their conditions of existence and activity by virtue of their being self-conscious social beings is thus the basic condition that makes an ethically relevant materialism possible. Since ethics exists only within the social field of life-activity and interaction, the argument must shift to examine how an ethically relevant materialism understands social relations and institutions.

1.3 MATERIALISM AND HUMAN SOCIETY

Life and life-activity are arrayed along a continuum ranging from simple drives for self-reproduction typical of the life of viruses and bacteria to social self-conscious struggles of groups of human beings to change the ruling value systems and institutions of their societies. Without invidiously contrasting human to non-human life or being dismissively anthropocentric, we know of nothing else in the universe able to treat the development and enjoyment of its sentient, emotional, cognitive, imaginative, and creative capacities as goals either advanced or impeded by social institutions and value-systems. Life-grounded materialist ethics understands these human capacities as rooted in our natural history but not reducible in their ethical meaning to mere adaptations to environments. As Joyce argues, "This seems to be what sets us apart from the rest of the animal kingdom: our capacity to work out how to do things 'on our own,' to operate successfully in living conditions that bear little resemblance to the environments [of our primate ancestors]."[30] The physiological and neurological bases of human capacities have an evolutionary explanation, and this explanation might be extended to explain some of the psychological dispositions at work in caring, evaluating, and struggling for better societies. As Marvin Harris's cultural materialism argues, the complex symbolic structures of rituals of different societies "rest on the ground and that [they are] built up out of guts, sex, energy, wind, rain, and other palpable and ordinary phenomena."[31] Yet, there remains an irreducible normative core to these dispositions when they are lived from the inside. This inside is what life-grounded materialism aims to understand.

Thus, life-grounded materialist ethics differs from Harris's cultural materialism not in denying that all higher expressions of human emotional, cognitive, and creative capacities are built up out of these elements, but by insisting that the intrinsic meaning and value people assign to these higher-level constellations of expressed capacities are as material and real and important as the elements of which they are composed. For life-grounded materialist ethics, society is essentially a field of life-*development* which emerges from our metabolic interchange with the natural field of life-support. But society's institutions and the goals they serve are not reducible in understanding to mere life-support. Art, ethics, political struggle, and other uniquely human practices depend directly on the organization of that social field. Good human lives depend on good social institutions, and good social institutions ensure not only survival but the wider and deeper expression and enjoyment of the full range of human capacities. While the struggle for *life* occurs in unmediated nature, the struggle for a *good* life occurs in society.

Society is not, like the natural field of life-support, a fact given independently of human action but is itself the product of human action. Human action is the highest known form of organismal action. In the preceding section, I distinguished organismal action from mere mechanical response by reference to the information-processing capacities of living things. I noted that the greater the scope of this processing

30 Joyce, *The Evolution of Morality*, 7.
31 Harris, *Cows, Pigs, Wars and Witches*, 5.

capacity, the greater the range of activity possible for that organism. Human beings have the greatest scope for activity because alone among the known life forms, we are capable of processing information *of our own creation.* This self-created information is, in general, the substance of human social life: the self-determined goals we posit as essential to a meaningful life. Again, the insistence on the reality of *meaning* as a motivating material force in human social life distinguishes life-grounded materialist ethics from reductionist materialisms.

The problems with reductionist attempts to explain human action have been well known since Aristotle. Consider his critique of Democritus's attempt to explain voluntary motion as the simple consequence of the shape and behaviour of soul atoms. "Democritus says that the spherical atoms, which according to him constitute soul, owing to their ceaseless movement, draw the whole body after them and so produce its movement. We must urge the question whether it is these same atoms which produce rest also – how they could do so is difficult and even impossible to say. And in general we may object that it is not in this way that the soul appears to initiate movement in animals – it is through intention or process of thinking."[32] Aristotle identifies the key limitation of the reductionist account: the same mechanism cannot account for opposite actions unless that mechanism *is made subordinate to a higher-level control system: the positing of goals that mechanical action obeys.* Action in general is distinguished from pure mechanical behaviour by the fact that action follows the processing of environmental information. Human action is distinguished as a higher-level emergent property of organismal action by the fact that human action occurs within social institutions and serves consciously posited goals.

Thus human beings live not only within nature, not only within social institutions as functional assemblages that assist the reproduction of human life, but within societies as normative systems. In general, the value systems that legitimate social orders are the highest-level creation of the human organism. Value systems "connect together goods that are affirmed and bads that are repudiated as an integrated way of thinking and acting in the world."[33] Thus human social self-conscious action, though made possible by our organism and the genetic code that helps construct it, is not ultimately governed by the goal of physical survival, but treats physical survival as a necessary condition of higher-level struggles to make life worth living. Life-grounded materialist ethics is, in the most general sense, an inquiry into the comprehensive material conditions,

32 Aristotle, *On the Soul,* in McKeon, *The Basic Works of Aristotle,* 544.
33 McMurtry, *Unequal Freedoms,* 7.

including the content of ruling value systems, which make life better or worse, and the practical means by which these conditions can best be institutionalized. The ultimate goal is not simply the historical goal of "leftist and progressive politics," to "improve the material conditions of life" in the sense of the usual measures of standard of living (income, levels of commodity consumption, and so on), but to ensure the satisfaction of the comprehensive conditions for the fullest possible freedom of human action.[34] As I argue in part three, historical struggles against exploitation and oppression are unified by the conscious goal of freeing human action from unnecessary and unjustified external constraints.

If conscious goals have such importance for a life-grounded materialist ethics, might it not be objected that it is not really materialism? Would not idealists be correct to argue that if life-grounded materialism must draw on Aristotle to support its conclusions, perhaps it is inadvertently proving that materialism is incapable of providing a cogent account of human action? For *real* materialism, the opponent might continue, what appears as action must always reduce to genetically or environmentally programmed behaviour. It is just because "matter" is always determined by proximate efficient causes that it cannot be the ground of explanation for action, thus forcing Aristotle to posit the existence of immaterial final and formal causes. If life-grounded materialist ethics draws on Aristotle's explanation of action, it must draw on the metaphysical basis of that explanation – form as an immaterial power that shapes matter. This is an important objection. A careful response is necessary, not only to obviate its immediate effects on the validity of the argument but also to clarify the meaning of "material" at work here and throughout the remainder of the argument.

I respond to the objection by first claiming that the real importance of Aristotle's account of action is that it focuses attention on the irreducible function of goals. His particular metaphysical explanation of the nature of thought which posits the goals is secondary and anachronistic. Thought, including the capacity to posit goals that it enables, is an emergent property of neural organization. Goals and values can be shown to derive from terrestrial, human sources, without the need for ultimate recourse to a divine principle. In sum, the possibility and the content of the values that guide human action can be explained without the need to posit immaterial formal powers. This reinterpretation preserves the essential point that Aristotle is making – that action cannot be understood on the basis of knowledge of the physical structure of the organs that make it possible because it is caused in part by self-given goals – without requiring recourse to immaterial causes.

34 DeLanda, *Deleuze: History and Science*, 29.

Instead of immaterial forms, the explanation of the possibility of action proper must pay attention to the unique evolutionary history of human beings, and in particular the processes by which language developed. The development of language, as Terence W. Deacon argues, transformed the subsequent evolution of the human brain, producing an organ unique in the realm of known life which has made possible a world of symbolic meanings and interactions closed to other life forms. The development of language may thus be posited as the crucial mediation between the natural and social history of humanity, i.e., the mediation through which human beings became capable of free, self-determined, action. Deacon argues, "we live in a world that is both entirely physical and virtual [symbolic] at the same time. Remarkably, this virtual facet of the world came into existence relatively recently, as evolutionary time is measured, and it has provided human selves with an unprecedented sort of autonomy or freedom to wander from the constraints of concrete reference, and a unique power of self-determination that derives from this increasingly indirect linkage between symbolic mental representation and its grounds of reference."[35] When we act we are determining ourselves through the irreducible mediation of symbolic meaning. We are free to posit goals for ourselves precisely because the material organ responsible for positing the goals mediates the physical world through its own symbolic constructions. We *act*, therefore, on what we *think, believe, imagine, hope, or intend* to be the case.

To the extent that this response succeeds in explaining how the teleological determination of human action is possible on the basis of language-based thought as an emergent property, it answers the objection that life-grounded materialism is implicitly idealist. However, the answer to that objection leads directly to a second. One can imagine a reductionist materialist asking: if it is not the case that the physical environment and human genetics determine all human action, if human thought creates spaces for human action proper, and this action creates social institutions which further widen that space, does not life-grounded materialism turn into uncritical voluntarism? My response is that it does not. Both nature and society are limiting frames on activity; freedom of a human form, as we will see more fully in part three, is always freedom to act within and against given natural and social constraints. As Marx, for example, famously argued, "men make their own history, but they do not make it just as they please; they do not make it under circumstances chosen by themselves, but under circumstances directly encountered, given and transmitted from the past."[36] He then elaborates: "when ... we ask ourselves why a particular principle was manifested in the eleventh or in the eighteenth century rather than in any other, we are necessarily forced to examine minutely what men were like ... what were their respective needs, their productive forces, their mode of production ... [and thus] present men as the authors and actors of their own drama."[37] Life-grounded materialism is thus as incompatible with abstract voluntarism as it is with physicalist reductionism. The motive force of human history and human society is human action. However, human action never occurs in a vacuum but always in definite natural and social frames which set the problems that agents confront and constrain the range of immediately available solutions. At the same time, because there is always ongoing action, these frames of determination are not absolutely fixed. The natural frames are more fixed than the social, but they too can widen under the impact of new knowledge. In a general sense, history from the life-grounded materialist perspective may be understood as the progressive widening of the social spaces for human action.

For example, the level of technological development in the early modern world meant that it was impossible for scientists to build an aircraft. Hence the problem of travel over great distances could not be solved with passenger jets. This limitation has subsequently been overcome because of developments in engineering, aerodynamics, and so on. "Society" did not produce these new insights by some automatic force; they were achieved by ongoing work by engaged scientists within more highly productive economies. The change from a society without air travel to a society where it is a banal fact of life thus requires an understanding of material limitations (the law of gravity, aerodynamic principles, etc), but equally an account of the capacities of human thought and practice to understand these limitations and work creatively within them. The life-grounded materialist understanding of society does not ignore the framing function of natural forces and social structures so much as it emphasizes the ability of collective human action to widen those frames by understanding the relevant forces in order to see how much, rather than how little, we can do within them.

When we focus on the way in which human understanding can widen the spaces for action, we are dealing with a collective and not an abstractly individual capacity. Just as social structures are not reducible to

36 Marx, "The Eighteenth Brumaire of Louis Bonaparte," in *Karl Marx and Friedrich Engels: Selected Works*, 1: 398.
37 Marx, *The Poverty of Philosophy*, 107.

their natural bases, so too they are not reducible to individual actions and intentions abstractly conceived. Instead, as Callinicos argues, both structures and agents are understood as emergent properties. Social structures "[arise] from, but [are] irreducible to the actions and mental states of individual human beings."[38] Society develops out of individual human responses to environmental challenges, but the nature and effects of emergent social structures like government or law cannot be understood through any methodological individualist reduction to abstract intentions of individuals seeking to maximize their own advantage. The behaviour of governments, for example, cannot be understood simply by reference to the organism of the human beings that compose these institutions precisely because, as officers of government, they have powers that they do not have as organisms. For example, it is only by occupying the office of prime minister that the empirical individual Stephen Harper can use his larynx to ask the governor general to prorogue the Parliament of Canada. What human beings do as officers of government, or members of social institutions more generally, is *understandable* in light of the social position they occupy, the social forces they must interpret and respond to, their particular goals, and the social and historical influences that shape them. This social understanding is quite distinct both from prediction in a mechanical causal system and from methodological individualism.

Individual agents are always socially located and influenced by the prevailing norms and institutions of their society. The outer limits of possibility of action are framed by the physical reality on which they depend. However, what they are capable of doing is determined by their actions and interactions, within these determining frames. Thinking opens up new fields of possibility because it is capable of novel insights and genuinely creative responses that change the social frames of future action. As Margaret Archer, from whose work Callinicos draws, argues, "the properties and powers of the human being are neither seen as pre-given, nor as socially appropriated, but rather these are emergent from our environment. As such they have relative autonomy from biology and society alike, and causal powers to modify both of them ... Thus ... mind is emergent from neurological matter, consciousness from mind ..."[39] Life-grounded materialism does not ignore, as an abstract voluntarism would, the limiting power of social and natural frames on activity, but instead judges the relationship to be dialectical and, as such, ultimately open. What human beings are capable of doing as agents is limited but not

38 Callinicos, *Resources of Critique*, 184.
39 Archer, *Being Human*, 87.

determined by social structures, which are themselves not fixed realities but change in response to changed forms of action and interaction, changes which are not programmed but result from novel thinking in given contexts.

Yet, it might further be urged against life-grounded materialism that its response to the problem of voluntarism is scientifically naive and thus still too voluntaristic. For example, in *Freedom Evolves* Daniel Dennett cites experiments that purport to prove that what manifests itself as a consciously chosen action has already been determined unconsciously by the brain a few microseconds before any choice registers in consciousness.[40] If these experimental results are sound, it would seem to follow that the intentionality normally linked with the causal efficacy of deliberation and decision is nothing more than a reflex of neural activity, which is itself a reflex of sensory stimuli. However, even if these experiments prove what the experimenters think they prove, it does not follow that consciousness is otiose in the process of action formation. In order to understand this rejoinder, recall Korn's comment cited above that life cannot be understood unless the way organisms act on information is understood. For human beings, as Deacon argued, raw sensory information is, except in extreme circumstances, filtered through interpretations and background knowledge that have an irreducible social and symbolic content. If that is true, then it follows that even if conscious decisions are already "taken" unconsciously by the brain, consciousness itself cannot be removed from the complete account of the complex of processes that results in decisions and actions because the content to which the brain responds is not raw data from the environment but already symbolically processed and mediated. An example will help to spell out the point more clearly.

A thermostat switches on the furnace when the ambient temperature of the room falls to a predetermined level. The person who sets the thermostat, however, does not do so in mechanical response to abstract bodily states but in accordance with an interpretation of various temperatures according to the potentially conflicting criteria of comfort, affordability, and energy use. If I feel cold, but have already spent my heating budget for the month, I might decide not to turn up the heat. Likewise, if I am cold but am also politically and ethically committed to reducing my natural gas usage, I am capable of overriding the sensations of physical discomfort for the sake of satisfying my political and ethical goals. There may come an extreme point of discomfort where that ethical and political commitment is itself subject to physical override, but for purposes of

40 Dennett, *Freedom Evolves*, 227–42.

the argument let us restrict ourselves to normal conditions. Since economic and ethical commitments have no meaning to the neurons that "make" the decision, and yet it is impossible to understand what I in fact decide to do without reference to one or the other, there is no strictly reductionist way to understand my decision. If I were a behaviour machine I would raise the temperature until I was comfortable. The decision that I in fact make, however, cannot be understood outside the meaningful social matrix of my life and involves knowledge of the nature of money, the realities of having to pay for necessities in a capitalist economy, the consequences of not paying my bills; or, on the other hand, the state of the environment, my political and ethical concern to improve it, and so on. This meaningful social matrix is not some ideal world apart but is the essential structure of social self-consciousness in which I live my life, a structure that has emerged out of the more basic material of human natural history but is irreducible in understanding to it.

Since the emergentist understanding of consciousness does not deny that consciousness develops out of neural organization, it is simply not a problem for it that the brain might "make" decisions that then register in consciousness. Since there is no ideal substance making the decision, there is only the material organ that generates my conscious states. The relevant point concerns not the lines of causation connecting environment, brain, and consciousness, but the conditions of understanding human action. Brain activity is the material condition of there being intentions and actions, but being a material condition is distinct from being a mechanical determining force. In order to light a match, the match must be dry and the surface upon which it is struck sufficiently rough to generate friction. But given these two material conditions it does not follow that the match will be struck. Even if it is the case, therefore, that a few microseconds before I decide to not raise the setting on the thermostat the relevant neural interactions have "made" this choice which then registers "in mind," it does not follow that I have not made that choice: the choice is whatever the neural interactions have produced through their mode of activity, *but on the basis of how I have already linguistically interpreted the situation.* The *decision* is between meaningful alternatives and can only be expressed in the language of conscious thought. There is no ontological gulf between the operations of the neurons and the language of self-conscious thought, but a process of transliteration between self-conscious states and neural operation and back again. That this must be the case is proven by the fact that no simple understanding of the ambient temperature and my sensations of mild discomfort would be able to predict what my decision will be, just as the presence of the material conditions of combustion is not sufficient to predict that the match will be lit. Without the relevant economic, political, and ethical information *that I act on,* no one would be able to even understand what I chose to do and why I chose to do it.

In sum, human action is a complex whole whose complete understanding requires not only an understanding of environmental conditions, neural systems, and the sensory connections that link them, but equally the socially and symbolically (linguistically) structured matrix which always mediates human beings' relationships and interactions with their environment. If action is understood as a complex whole then there is no warrant for arbitrarily selecting one element of this complex whole and establishing it as the decisive factor. That approach to understanding action makes as much sense as asking whether the respiratory or nervous system is more fundamental to human life. The answer is that neither can even be understood outside the complex whole which is the human organism. Without the autonomic nervous system, the heart would not beat nor the diaphragm contract; without the respiratory system, the nervous system would not receive the oxygen it requires to function. The same holds with regard to the whole that is action. Understanding why human beings do what they do as human beings requires an integrated understanding of how the different elements come together to form a whole.

The general conclusion to be derived from this discussion of action is that human life cannot be understood *as human* outside the social-symbolic systems in which actions and interactions take place. This conclusion does not violate the primacy of the natural world central to materialism. Ultimately, human life depends on definite relationships to the natural world as the foundational life-support system. Human beings live on nature, but they act in society. At the root of social organization one finds natural life-requirements, but natural life-requirements alone cannot explain the more complex institutional orders that are created by human action. Action responds to given contexts (and in this dimension is constrained) but also opens up new avenues for wider fields of action in the future (and thus widens the social space for human self-determination). Marx makes this point effectively in *The German Ideology:* "Men can be distinguished from animals by consciousness, by religion, or anything else you like. They themselves begin to distinguish themselves from animals as soon as they begin to produce their means of subsistence, a step which is conditioned by their physical organization. By producing their means of subsistence men are indirectly producing their material life."[41] This material life is not confined to means of

41 Marx, *The German Ideology,* 37.

physical subsistence but includes, as even very early human communities prove, complex symbolic and aesthetic mediations with the environment. If simple predictions of the forms of human action within the natural field of life-support are impossible for very early human communities, they are, a fortiori, impossible for more complex social formations. Viewed generally, human historical development is the development of more and more complex sets of mediations between human beings and nature which create wider and wider scope for human action proper.

This collective capacity for social world creation distinguishes social forces and rules from natural laws. Whereas natural forces and laws are fixed independently of human activity, social forces and rules ultimately derive from human action and interaction, and are therefore always, in principle, alterable in response to changed goals. Although Marx is not always consistent in his treatment of the difference between natural and social laws, his work is nevertheless a solid basis from which to understand it. Whenever Marx criticizes (as opposed to analyses) bourgeois political economy, the core of his critique is that it illegitimately converts mutable social principles into eternal laws of nature. For example, in *The Poverty of Philosophy*, Marx argues that bourgeois political economy expresses "the relations of bourgeois production ... as fixed, immutable, eternal, categories ... [these categories explain] how production takes place ... but what they do not explain is how these relations themselves are produced, that is, the historical movement which gave them birth."[42] Since history for Marx is nothing but the cumulative results of the social actions of human beings acting in the material conditions that are given to them ("history is not a person apart, using man as a means to achieve its own aims, history is nothing but the activity of man pursuing his aims") it follows that the frames imposed on human activity by given social forms are alterable through altered social activity.[43] "The materialist doctrine concerning the changing of circumstances and upbringing forgets that circumstances are changed by men and that the educator himself must be educated."[44]

Marx himself often falls back on explanations of social change which more closely resemble the mechanical materialism that he criticizes. This inconsistency becomes most pronounced whenever he tries to account in a systematic way for the objective conditions of social revolution. As he argues in his oft-quoted introduction to the *Contribution to the*

42 Marx, *The Poverty of Philosophy*, 97.
43 Marx, *The Holy Family*, 116.
44 Marx, "Theses on Feuerbach," in *The German Ideology*, 615–16.

Critique of Political Economy, "It is not the consciousness of men that determines their existence, but their social existence that determines their consciousness. At a certain stage of development, the material productive forces of society come into conflict with the existing relations of production ... From forms of development of the productive forces these relations turn into their fetters. Then begins an era of social revolution."[45] What is most problematic from the perspective of life-grounded materialist ethics is not the implicit premise that social development can be contradictory but the explicit reduction of political action to predictable behaviour. A complete historical survey of the history of capitalism is not possible here, but even common historical knowledge is sufficient to refute Marx's claim that periods of social *revolution* can be predicted on the basis of knowledge of the state of the contradiction between the relations of production and the forces of production. Who of any political stripe predicted the revolutions that erupted across North Africa in January 2011?

Nevertheless, the general idea of social contradiction that Marx develops is essential to the life-grounded materialist explanation of human self-determination. Without a doctrine of social contradiction life-grounded materialism would risk lapsing back into an abstract voluntaristic understanding of social change, a doctrine which is as unsupported by historical evidence as its mechanical materialist opposite. The argument that social structures are contradictory provides the basis of explanation of why human action can be causally efficacious in history. Were social structures entirely harmonious, facing no internal barriers to their reproduction, they would foreclose all space for novel social, political, and economic activity. Individual activity would be determined by the forces of the social system, people would quietly occupy the place those forces assign to them, and social life would simply reproduce itself from generation to generation. But, because the normal operation of social forces and institutions breaks down, society itself creates the space in which novel thinking, which can generate novel practices (including revolutionary practice), can emerge and become effective. Callinicos articulates this point clearly: "strains within and between [social structures] may destabilise existing social relations and, directly and/or as a result of this destabilisation, motivate actors to seek change."[46] Social contradiction thus explains how the spaces for "change seeking-behaviour" develop. People trying to understand their society and its justifications encounter problems when the actual operation and results of social

45 Marx, *Contribution to the Critique of Political Economy*, 21.
46 Callinicos, *Resources of Critique*, 191.

dynamics fail to conform to ruling value system principles. In this case, intelligence is confronted objectively with a contradiction, which it can either try to ignore (until it is too late) or come to grips with by developing new concepts and initiating new collective practices. An understanding of the direction of change, however, can never be predicted from one-sided knowledge of the objective state of social dynamics.

If social contradictions alone produced periods of socialist revolution, Marx's own critique of capitalism would be useless. What need would there be for a *critique* of capitalism if capitalism's own contradictions will eventually produce a socialist revolution? From the life-grounded materialist perspective, social contradictions produce life-crises which spur people to critical reflection on what has gone wrong with "ordinary life." Political mobilizations follow from the activation of critical consciousness in the context of life-crisis. Thus, one might agree with Marx to the extent that his argument holds that social contradictions can produce periods of social *crisis*. Social crisis, however, is a time for decision between different possibilities for social action. Decisions about how a crisis is to be solved cannot be fully understood without reference to the values that ultimately win out. Once we have entered the field of values we have left the field of external social and natural forces. When people begin to justify their alternatives as good or bad, these claims must be assessed in terms of the lived valuations of alternative forms of life-organization.

As soon as political change is on the agenda, an ethical assessment of alternatives becomes inescapable. In the absence of an ethical moment, political change would be nothing but mechanical behaviour, but mechanical behaviour cannot explain what is unique to political action, namely, the requirement that it not only be possible but legitimate. McMurtry explains the significance of this claim on the basis of an analogy between the role of values in human life and the laws of nature in the field of physical reality. "Because our lives, our social orders and our civilizations themselves are all embodiments of values we consciously or unconsciously bear, we might best understand our human reality as a vast and complex *world field of values* whose inscriptions constitute the human meaning of both our individual and collective lives. Values are to humanity as the laws of physics and chemistry are to inanimate matter."[47] Just as the laws of physics and chemistry are constraints on what it is objectively possible for human beings to *do*, so too values are constraints on what it is materially rational for human beings to *choose*.

By focusing on what it is materially rational to choose, in terms of both social policy and individual life, life-grounded materialism is an ethics of

47 McMurtry, "What is Good, What is Bad," 4.

realizing the good through social- and self-limitation. This focus is in contrast to classical liberalism, which is an ethics of self-maximization. As Collier rightly argues, the real social and natural implications of self-maximizing behaviour have proven to be both "destructive and irrational."[48] "Irrational" should be read as "materially irrational." "Materially irrational" means the failure on the part of a system of human thought and action to distinguish between the life-requirements of human beings and the contingent ends that they may form assuming they are alive and able to think. Such a failure contradicts the material (natural and social) conditions of possibility of that very system. Such a system of thought and action ignores what Keith Graham aptly calls "constraints of precondition," material foundations which must be in place before any thought, choice, or decision can be conceived or taken.[49]

In order to understand the difference between the material rationality of life-grounded self-limitation and the material irrationality of liberal self-maximization, we need to examine the relation between the object and subject of value judgments. A consistent error of liberal philosophy has been to assimilate the object of value to the subjective act of valuation, such that the objective ground of value in service to life-support and life-development disappears in the subjective judgment. The incalculable variety of subjective judgments is then employed as a refutation of the possibility of objective, material values. It is empirically true, as Hobbes argues, that anything at all may be made an object of a value judgment provided only that some person desires the object.[50] It does not follow that everything so judged *desirable* really is of *value* for the living subject who makes the judgment. For finite living beings, consistently judging desirable objects as of value when their consequences for the life-activity of that subject are deleterious is self-undermining and ultimately materially irrational. Only those objects, resources, institutions, practices, and relationships are actually valuable that enable life to survive, reproduce, develop, and freely express and enjoy its life-capacities. As I argue more fully in chapter 2, this life-ground establishes a non-authoritarian, non-ethnocentric baseline of objective judgment that enables people to decide between what is and what is not life-valuable. In the reality of harms to life and life-activity lies the proof of the objective basis of life-value. When value judgments become alienated from this underlying life-ground, they tend to generate more or less life-destructive effects, on individuals, social fields of life-development, and natural

48 Collier, *Being and Worth*, 70.
49 Graham, *Practical Reasoning in a Social World*, 152–8.
50 Hobbes, *Leviathan*, 42.

fields of life-support. The more intense the life-destructive effects generated, the more materially irrational such judgments are, i.e., the more
they tend toward the destruction of the objective material conditions of
the subjective possibility of making any sort of value judgment at all.

Life-values are thus not determined by sovereign individual judgments
about what is desirable. Materially rational value judgments always develop from consciousness of the life-ground of value. In the case of natural
life-values, this ground is first of all discovered and not produced.
However, human life, I have been stressing, is not simply organic but synthetically organic-social. Hence social organization, too, forms a moment
of the life-ground of value which is distinct from nature insofar as it is
produced by human interaction and concerned with life-development,
not simply life-support. Both nature and society, we will see, are sources
of instrumental life-values insofar as they satisfy natural and social
life-requirements respectively. Through the satisfaction of these life-
requirements, intrinsic life-value is produced in the leading of lives
rich in expressed and enjoyed human capacities to feel and sense, think
and imagine, and act and create. Life-value is thus both discovered in
nature and produced in society. As instrumental, it is the material condition of all forms of experience and human action. As intrinsic, it is the
substance of a life worth living. If intrinsic value presupposes instrumental value and is what makes life worth living, it follows, as we will see, that
if people are systematically deprived of instrumental life-values, life can
cease to be worth living. Avoiding that outcome is the most basic goal of
life-grounded materialist ethics.

Before moving forward to the next step in the argument, let me sum up
this opening section. The first premise of life-grounded materialist ethics,
one which has been implicit in preceding materialism but never coherently explicated, is that the basic condition of the material universe's being valuable is the existence of living things who *care about being alive and
maintaining their lives*. Thus, there is instrumental life-value in the material
universe insofar as it provides the environments and the resources all living things require to exist, reproduce, develop, and act, to the extent of
their range of capacities for action. The range of organismal action extends from mechanical response to chemical signals to the socially self-
conscious creation and transformation of human value systems.

While all organisms partake of instrumental life-value in the resources
that support their lives, only in human life does intrinsic life-value arise
as an explicit problem. This problem is posed as the degree to which the
ruling value system recognizes life-value as fundamental. The most important ethical question to be asked of any socially contingent value system is not whose class-interest it serves, as in classical Marxism, but the

deeper question of whether it recognizes and satisfies the comprehensive range of human life-requirements, or whether it confuses these life-requirements with the system-requirements of its own reproduction. Hence the main concern of life-grounded materialist ethics is the degree to which any social value system promotes or inhibits materially rational choices and materially rational patterns of collective activity. Choice and collective activity are materially rational when they comprehensively but sustainably satisfy everyone's life-requirements for the sake of enabling the intrinsic value (i.e., goodness) of their lives. Before we can understand the general structure of a good human life, its natural and social instrumental conditions must be explicated and defended. To this task the argument now turns.

2

The Life-Ground of Value
in Human Life-Requirements

CHAPTER ONE CONCLUDED that the fundamental concern of life-grounded materialist ethics is the extent to which ruling value systems recognize and satisfy the comprehensive requirements for the free development of human sentient, emotional, cognitive, imaginative, and creative capacities. Thus the first step in explicating the life-grounded materialist ethical conception of the good life is to inquire into the full range of human life-requirements. Before the full range of life-requirements can be explicated, the distinction between life-requirements in general and consumer demands needs to be rigorously drawn. Once this core distinction has been established, the comprehensive set of human life-requirements can be systematically derived and defended.

2.1 LIFE, LIFE-REQUIREMENTS, AND THE LIFE-GROUND OF VALUE

The ethical argument of life-grounded materialism rests on the claim that there are life-interests common to all human beings. These common life-interests are defined by the requirements of human life. The problem is not to conceptually link common life-interests and life-requirements: what else would a common life-interest be other than a life-requirement? The problem is to distinguish life-requirements from the extraordinary range of demands people place on their natural and social environments. The first step toward solving this problem is to remind ourselves of the meaning of the life-ground of value.

The life-ground of value was defined as the connection between life and life's requirements. The reality of this ground of value is found in the observable fact that all living things, and not just human beings, struggle to maintain connection to that which sustains their lives. In human beings, as Marcuse argues, this striving takes the higher form of the conscious valuation of life "as worth living," or capable of being made into a form worth living.[1] Humans, like all living things, must maintain connection to the life-ground. Thus, if we want to distinguish in general between what all human life requires to survive and develop and what particular human beings as a matter of fact demand, even though their lives do not require the object of the demand, we need to ask the following: what, above all, do people strive to avoid losing connection with?

To understand what people strive to avoid losing connection with above all it is not enough to simply canvas history for examples of struggles. We must approach history with some sense of the accumulated scientific and philosophical knowledge about the physical nature of our organism. The history of medicine in the widest sense has generated extraordinary insights into the different sorts of physical harm to which humans are liable. The history of political struggles supports these insights to the extent that we see various uprisings and revolts motivated by deprivation of basic physical requirements of life and health. However, history also bears witness to struggles for the social conditions of free life-capacity development. In both cases what humans are struggling to avoid is harm, whether to their organism or to their humanity. This provisional conclusion leads us to a general criterion by which to distinguish life-requirements from consumer demands. In its original formulation by McMurtry, the criterion states that "N is a need, if and only if, and to the extent that, deprivation of n always results in a reduction of organic capability."[2] What was originally called "need" was later reformulated as "life-requirement" to avoid the ambiguities of the term "need" that I will examine below.

Having now defined needs as life-requirements, and life-requirements as anything which, if we are deprived of it, results in harm to our organism or our humanity, the next step is to see how this criterion helps us to distinguish life-requirements from consumer demands, and why this distinction is important to life-grounded materialist ethics. The key difference between life-requirements and objects of consumer demand is that deprivation of the latter might produce subjective *feelings* of harm in some people in wealthy societies, but these feelings are not objective harms. I take an easy case for purposes of initial illustration. (I consider more difficult cases below).

If a human brain is deprived of oxygen for several minutes it will suffer damage to its cognitive capacities. These capacities may be damaged to such an extent that the person in question may not realize or be able to articulate the full range of what she has lost. Perhaps the victim is no longer subjectively aware of the real harm that she has suffered, but her

---

1 Marcuse, *One-Dimensional Man*, x.
2 McMurtry, *Unequal Freedoms*, 164.

lack of awareness does not change the fact that she has suffered the objective harm of loss of cognitive capacity which she formerly enjoyed. The harm is measured by the objective loss, not one's feelings toward this loss. By contrast, someone whose television set breaks, thus depriving him of the instrumental condition of satisfying his desire to watch the hockey game, might feel harmed. Unlike the loss of cognitive capacity, this man's *feeling* of being harmed can be overcome. All the man need do to stop feeling harmed is to reinterpret his desires. Perhaps he discovers (as sports fans generally do when the players in their favourite sport strike) that sitting inert on a sofa passively absorbing a spectacle is not a valuable mode of realizing one's sensory capacities.[3] Hence there is no objective harm in this case, and no life-requirement for the television set.

Admittedly, this is an easy case, but its only purpose here is to clarify the difference between life-requirements in general and consumer demands. A more difficult problem is the distinction between life-requirements in general and the instrumental requirements for successfully realizing particular individual projects. This case is more difficult since if the goal of life-grounded materialist ethics is to enable the free realization of life-capacities, it would seem obliged to include under the set of life-requirements *any* object instrumentally required by any project through which life-capacities are expressed and enjoyed. That McMurtry's criterion is able to make this distinction gives it a significant advantage over other attempts to ground ethical claims in needs or life-requirements.

In order to understand this advantage, McMurtry's criterion can be contrasted with Doyal and Gough's semantic approach to distinguishing needs from other sorts of demands. Doyal and Gough attempt to understand needs by analysing needs-statements.[4] They discover that needs-statements are more exigent than other sorts of statements that make claims on goods. A needs-statement asserts that unless the stated condition is met, the goal relative to which the condition is a need cannot be realized. This approach accurately captures the necessity that characterizes

---

3 Of course, there will always be cases that cannot be solved by philosophy operating in a social and political vacuum because they involve conflict between two contrasting but equally plausible arguments about the most life-valuable use of a resource. The only solution to these cases is actual debate and compromise in concrete political contexts.

4 Doyal and Gough, *A Theory of Human Needs*, 35–46. David Braybrooke comes closer to a life-grounded definition of need, developing a similar argument against semantic approaches. The problem with Braybrooke's position is that he ultimately concedes to most of the skeptical arguments that he initially contests. See Braybrooke, *Meeting Needs*, 29–49. Martha Nussbaum's work implies that there exists a class of objects which are of essential life-value because they are life-requirements, but the concept of need or life-requirement is nowhere defined in her work. I examine Nussbaum's work in greater detail below.

needs-claims but leaves open the crucial question of how to distinguish, within the set of all possible needs-claims, between those which are of objective life-value because they refer to universal life-requirements, and those which may or may not be of life-value because they refer to instrumental inputs into particular projects whose life-value is an open question. If the argument is left at the semantic level, there is no way to distinguish universal life-requirements from any object that is a necessary instrumental condition of the successful realization of any project whatsoever. It is equally true that I need oxygen in order to live and that I need a television set in order to watch the hockey game. If life-requirements are distinguished from consumer demands only in virtue of their necessity relative to a given project, then any object that is necessarily required to complete any particular project is an object of need. Though this conclusion may be true semantically, it does not follow that an object of need in this semantic sense is at the same time an objective life-requirement.

The ethical difference between needs as universal life-requirements and needs as instrumental necessities relative to particular projects resides in the fact that the realization of some projects can have life-destructive consequences. It would be self-contradictory, therefore, to define universal life-requirements in terms of their instrumental necessity to any project whatsoever. While it is of course true that even destructive projects presuppose life, and therefore the satisfaction of life-requirements, it is not the case that a good society is obligated to satisfy life-requirements *for the sake of enabling some people to destroy the life or life-conditions of others*. On the contrary, the goal of satisfying *universal* life-requirements is to enable everyone to express and enjoy their capacities, a goal which presupposes that the projects people engage in are consistent with the health of the natural field of life-support and other people's projects.[5] Without the limitations imposed by the natural field of life-support and other people within the social field of life-development, the social obligation to meet universal life-requirements would undermine itself by licensing unlimited claims on natural and social wealth. Thus, people have a legitimate claim that the ruling value system under which they live ensure the satisfaction of universal life-requirements but *not* any and every instrumental input required by any individual project whatsoever. Given the conditions of human life, the contingencies to which it is subject, the different demands placed on natural resource bases, and the social institutions that produce and distribute different products out of that resource base, no society can guarantee to everyone the particular instrumental conditions

5 McMurtry, "Human Rights Versus Corporate Rights," 4.

of success in every project, even if that project is life-valuable. Finding a cure for all cancers would indeed be a life-valuable achievement, but if its realization meant that everyone beyond a handful of top scientists would be forced to live at a subsistence level, the life-value of that goal would come at too high a cost for the overall life-value of everyone in society. What is of general social importance, therefore, is ensuring the comprehensive satisfaction of universal life-requirements.

Yet, if society is *mandated* by its ruling value system to ensure the satisfaction of people's fundamental life-requirements, is it not the case that this mandate undermines rather than ensures the material conditions of human freedom? Classical and neo-liberal critics might indeed launch this sort of argument. Since the highest goal of life-grounded materialist ethics is the free expression and enjoyment of life-capacities, it is essential that it be able to answer the charge that it could be, in Steven Lukes's words, "paternalist licence for tyranny."[6] Friedrich von Hayek provides a robust expression of this argument in his work.

According to von Hayek, "there can exist ... no single ordering of needs" because no individual or collective agent has all the information necessary to provide an overall convincing ranking of the different sorts of demands that people make. However, von Hayek makes no distinction between needs and expressed consumer demands.[7] He does not make the distinction because capitalist markets respond only to price signals. Price signals are generated by people's purchases, and people purchase all sorts of things. What people "need" in this view is neither more nor less than what they spend their money on. As an argument against centralized bureaucratic planning of an economy, von Hayek's argument ought not to be dogmatically dismissed. I have considered it as an economic argument elsewhere.[8] Here I am concerned with its underlying normative implications, implications which are problematic.

The problem with von Hayek's argument is that it is articulated in abstraction from the life-ground of value that he himself presupposes as a well-fed, articulate critic of centralized planning. Abstraction from the life-ground can only be done in theory since to really abstract oneself from the life-ground of value is to abstract oneself from the field of

---

6 Lukes, *Power: A Radical View*, 8. McMurtry himself is sensitive to this problem. He argues against Marcuse, for example, that the vagueness which attached to Marcuse's distinction between true and false needs in *One-Dimensional Man* left him open to charges that he was arrogating to himself the right to dictate to everyone what they ought to desire. McMurtry, *Unequal Freedoms*, 209n9. See also Noonan, "Marcuse, Human Nature, and the Foundation of Ethical Norms," 267–86.

7 Von Hayek, *Law, Legislation, and Liberty*. Volume 2, *The Mirage of Social Justice*, 113.

8 See Noonan, *Democratic Society and Human Needs*, 227–47.

life-requirements, and thus from life altogether. Von Hayek and others who appeal to the diversity of human desires, drives, and demands as a knockdown argument against universal life-requirements as normatively prior to other ends presuppose the material conditions of the existence of the people to whose diversity they appeal; people are simply assumed to be there with competing ends. By assuming what must be explained – how these people with competing ends came to be, how they were fed, clothed, housed, educated, etc. – von Hayek makes it appear that competing ends and difference are natural facts about human life. Obviously, however, infants do not have ends that differ from one another. Their initial goal is to eat, sleep, and expel waste. Infancy thus tells us something of importance about all subsequent life – the differences that distinguish empirical people from one another *develop in society* and are not, therefore, natural facts. Von Hayek's theory ignores the fact that (at the very least) the natural life-requirements of people must be satisfied by the natural environment and other people's productive activity as a necessary material condition of there being any adult egos with competing ends. To have a social commitment to the comprehensive satisfaction of life-requirements is thus not to impose alien ends on people; it is to satisfy the fundamental conditions of their positing any other ends for themselves to pursue.

An analogous response can be made to the objection that the objective harm criterion of life-requirements has ethnocentric implications. The implications of the criterion are no more ethnocentric than they are authoritarian because the criterion does not dictate what concrete groups of people employ to satisfy their life-requirements, or how in particular they should organize themselves so as to ensure their satisfaction. In other words, the criterion does not determine the content of what Doyal and Gough call "need-satisfiers," or what in the object, resource, etc., actually satisfies the life-requirement in question.[9] The criterion is to be *applied* by real people reasoning in the definite contexts in which they find themselves about what is and is not a real life-requirement satisfier. Obviously, however, the underlying question of the connection between life and life's resources is not a problem upon which any set of people, regardless of their culture, awaits philosophical instruction. People know in general what they require to continue to live, and these requirements come in culturally concrete forms. In this sense, what is valuable as a life-requirement satisfier is anything that satisfies the requirement. The culturally concrete differences between the contents of life-requirement satisfiers do not express fundamental differences of life-requirement across cultures. As Ruth Benedict, purportedly a paradigmatic "cultural

9 Doyal and Gough, *A Theory of Human Need*, 69–75, 168.

relativist," argued, different cultural constructions can have the same value insofar as they "serve a society to live by."[10]

Thus, if humans are liable to shared forms of harm, it is because they have shared life-requirements. While life-requirements have been distinguished in general from consumer demands, the more difficult task lies ahead. That more difficult task is to convincingly explicate a comprehensive set of human life-requirements. My approach is to derive the comprehensive set from three dimensions of human nature which I take to be universal. All human beings are organisms, and our organism encodes physical-organic requirements of life. All human beings are also potentially socially self-conscious agents. The realization of this potential depends on the satisfaction of definite socio-cultural requirements of human life. Finally, because the life-time of all human beings is finite, the free realization of our human capacities depends on both the quantity and the quality of life-time we are able to experience and enjoy. I thus contend that there is a distinct life-requirement for free time without which the free realization of human capacities is impossible. I will now explain and defend each class in turn.[11]

2.2 ORGANIC LIFE-REQUIREMENTS

All life exists within definite ranges of tolerance, depends on specific environmental conditions, and requires regular inputs of natural resources. Each factor is affected by the structure of social organization and the ruling value system that legitimates that structure. Every human being will eventually die, but thirty thousand children die of preventable causes every day. Hence, the material conditions of life are not only environmental but include the ruling value systems that legitimate certain uses of environmental resources and rule out others. In the past it was possible to regard mass deprivation of organic life-requirements as natural accident. Living in local communities immediately dependent on the vagaries of weather, the health of the crops they had planted, and other factors that were beyond their control, our ancestors depended in a more direct way on the strictly local conditions of natural life-support.

10 Benedict, *Patterns of Culture*, 23. On the charges of cultural relativism as largely a strawperson distortion, see Geertz, "Anti-anti-Relativism."

11 Compare the related but distinct typology in McMurtry. McMurtry divides life-requirements into seven classes of goods, whereas I operate with a simplified typology of three classes, derived from what I take to be the three universal dimensions of human being. As regards content, McMurtry does not recognize a distinct life-requirement for free time but only limitations on the hours worked each day. See McMurtry, "Human Rights Versus Corporate Rights," 22–6.

The failure to satisfy basic organic life-requirements because of a poor harvest or because some catastrophe spoiled food reserves was not an ethical problem. Today people are interconnected by trade, by communication technologies, by the means to transport resources quickly around the globe; improved methods of production mean that the global economy produces more than enough food to satisfy everyone's general requirements. Thus, the provision of organic life-requirements has become a matter of the value system that governs the production, distribution, and use of resources.

I have introduced the question of organic life-requirements in this way to emphasize that today the basic material conditions of life are not a presupposition of ethics but the first level of life-grounded materialist ethics. The satisfaction of physical-organic life-requirements is not simply a presupposition of a good life; the degree to which these requirements are satisfied is the most basic content of the good life. In order to understand this component of the good life it is essential, therefore, to know more precisely what the core physical-organic requirements of human life are.

The life sciences have produced an extraordinary wealth of insight into what fundamental organic life-requirements must be satisfied if human life-capacities are to develop more rather than less fully. The metabolic functions of the human body require inputs about which we know a great deal because we have learned a great deal about the body's organic chemistry. The body must be hydrated; it must be able to breathe air that contains sufficient oxygen but is free of fatal levels of deadly toxins. It requires a definite caloric value in the food that it eats, as well as protein, minerals, and vitamins in known amounts. It requires clothing and shelter appropriate to the climate and means to travel the distances required to access the life-requirement satisfiers not immediately at hand. Infants and children require special physical protection from the natural and social environment and humans of all ages require protection from violent traumas. Finally, the maintenance of life can require periodic health care relative to the objective disease problems that arise in the course of life. These resources and forms of protection are material requirements of *life*. They are shared by human beings because human beings share an evolved organic material nature.

The bearer of our organic life-requirements is the same across the globe – the human body. In this regard, life-grounded materialist ethics concurs with Nussbaum that "prior to any concrete cultural shaping, we are born with human bodies, whose possibilities and capabilities do not as such belong to any culture. The experience of the body is culturally influenced, but the body itself, prior to social experience, provides limits and parameters that ensure a great deal of overlap in what is going to be experienced where hunger, thirst, desire, and the five senses are concerned."[12] Such a claim may appear to be so obvious as to be beyond challenge. Yet the same social mediations that make the problem of organic life-requirement deprivation an ethical question can be appealed to in criticism of the objectivity of these requirements. If even the basic requirements of human life turn out to be not universal but variable cultural constructs, then the most basic claim of life-grounded materialist ethics is undermined. The strongest challenge to my position of which I am aware is mounted by Jean Baudrillard.

For Baudrillard, human societies are institutional structures that subsume and transform the material conditions of human life into symbolic conditions of their own reproduction. Since human beings relate to nature through different social-symbolic constructions, it follows that these constructions subsume and transform the body's physical-organic requirements as well. Baudrillard concludes that there are no universal physical-organic life-requirements because there is no direct experience of life at this material level, but only different symbolic constructions. "Needs" he claims, "can no longer be defined adequately in terms of the materialist-idealist thesis – as innate, instinctive power, spontaneous craving, anthropological potential. Rather, they are better defined as a *function* induced (in the individual) by the internal logic of the system: more precisely, not as a *consummative force liberated by* the affluent society, but as a *productive force* required by the functioning of the system itself, by its process of survival and reproduction. In other words, there are needs only because the system needs them."[13]

The life-grounded materialism that I constructed in chapter 1 does not deny the reality of human symbolic constructions. However, it does not follow that because we relate to the body through different social-symbolic constructions, the body is nothing real apart from these constructions. Sebastiano Timpanaro puts this point very clearly. Human biology, he reminds culturalist critics of materialism, is "not an abstract construction, not one of our prehistoric ancestors ... now superseded by historical and social man, but still exists in each of us."[14] Baudrillard's argument ignores this reality. It is thus politically and ethically self-undermining and based on a category mistake.

If it is true that human life-requirements are nothing but functions of the social system's reproductive requirements, then there is no ground

---

12 Nussbaum, "Non-Relative Virtues: An Aristotelian Approach," 263.
13 Baudrillard, *For a Critique of the Political Economy of the Sign*, 82.
14 Timpanaro, *On Materialism*, 45.

to criticize even massive failures of life-requirement satisfaction. If "eating" is a social construction then so too is "mass starvation." Hence it follows from Baudrillard's argument that starvation has no more material reality than eating. Feasts as well as famines would be social constructions. Therefore, mass starvation cannot be criticized on the basis of the life-destruction it causes because for Baudrillard there is no material reality to life that could be damaged. Consistently interpreted, Baudrillard's argument entails that the starving are not deprived of anything their lives actually require because their function within the given social system is to not consume. They thus fulfill their function by starving to death. The political and ethical absurdity of this conclusion is evident.

The category mistake requires more philosophical work to explain. The basic problem is that Baudrillard ignores the difference between a construction and the materials out of which the construction is built. A home, I noted in chapter 1, is not identical to the material out of which it is built. Being a home equally depends on the structure imposed on those materials and the emotional disposition of the person who lives in the home toward this physical structure. The home is the complex whole formed from these materials, according to this plan, and that evokes these feelings in the person who dwells within. Baudrillard reduces this complex whole to architectural plans. He thus mistakes complex material structures, human bodies included, for symbolic interpretations of them. By eliminating the material moment of the structure, Baudrillard eliminates that which is the object of interpretation. A coherent understanding of these structures, by contrast, must be synthetic and embrace both the matter and its meaning.

The sort of category mistake involved in Baudrillard's argument can be made vivid by asking the skeptic to put the theory into practice and demonstrate that it is possible to live without nutritious food, water, shelter, and so on, or to find a society in which these are not produced in any form. Articulate skepticism would cease after a few minutes of oxygen deprivation. It is clear therefore that the skeptic is able to make a plausible case only by abstracting herself from the life-ground of value, i.e., by ignoring the real material conditions of her being alive.[15] Since actual ignorance of these material conditions would kill the skeptic, the robust skeptical argument either presupposes the truth of the life-requirements it denies, or proves materially irrational, i.e., fatal to the skeptic if acted on.

Strong culturalist arguments, such as Baudrillard's, against the universality of organic life-requirements are also rooted in a reified conception

15 I draw here on arguments jointly developed with Alison Assiter. See Assiter and Noonan, "Needs: A Realist Perspective."

of culture. Cultures tend to be read as fixed and static wholes determining individual life absolutely. How cultures come to be and change remains unexplained. Cultures are not reified wholes determining individual life from the outside, but, as I argued in chapter 1, products of collective labour on the natural life-support system. No matter how extensive the development of human productivity, including symbolic construction, nature remains the primary material reality underlying human thought and practice. Human activity modifies and transforms natural substances, but this modifying and transforming activity, while productive of a truly human world out of the givenness of nature, never entirely "socializes" the natural world, as even Marx sometimes seems to argue.[16] If we overemphasize the degree of independence of culture from its bases in nature and human labour, we cannot account for the fact that cultures change their practices on the basis of new information about physical-organic life-requirements. For example, mothers in parts of Africa organized themselves to distribute vitamin A to their infants after it had been explained to them that the night blindness that their infants suffered could easily be corrected by taking a vitamin supplement. Pills were not a culturally sanctioned form of vitamin distribution, but these women adapted their traditional practices, after a period of trepidation, once they became convinced that their babies were being deprived of a life-requirement.[17] The mothers *learned* the material reality of a life-requirement that had not formerly been symbolically acknowledged in their culture. On the basis of this new information they chose the health of their infants over the strict replication of older cultural practices.

Nor can skepticism about organic life-requirements explain the history of struggles against different social practices that cause the same sorts of physical-organic life-requirement deprivation. Of greatest salience here are the struggles of indigenous peoples around the world to

16 On this subject, Marx seems to adopt different views in different works, and sometimes even in different paragraphs in the same work. In *The German Ideology*, for example, he excoriates Feuerbach for thinking that there is a "nature" independent of human productive activity, arguing on the one hand that productive activity is the "foundation of the whole sensuous world," but then adding, a few sentences later, that this claim does not undermine the priority of external nature over human society. Clearly, however, if social activity is the *foundation* of the whole sensuous world, which would include nature, it must be primary, the foundation being more basic than that which it founds. Much later, however, in *Capital*, Volume 3, Marx adopts a different, and truer position, recognizing that while social development changes our relationship to the natural world, natural necessity never disappears from human life but remains as a historically constant underlying set of organic life-requirements. See Marx, *The German Ideology*, 46, and Marx, *Capital*, 3: 820.

17 Haselow, Obadia, and Akame, "The Integration of Vitamin A Supplement into Community-Directed Treatment with Ivermectin: A Practical Guide for Africa."

reclaim control over the lands lost in the long, brutal history of colonial conquest.[18] What are these culturally distinct groups of people fighting for if not the same material conditions of life-support? As the history of Canada's First Nations proves, a vital symbolic culture cannot be maintained in material conditions of absolute dependence caused by loss of the land to colonial forces. Consider just one example: the confrontation between the Canadian government and the Mohawk Nation in Oka, Quebec, in 1990. Johnny Cree, a member of the Mohawk Nation, notes how the political organization that led up to the struggle against the Canadian government had ameliorated the often serious drug and alcohol problems that have afflicted many of Canada's First Nations: "people of the Longhouse do not believe in the use of alcohol or drugs ... they do not belong in any society ... Actually it has cut down a lot among our young people because there is pride. Our young people are finding out who they are. There is no more shame."[19] The loss of pride followed the loss of control over the life-sustaining earth. The recovery of pride, as Cree explains, developed through the struggle to re-establish control over it. Thus, whatever value one wants to assign to symbolic differences between different cultures, the history of indigenous oppression at the hands of colonial forces proves that symbolic richness dies with loss of control over the life-sustaining land and waters. Whether one looks to Canada, or Nigeria, or Bolivia, wherever indigenous life-ways are struggling to recover from five centuries of colonial oppression, one will always find those struggles to be focused on reclaiming control over the natural bases of life-support.

The evidence of biological and medical science, philosophical reflection, and political struggle strongly supports the conclusion that there are fundamental organic requirements of human life underlying its symbolic richness and diversity. But what of this diversity and richness itself? Does it too require the satisfaction of universal socio-cultural requirements of *human* life? Prima facie, the answer would seem to be "no." What makes a life truly human is precisely the symbolic richness of cultural difference. These cultural differences arise from different institutions, and this seems to imply that there are no *social* bases for shared

18 For examples of these movements for control over basic life-resources, see the examination of Bolivian peasants' struggle to reclaim control over their water from the Bechtel Corporation in Jim Schultz, "Bolivia's War over Water"; and Vandana Shiva's examination of the struggles of Indian peasants to resist agribusiness in *Biopiracy: The Plunder of Nature and Knowledge*; and the struggle of Canadian First Nations to re-establish control over the resources on their traditional lands in Noonan, "Need-Satisfaction and Group Conflict: Beyond a Rights-Grounded Approach."

19 Maclaine and Baxendale, *This Land is Our Land: The Mohawk Revolt at Oka*, 41.

socio-cultural life-requirements. The requirements of social life are relative to distinct societies, and all attempts to insist on the objective reality of shared socio-cultural life-requirements have been imperialistic. I will argue, on the contrary, that the very development of distinctive symbolic systems proves the objective reality of universal socio-cultural requirements of *human* life.

2.3 SOCIO-CULTURAL REQUIREMENTS OF HUMAN LIFE

Life-grounded materialist ethics treats the satisfaction of organic life-requirements as the first element of a good human life. However, the comprehensive conditions for the good life for human beings are not reducible to the physical-organic requirements of life. The difference between physical-organic and socio-cultural life-requirements is implicit in Marx's distinction between natural needs and the "human form" of needs. One can satisfy the former and yet fail to live a fully human life. "The sense caught up in crude practical need" he argued, "has only a restricted sense. For the starving man, it is not the human form of food that exists, but only its abstract existence as food ... The care-burdened, poverty-stricken man has no sense for the finest play."[20] Humanity's highest potential, "free, conscious activity," thus demands the satisfaction of needs that develop out of the physical-organic foundations of life but are not reducible to them.[21]

If we distinguish human life by its collective capacity to freely create its own social worlds, then the plurality of social worlds that it has built, with their different languages, institutions, and value-systems, seems to rule out from the beginning the possibility of there being common socio-cultural requirements of human life. Any reference to *human* life will have to make reference to the symbolic contents that make it meaningful for real people, and those symbolic contents can differ radically from culture to culture. Nancy Fraser, for example, argues that socio-cultural needs are always interpretations generated by differently situated groups on the basis of their distinct, concrete life-experiences.[22] Given the fact that these life-experiences are group-relative, so too are the social needs

20 Marx, "Economic and Philosophical Manuscripts of 1844," 302. I return below to fundamental problems in Marx's conception of the "human form of needs," but my general focus is not on Marx's conception of need as a distinct and abstract problem. Two excellent studies exist. See Heller, *The Theory of Need in Marx*, and Fraser, *Hegel and Marx: The Concept of Need.*

21 Marx, "Economic and Philosophical Manuscripts of 1844," 276.

22 Fraser, "Women, Welfare, and the Politics of Need Interpretation," in Fraser, *Unruly Practices*, 153–4.

that people feel and express. While different groups might, through processes of dialogue and deliberation, come to make similar demands, any
common needs would be deliberate constructions and not, as I will argue, presuppositions of the existence of different groups.

While I agree with Fraser that socio-cultural life-requirements are always *interpreted*, it does not follow that they are *interpretations*. Thus Fraser
makes a category mistake similar to the category mistake that undid
Baudrillard's argument. It is, of course, undeniable that the symbolic
contents that make life meaningful differ from culture to culture, group
to group, and in liberal cultures, even from person to person. It is equally true that these interpretations, as products of human action and interaction, have shared general conditions in the institutions, relations, and
practices without which the symbol-producing, interpreting, and creative capacities of human beings cannot develop. If human social self-
consciousness is to be able to produce meaningful constructions and
interpretations, it requires access to definite relationships and institutions without which these uniquely human capacities cannot develop.
Since our meaning-generating capacities distinguish the *human* form of
life, it follows that these institutions are every bit as necessary to us as
humans as oxygen and water are to us as *organisms*. Life-grounded materialist ethics is thus concerned to understand the general socio-cultural
conditions for the development of the human capacity for socially self-
consciousness. meaning creation, interpretation, and action. I argue
that, where certain groups of people are denied access to these institutions, they are harmed in their humanity, just as those who are deprived
of organic life-requirements are harmed in their organism.

The social self-consciousness that enables humanity to generate meanings is not a world apart but a development out of our organic nature. As
Reid argues, "Human social and cultural evolution does not arise from
the accumulation of behavioural adaptation, but from the *adaptability* of
our species ... although adaptability is grounded in the genes, it operates
at higher levels of organization ... [especially] the central nervous system, the brain, and the conscious and subconscious mind. These are
what free us from the automatic responses of our primitive ancestors."[23]
Human nature is synthetically organic-social. To be a human being is to
be a member of a species which builds its own social world, evaluates it
according to theoretical, ethical, political, and aesthetic standards, and
changes it in response to systemic problems and contradictions. The
natural ties established between human beings and nature by our organic life-requirements are also *social ties* binding us one to the other in

23 Reid, *Biological Emergences*, 100.

different forms of collective labour through which these worlds are built, interpreted, and changed.

Marx's account of the development of the "productive forces" in *The German Ideology* can help us understand this complex relationship between humanity, the natural life-support system, and the social life-development system. Marx argues that "the social structure and the state are continually evolving out of the life-process of definite individuals, however, of these individuals not as they may appear in their own or other people's minds, but as they actually are ... under definite material limits."[24] Since reflective collective and individual intelligence is brought to bear on these tasks, knowledge accumulates about how best to accomplish them, which in turn generates second-order forms of production: production of tools which aid the primary forms of metabolic interchange with nature. "The satisfaction of this first need (the basic organic needs of life)," writes Marx, "the action of satisfying it and the instrument of satisfaction which has been acquired, leads to new needs."[25] Over time, entire social worlds are built up out of nature, which makes possible the cultivation of human capacities as ends in themselves. That is, society generates a life-purpose unique to itself: the cultivation of social self-conscious agency, not as an instrument of survival but a good in itself. In order to develop, social self-consciousness has ongoing natural conditions of *existence* and socio-cultural conditions of *development*.

Because human beings evaluate their lives according to normative and not just survival principles, human action must be understood through social, not abstractly natural, categories. Marx again helps in understanding this point. "Consciousness is at first ... merely consciousness concerning the *immediate* sensuous environment and consciousness of the limited connection with other persons and things outside the individual." As productivity increases and the division of labour develops, the hitherto hidden potentialities of raw consciousness emerge, and a new reality in the universe is born: human symbolic life. "From this moment onwards consciousness *can* really flatter itself that it is something other than consciousness of existing practice, that it *really* represents something real; from now on consciousness is in a position to emancipate itself from the world and to proceed to the formation of 'pure' theory, theology, philosophy, morality, etc."[26] There is no doubt that on one level Marx is mocking the idealists with whom he is arguing. At the same time, as there is some truth in all jokes that work, there is an insight here which is

24 Marx, *The German Ideology*, 41.
25 Ibid., 48.
26 Ibid., 50.

important for life-grounded materialist ethics. At a certain point in social development the world of human consciousness becomes a *material reality*, insofar as the ideas of theology, philosophy, politics, law, and so forth enter into the structure and dynamics of social life as part of the field of determinations acting on human beings. The natural problem of human life – how to survive – becomes the social problem of how to live well.

Since these two sides of human life cannot be coherently separated from each other, i.e, because the life-ground of value for human beings is inextricably natural and social, the most basic socio-cultural requirement of human life must be a hinge connecting the natural and social sides of our being. This hinge is the economic system understood in its instrumental life-value as the instituted practices through which human beings work on nature for the purpose of ensuring the satisfaction of organic life-requirements. "The labour process," Marx writes, "is human action with a view to the production of use-values, appropriation of natural substances to human requirements; it is the necessary condition for effecting a change of matter between man and Nature; it is the everlasting, nature-imposed condition of human existence, and is therefore independent of every social phase of that existence."[27]

Marx implies but does not explicate the deeper principle most salient for present purposes. Any materially rational economy must prioritize the production of use-values which have life-value, and not use-values of any sort whatsoever. Unless use-value is itself life-grounded, energy and resources can be wasted on pursuits that contribute nothing to life or, worse, damage or destroy it. Since human life cannot persist without the production of life-values, the first shared socio-cultural requirement of human life is an economic system that is in fact life-grounded. As McMurtry argues, "production and distribution for life-need, and that, in turn, for life-capacity and experience in more comprehensive ranges of enjoyment and expression – this is the only ultimate value on earth. Any sane economy is there to serve it in opening horizons of life-worth."[28] Thus, the first socio-cultural life-requirement is an instituted economic system which ensures that collective labour produces use-values which have instrumental life-value as organic life-requirement satisfiers.

Essential as this role is, economic systems are not only the hinge between nature and human society. They are also social institutions in which "free, conscious activity" can be expressed and enjoyed. As Sean Sayers argues, "all human labour is social and involves a communicative

---

27 Marx, *Capital*, 1: 179.
28 McMurtry, *Value Wars*, 124.

element."[29] The life-value potentially produced within economic systems is thus not only instrumental but also intrinsic. Economies are also spaces of social interaction within which intrinsically life-valuable cognitive and creative capacities can be developed. Since all work involves some degree of transformation of existing materials, and therefore some degree of ingenuity and creativity, work can have intrinsic as well as instrumental life-value. This intrinsic life-value is not confined to the particular capacities developed in work life but in work's being the way in which our ethical commitments to others' well-being become real in the contribution our particular work makes to the overall society. There is thus intrinsic life-value in the capacities that work allows one to develop, in the extent to which it allows one to develop them, and in the social self-consciousness of oneself as a contributing member of society. One does not have to be a Marxist to appreciate this point. Alan Gewirth clearly understands the importance of work as a social practice that allows people to "see themselves as part of a larger whole to which they are bound by ... social, political, and cultural values," and thus become "motivated by their obligations to their nurturing society."[30] Where work is alienated in Marx's sense, the life-value of work is compromised. It might produce use-values with no life-value, it might not develop any individually meaningful capacities, and it might be experienced as an oppressive burden that ruins the worker's life while contributing nothing of significance to society.

To suffer forms of work that are devoid of intrinsic life-value for oneself and one's society is to suffer in one's humanity. If we are alienated in our working lives we cannot, as Marx says, "contemplate ourselves in a world we have created" and value ourselves as a contributor to this creation.[31] To become fully life-valuable, the labour that people perform as individuals must not only contribute as a *function* to social reproduction, it must be expressed and enjoyed as an individually meaningful human vocation that consciously contributes something that others' lives require. Since so much of our life-time is given over to labour, the quality of its activity is an essential ethical problem for human beings. For any person or group to be reduced in their labouring activity to a mere tool of system-requirements is to be harmed in their human capacity for creative self-realization and productive commitments to the well-being of others. It follows from McMurtry's harm criterion of life-requirement that intrinsically life-valuable work is a second universal socio-cultural requirement of human life. Where this life-requirement is not satisfied

29 Sayers, "Labour in Modern Industrial Society," 153.
30 Gewirth, *The Community of Rights*, 151.
31 Marx, "Economic and Philosophical Manuscripts of 1844," 277.

because economic institutions are indifferent to the life-value of work, life-grounded materialist ethics concludes that those economic institutions are contrary to the comprehensive conditions of good human lives.

If one rejects the claim that intrinsically life-valuable labour is an objective and universal socio-cultural requirement of human life, then one must agree that de-skilled and routinized behaviour within authoritarian workplaces is not a harm to human beings. As an ethical problem, alienated labour is essentially a problem of the structure of rule over life-activity. Labour can be dominated in many different ways in many different types of society but, since the argument aims at shedding light on contemporary problems, I confine my discussion to capitalism. Within capitalism, the content of life-activity is determined by the commands of the ruling class, who in turn are responding to the reified power of market forces, which in turn are generally treated as both an irresistible natural force and a universally legitimate moral imperative.[32] There is no recognition from within this system of command that the primary value of labour is not its economic value in the narrow sense (the production of exchange values) but its instrumental and intrinsic life-value. Despite Marx's off-hand dismissals of Kant, it is clear that the problem of alienated labour, of the failure to develop the intrinsic value of labour, is essentially a social problem whereby ends and means, intrinsic and instrumental values, are inverted.[33] Alienated labour reduces some people to the status of mere tools of ruling classes, ruling value systems, and ruling social forces. Where people are reduced to mere tools, they are objectively harmed in their human capacity for intrinsically life-valuable activity. There is therefore a shared human life-requirement for economic systems that satisfy the conditions for labour's realizing its intrinsic life-value.

The life-value human beings have for one another within the social field of life-development is not limited to the contributions that we make to each other through our labour. Our emotional lives are enriched by the intrinsic value of relationships of all sorts (familial relationships, friendship, sexual relations, long-term committed love, and so on) in

32 The model for this contradictory synthesis of natural force and moral imperative is Adam Smith's idea of the invisible hand. He treats it as both a natural outcome of human nature, i.e., the propensity to work for one's own self-maximization, and a moral imperative, a sign of the work of providence in human affairs. See Smith, *The Theory of Moral Sentiments*, 303–5.

33 See, for example, Marx, "Economic and Philosophical Manuscripts of 1844," 306–8, 314. The relationship between Marx's critique of capitalism and Kant's critique of the instrumentalization of humanity has been the subject of two recent illuminating studies. See Van der Linden, *Kantian Ethics and Socialism*, and Karatani, *Transcritique: On Kant and Marx*.

which the aim is reciprocal enriching of each member's emotional life, as opposed to the exclusive pecuniary gain of one member. The reality of the life-value of these relations is the joy one feels at another's joy, the sorrow one feels at another's sorrow – in general, the capacity to identify with others we care about. For people mutually attuned to each other in this way, their own good does not form a world apart from their relationship but crucially involves their connection with others. Far from making this sort of mutuality impossible, as Kasser claimed above, materialism, at least in its life-grounded variant, affirms these connections as of essential importance to human life. Among its key interests are the general social conditions required to develop the individual capacity to identify with and care about others. In order to gain insight into the relevant life-requirements involved in the development of this capacity, I begin by examining the extremes at either end of the range of possible human relationships.

At one extreme is overt physical violence intended to destroy the other insofar as the other is judged a barrier to one's own experience and activity regarded as good if and only if not shared in any way with others.[34] At the other extreme is the relationship described movingly by Nel Noddings as a structure of care for the well-being of the other.[35] Thought to their ultimate implications from the life-grounded perspective, only the latter and never the former can be coherently affirmed as life-valuable. If all social relations were actually zero-sum conflicts, then the human species would soon destroy the social conditions for its human (although perhaps not its organic) existence. If each really treated his own good as private and others only as threats to this good, human collective life would be incapable of the sorts of co-operation and mutual commitment that enable the growth of higher-level human thought and creation. How could anyone teach others what they know, for example, if others are assumed to be competitors who will employ this knowledge to undermine the teacher? Even if the more extreme problems were avoided, zero-sum competition as the dominant mode of social relationship must produce over time less rather than more life-value than co-operation and care; in competitions there must be losers, and to lose when life-value is at stake is to suffer a diminution of life-value. Caring relations as a model for social relationship, by contrast, always increase overall life-value because the outcome of successful caring is the elevation of the object of care to a better life-state without loss of life-value of

34 This pole and its contradictions are incisively grasped by Hegel in chapter 4 of the *Phenomenology of Spirit*, 109–11.
35 Noddings, *Caring*, 83.

the one caring. If one has two grandparents who require one's care, will they be better served by putting them in competition with each other, with the winner getting all the care and the loser none? Or are they better served through co-operatively organizing their schedules so that each receives sufficient care? Since in the former case the loser loses all life-value, the second alternative, in which each receives sufficient care, is clearly the more life-valuable and coherent solution.

Moreover, just as there is intrinsic life-value to labour beyond its instrumental value, so too is there intrinsic value to caring in the life of the one who cares. When human beings care about one another, they increase their own life-value by expanding the number of affirmative connections between themselves and other humans, and they increase the life-value of others by acting toward them in such a way as to enable them to express and enjoy more life-value in their own lives. It is no objection to this argument to insist that it is impossible to care for everyone in the way we care for those closest to us since it is by definition possible to care only for those with whom we come into contact, and we do not come into contact with everyone.[36] The point is to establish caring relations as the model of human relations, whether they be familial, romantic-sexual, or friendly, such that when we do encounter others, we encounter them as people about whom we care, and not as threats to be destroyed. The general capacity at issue in this dimension of experience and activity is the capacity to live in reciprocity with others, to care about others as unique and unrepeatable bearers of life, to allow oneself to be so cared for, and thus to govern social relationships, as far as possible, by the goal of expanding mutually enriching forms of interaction. The socio-cultural life-requirements for the expression and enjoyment of this capacity to care can be determined by asking which social-institutions are involved in the development of a caring personality.

Just as economic institutions are the hinge between the natural life-support system and human social life-development systems, so family institutions are the hinge between the instinctual inheritance of human beings and the social cultivation of human emotions. Before spelling out the argument further, two qualifications are in order. First, while I argue that some form of systematic, caring, and loving structure is a requirement of healthy emotional development, it does not follow that this implies that all adults must form families and have children. Since all humans begin life as children, all need systematic love and care. It does not follow that once we have become adults we must have children in turn. Second, I understand family institutions broadly and I do not privilege any one

36 Ibid., 86.

particular mode of satisfying this socio-cultural life-requirement for caring familial relations. "Family" in the life-grounded sense means "institutionalized structures of adult care and concern for children" and not a biosocial unit of genetic-legal relationship. I make this distinction to obviate objections that my argument relies on a conservative conception of "family values." It does not. Gays, lesbians, single women, and unrelated but genuinely caring adults can all satisfy the socio-cultural life-requirements of children to be cared for and loved. Human beings do not require a nuclear family in order to develop their capacities for caring, non-exploitative relationships with others, but we do clearly require some form of loving adult care while we are young.

The forms of physical protection required by our organic nature are not sufficient for the development of the emotional dispositions required if people are to "live with and toward others, to recognize and show concern for other people ... [and] to be able to imagine the situation of another."[37] If people are to be able to form non-violent, non-exploitative, non-instrumental, caring relationships with other people, they require non-violent, non-exploitative, and non-instrumental care and love from adults while they are young. Tim Kasser presents a wide spectrum of psychological research carried out in different cultural contexts to support the claim that structures of adult care and love are life-requirements for healthy emotional development. Healthy emotional development means, for a human being, developing the capacity to interact with others in a way that demonstrates genuine concern for their self-development. Children who are cared for and loved prove much more able to value others as subjects in their own right.[38] A society in which this disposition widely prevails will tend to be less violent and destructively competitive.

Thus, being loved and cared for, especially while young, is a shared socio-cultural life-requirement because without it the human capacity to love and care for others is degraded. Since the degradation of this capacity does not eliminate the existence of others from one's life, the lack of development of this capacity entails constant conflict and the social pathologies of violence and indifference to suffering it engenders. Just as organic life-requirements can be satisfied in multiple ways, so too can this human life-requirement. Since the structures of relationship in which adult care and love are manifested toward children can vary, it follows that the ways in which this socio-cultural requirement of human life may be satisfied can vary, from culture to culture and within cultures.

37 Nussbaum, *Frontiers of Justice*, 77.
38 Kasser, *The High Price of Materialism*, 30–2, 61–4, 67–72, 88.

What matters is not the genetic connection or lack thereof between care-givers and children, but that the child is loved.

Finally, I do not believe that the ability to love and care for what is not-self is an altruistic virtue which people are to be commended for developing but which is not a fundamental human capacity. A society in which everyone really did seek in others only an opportunity for conquest would be so emotionally impoverished as to be intolerable to its members. Such a society would be without love, care, friendship, mutual laughter, trust, concern for the pleasure of others, delight in others' success, disappointment in others' failures, real co-operation, solidarity, and that ineffable electric feeling of excitement when one finds oneself in the company of friends who care about each other. It is not coherently possible to affirm such emotional impoverishment as a better society than one in which emotional life is cultivated in these multiple dimensions. Thus, our capacities for reciprocal caring are essential intrinsic life-values whose development depends on the satisfaction of the life-requirement for loving and caring family relations.

As we develop our capacity to identify with others, we begin to carve a space of life for ourselves. As we grow in independence, we encounter more of the world, and as we encounter more of the world, ever new questions touching on all dimensions of existence arise. The cognitive and imaginative capacities required to pose answers to these questions (and pose new questions in turn) cannot develop simply on the basis of caring relationships. The higher-level capacities of human thinking and imagination require education. I thus argue that education is a socio-cultural life-requirement without which our cognitive and imaginative capacities cannot develop fully. Because our practical and creative capacities depend on our cognitive and imaginative capacities for the human form of their expression, if the former are constricted, so too will the latter be constricted. As with the nature of families, so too with the nature of education: it can take different forms. To argue that education is a life-requirement is not to argue that a specific institutional-bureaucratic form is required. Nor is it to argue in favour of one mode of pedagogy to the exclusion of other modes. By the term "education" I do not refer to any particular learning institution or teaching method. I regard as "educational" any institution, method, relationship, or practice through which the cognitive and imaginative powers of the human intellect grow in scope, depth, and rigour of employment.

What distinguishes education from indoctrination or programming is its goal. The goal of education is the richer development and more rigorous employment of the cognitive and imaginative capacities of human social self-consciousness. Therefore, education is distinct from assimilation of facts, folk beliefs, cultural prejudices, chauvinistic attitudes, or a generalized grasp of "how things are done around here." An educated person is not someone who knows a large number of disconnected facts with a retrieval algorithm, like Watson the *Jeopardy*-playing computer. Nor is an educated person someone who knows how to "find their niche" by exploiting available opportunities for private gain. The truly educated person is, to borrow a phrase from Hegel, the person who can adopt a negative disposition toward things. Educated people are thus able to think *otherwise* than is immediately given in experience, whether that experience is raw or socially mediated.[39] The objective world in which we live is complex, and education must develop the all-purpose cognitive means for understanding that complexity as well as the imaginative capacity to think it otherwise than it immediately presents itself to be. Without these capacities human life would not involve human activity but only machine-like functioning. It would devolve in the direction of the mechanical execution of programs imposed by social necessity.

The cognitive and imaginative capacities of human beings are not functions of particular social orders, although their elaboration in higher and deeper ranges of practice grows as social complexity grows. As a life-requirement, education is not a culturally relative goal; it is anchored in the fact that the latent capacities of human social self-consciousness do not unfurl like the petals of a flower in spring but require deliberate cultivation. The latent capacities of human social self-consciousness develop only in interaction with others whose vocation it is to assist in their cultivation for the good of the student. The goal of education is to enable the capacities of human social self-consciousness to develop in ways not yet expressed or even anticipated in any given society.

The cognitive and imaginative capacities through which human beings evaluate and judge worlds are the precondition of their becoming an active force in the creation of new and better forms of social relationship and activity. What matters here is not simply innovation, in the capitalist sense of creating new variations on old products. What matters far more is the creation of novelty of insight that enables the solution of collective problems, the deepening of understanding of our world as an end in itself, and the creation of new forms of beauty. The creation of life-valuable novelty, whether in art, science, or politics, depends on the general cognitive and imaginative capacities of human social self-consciousness exercised in relation to existing social relationships and practices. Of all the objects of thought and imagination, the social relationships and practices within which people exist are the most important; one's general

---

39 Hegel, *The Phenomenology of Spirit*, 20.

life-horizons are formed within the institutions that structure those relationships and the values that legitimate the institutions. To test these limits against imaginative and theoretical constructions of what is possible and better is the basis of intelligent social change, just as the ability to test the limits of established scientific knowledge is the basis of the progress of understanding in the sciences. Education is, thus, always about learning how to test and then go beyond established limits. This ability to question, understand, evaluate, and transform is the essential difference between an educated person, wherever she or he exists, and the person who has simply been programmed to think in expected ways. .

This critical dimension of education explains why conservative social forces are always afraid of it. Educated people do not comply with commands but only with reasons that withstand critical scrutiny. The authority of divine command as divine command, the authority of cultural codes presented to people as inviolable rules of conduct, the authority of political power as the exercise of threats and intimidation, all lose their efficacy in the face of a mass of educated people. This fact explains why totalitarian movements constantly struggle to reduce the educational system to indoctrination to cultural prejudices.

To be totally deprived of the ability to test the given against the possibly better is thus to be harmed in our human capacity to think and act in creative and novel ways that expand the life-value of society. Without the cognitive and imaginative capacities of social self-consciousness being developed through systematic interrogation of the given as an object whose most basic structures can be improved, not simply accepted, people completely deprived of education are trapped in the given, dependent on immediate experience or the content transmitted to them by political power as the only available sources of understanding. To be absolutely dependent on what is given is to be reduced to being the dependent of the powers that rule the given. It is to be cut off, as an individual, from becoming a socially self-conscious agent. But socially self-conscious agency is the distinguishing mark of *human* life, and thus to be deprived of education by the machinations of political power, hateful prejudice, or poverty is to be cut off from an essential social condition of living a fully human life. *Totally* uneducated people are reduced to a life of more or less mindless enactment of scripts written for them by the socially powerful for the sake of reproducing their own power. Hence deprivation of education is illegitimate on the same grounds as mindless and meaningless work – the uneducated person is always treated as a mere means to the reproduction of existing structures of social power. The reality of this harm is again supported by the reality of the changes that education introduces into people's lives. As soon as people's cognitive and imaginative capabilities have been educated, old social patterns and institutions appear questionable. Ancient structures of domination, such as the millennia-old and cross-cultural domination of women, rarely survive intact once the dominated awake to their domination.[40]

Love and care enable us to develop healthy dispositions toward other people – to value them as unique life-bearers and to develop mutual relationships with them. Education develops our capacities to understand and imagine, and thus to build and transform, the human social world. As rich as the capacities developed by care and love and education are, they do not exhaust the wealth of human potential. Human beings are also capable of experiencing both the natural and the social world as beautiful. The realization of this capacity certainly involves aesthetic education, but I distinguish the life-requirements involved in its realization from general educational requirements because the development of our capacity to experience beauty presupposes the preservation and creation of beautiful spaces, objects, and practices. The existence of these objects can be threatened by definite social processes. If there are no beautiful objects, there can be no experience of beauty. Hence the life-requirements involved in the development of our aesthetic capacities are both subjective (aesthetic education and cultivation) and objective (preservation and creation of beauty). It is on the objective side of this life-requirement that I focus.

It might be objected at the outset that there is no universal capacity for aesthetic experience and judgment. History seems to furnish the best rejoinder. Natural forms have inspired awe in people across time and cultural space. Art – visual, aural, movement-based – has been created in different human cultures for several thousands of years. By what physical law of nature could the profound emotional responses that nature and art invoke in us be explained? What evolutionary advantage does poetry confer on human beings? To anyone who has been moved by a painting, a symphony, a poem, a story, a dance, or, in the natural domain of beauty, a prairie field illuminated gold in the setting autumn sun, trees clinging to a cliff, the sea colliding with headlands on a blustery day, or a towering mountain range, such a question would sound senseless. The value of beauty cannot be understood reductively, since to reduce the beautiful object to its abstract material constituents (rock and water, trees and hills, sound waves, ink on a page, pigment on a canvas, etc.) eliminates the object of the aesthetic capacity. Yet the life-grounded argument does not take us beyond materialism to an idealism of Beauty in which Beauty

40 Nussbaum provides examples of the liberatory role of the education of women in India. Nussbaum, *Sex and Social Justice*, 152.

is an immaterial form elevating otherwise dead matter. Rather, it takes us beyond a narrow, impoverishing materialism that can recognize only physical forces to a materialism that understands beauty as an emergent property of material organization which requires human experience and interpretation in order to be drawn out from the material basis. The relevant material relation is not just between the paint and the painting, the light-wave and the image of the sea crashing against the rocks but between the living human being as the subject of experience and the natural and social worlds as beautiful and not just instrumentally useful. The aesthetic capacity is an opening of human sensibility and imagination beyond their original food- and mate- finding function. Its life-value lies in the potential doubling of the content of every human experience: every experience can be understood in its physical reality and in its aesthetic reality. The latter enriches our lives insofar as it frees thinking and activity from calculating the ways in which things may be useful to us. To see the beauty in something is to let it be. As Marcuse argued, "the aesthetic universe is the *Lebenswelt* on which the needs and faculties of human freedom depend for their liberation."[41]

As I noted above, the human aesthetic capacity requires for its cultivation more than education. It requires that social policy be freed from the tyranny of "useful" spending to include investments in the free (i.e., non-commercial) development of art in the widest possible sense and a social commitment to the preservation and creation of beautiful natural spaces. Both are threatened by the prevailing money-value system. Art today exists largely within the "art world," which is no longer the preserve of an avant-garde moved by aesthetic considerations but of collectors and curators, moved mostly by monetary calculations. The same tyranny of money-value threatens natural spaces. Wild spaces are threatened by real estate "developers" seeking to enclose the aesthetic commons and turn it into the preserve of those wealthy enough to be able to afford to live, or visit, or golf there.

Thus, the life-requirements that must be satisfied if our aesthetic capacities are to be developed and enjoyed are largely institutional commitments to invest in the creation of humanly created beauty and preserve already existing natural beauty. Concretely, this means the preservation as public trusts of those natural spaces not yet subsumed under commercial uses. Furthermore, it requires devoting social resources to the support of artistic labour as well as the institutions – public galleries, libraries, performance spaces – in which the products of human imagination are freely available for reflection and interpretation. Unless these

41 Marcuse, *An Essay on Liberation*, 31.

life-requirements are met, our aesthetic capacity does not develop, and if our aesthetic capacity does not develop, we are harmed by losing touch with all in nature and society which is not instrumentally useful or commercially exploitable. The harm lies in the impoverishment of our sensibility caused by a one-dimensional relationship with nature and society.

One might object that so long as mass poverty and other pervasive social problems prevail, a materialist ethics must prioritize the satisfaction of physical-organic life-requirements. This approach is often taken by policymakers, who invidiously contrast art as a "luxury" to "meat and potatoes" matters of economic policy. Philosophers rightly and understandably appalled by the "moral catastrophe" of absolute poverty also seem to imply that the overriding goal of social criticism ought to be to ensure the satisfaction of basic needs, with other issues of a less exigent nature left to be dealt with after the problem of physical-organic life-requirement satisfaction has been solved. Cosmopolitan liberal thinkers like David Held, Thomas Pogge, and Peter Singer, for example, seem to argue that there is a serial order of priority between physical-organic and socio-cultural life-requirements.[42] There is something like a stages theory of morality implied here, nicely summed up by Brecht: "food is the first thing – morals follow on."[43]

Of course, it is true, and life-grounded materialist ethics does not deny, that physical-organic life-requirements are basic to human life in a way that socio-cultural life-requirements for the existence of beautiful natural spaces and social artifacts are not. There is no dying from art-starvation. However, there can be death of the human forms of sentience and imagination where people acquiesce to sterility and ugliness because they feel that the duties of a life-grounded materialist ethics must be realized in mechanical stages. The duties implied by life-grounded materialist ethics are not resolvable into stages but are internally unified as the demand for the creation of the social conditions in which human life-requirements are treated and satisfied as a coherent whole. Life-grounded materialist ethics rejects both the reductionist demand that food be eaten before beauty enjoyed and the millennia-old class prejudices according to which beauty is the preserve of the rich and staying alive is the concern of the poor. One finds art among the poor and oppressed too. What form of life was harsher than the slave plantation? Yet even here humanity in its most brutalized condition was able to sing with such haunting beauty that the spirituals of the African slaves form the basis for almost every mode of popular Western music today. Those

42 Held, *Global Covenant*; Singer, *One World*; Pogge, *Global Justice*.
43 Brecht, *The Three Penny Opera*, 46.

anonymous singers must have said to themselves "We'll sing regardless." The persistence of art even in the most extreme forms of oppressive social domination is perhaps the strongest proof of the essential connection between our humanity and our aesthetic capacity.

Far from exposing a rift in the unity of our organic-social nature, the reality of our life-requirement for institutional commitment to natural and social beauty re-emphasizes its continuity. Nature provides us with vitamin C and the gnarled beauty of the north shore of Lake Superior. Well-organized societies ensure that physically necessary labour is performed and that people can study music. Whether these goals are accomplished in a coherent and comprehensive way obviously depends on the physical availability of resources. If there is sufficient wealth, the problem is not natural scarcity but the institutions and value systems that govern the use of that wealth. All societies have some instituted means of making collectively binding decisions on the use of social wealth. I call these institutions "political" to indicate that their function is to determine how collective life will be governed. The final socio-cultural life-requirement, the most fundamental, but also, for most of human history, the most rarely recognized and never fully satisfied, is the requirement for institutions that enable the effective participation of citizens in the governance of collective life.

Once again the harm criterion of life-requirements supports this conclusion. The general form of harm to which people are liable as socially self-conscious agents is to be reduced to the status of tools or instruments of social reproduction. With few exceptions, ruling value systems have typically justified the division of society into invidious hierarchies, with only a minority class assumed to be responsible enough to make decisions for the whole. For the rest, their lot was to serve and to be content with their servitude. The life-requirement to effectively participate in the governance of collective life entails the conclusion that people treated as mere tools of social reproduction, whenever and wherever this systematic instrumentalization takes place, are harmed. What is harmed is the human interest in the content of the regulations and laws that structure everyone's life in society and the human capacity to effectively participate in the determination of those regulations and principles. I thus claim that there is a shared human life-requirement for social institutions, and especially institutions of political rule, that enable all to participate as socially self-conscious agents in the ongoing process of determining the regulating principles of collective life.

To argue that human life requires democratic participation in major social institutions is not to argue that human life requires existing liberal-democratic capitalist institutions. While they are a partial realization of this human life-requirement, existing liberal-democratic institutions are not sufficient because they have evolved on the basis of separating the institutions of government (political democracy) from the basic means of life-maintenance and the economic institutions that convert these means into social wealth.[44] Liberal democratic institutions are thus not intrinsically life-valuable. Like all institutions that regulate social life, they are good or bad relative to the degree to which they enable the comprehensive satisfaction of life-requirements. Liberal political institutions, because their power to ensure the comprehensive satisfaction of life-requirements is limited by the normal operation of global capitalist market-forces, are not fully democratic. In their present form they cannot be the goal of life-grounded struggles to ensure that this final socio-cultural life-requirement is met.

On the other hand, to point out the democratic limitations of these institutions does not mean that more life-valuable forms of democratic institution cannot develop out of them. As I argue in chapter 7, more deeply and comprehensively life-grounded democratic practices can develop from existing political structures. This extension can be justified by the already legitimate principle that those who are affected by law and public policy ought to participate in its shaping.[45] This democratic principle exists today in tension with competing principles that justify the privileges of superior wealth generated by capitalist market dynamics. As the ongoing struggles in North Africa attest, struggles for democracy are not struggles for a set of political institutions that will leave class structures and gender relations alone. As David McNally observes about the role of Egyptian workers in the revolution, "they are fusing demands for economic justice to those for democracy, and they are among the hundreds of thousands building popular power and self-organization."[46] Mass democratic movements call into question the totality of established certainties and insist on the reconstruction of economic and cultural life as the real content of democratic transformation. In liberal-democratic societies, the legitimacy of these struggles for comprehensive participation is partially evidenced in institutions like unions, school boards, hospital boards, and so on, which at least acknowledge, if not fully realize, the principle that all affected by an institution ought to participate in its governance. If the capacity to participate is real, then the denial of the

---

44 See Marx, "On the Jewish Question," in *Karl Marx and Friedrich Engels: Collected Works*, 3: 146–74; Wood, *Democracy against Capitalism*, 181–237, 264–83; Noonan, *Democratic Society and Human Needs*, 10–58, 111–32.

45 This general criterion of democracy is borrowed from Beetham, *Democracy and Human Rights*, 4.

46 McNally, "Mubarak's Folly: The Rising of Egypt's Workers."

life-requirements instrumentally necessary to its development is a genuine harm to those who are so deprived.

Like the physical-organic requirements of biological life, the socio-cultural requirements of human life are defined by the objectivity of the harms that ensue for those who are systematically deprived of them. The specific forms of harm caused by deprivation of the different socio-cultural life-requirements find their common basis in the instrumentalization that anyone systematically deprived of them suffers. Failures to satisfy human socio-cultural life-requirements undermine our capacities to work in instrumentally and intrinsically valuable ways; to care about, relate to, and interact with other people as unique bearers of life-value; to think analytically and critically and imagine and plan for new possibilities of action and social organization; to perceive and appreciate the beauty of the natural world and social creations; and to work together to ensure that all social institutions are governed by policies and laws that ensure the ongoing, sustainable, and comprehensive satisfaction of the requirements of life and human life. Instead, peoples' lives are reduced to mere tools of the reproduction of the existing society. In contrast, if we assume that these first two classes of human life-requirements are satisfied, any particular life would have secure access to the means of biological life and health, and the institutions of life-valuable work, care and love, education, aesthetic cultivation, and democratic governance. By accessing these life-requirement satisfiers, the conditions for the life, health, and social self-conscious agency of human beings would be secured. However, there is a third class of human life-requirement which must be satisfied if social self-conscious agency is to be freely developed. I now turn to the temporal requirements of a free human life.

2.4 THE TEMPORAL REQUIREMENTS OF FREE HUMAN LIFE

Perhaps the most basic fact about human life from the materialist perspective is its mortality. For life-grounded materialist ethics the fact of mortality does not negate life-value but is itself an essential condition of life's being recognized as valuable. Life-grounded materialist ethics thus concurs with Camus that all people must "situate [themselves] in relation to time ... [everyone] must take their place in it ... [because everyone must] admit that [they] stand at a certain point on a curve that [they] acknowledge having to travel to the end." However, it disagrees with his ethical conclusion that in life's finitude everyone "recognises their own worst enemy."[47] Finitude need not be the enemy of life-value.

---

47 Camus, *The Myth of Sisyphus*, 11.

On the contrary, recognition of the fact that life-time is finite motivates the life-grounded materialist inquiry into the relationship between the extent of life-time, the organization of life-time in existing society, and the free expression and enjoyment of life-valuable capacities. The conclusion of this inquiry is that human freedom depends not only on the satisfaction of organic and socio-cultural life-requirements but also on the satisfaction of a temporal life-requirement. This temporal life-requirement has two sides: sufficient life-time for the comprehensive development of the intrinsic life-value of our capacities, and an experience of life-time as an open matrix of different possibilities of expression of those capacities. I treat each of side in turn.

With respect tong the quantity of life time, it might be thought at the outset that life-grounded materialism would insist on the maximal possible extension of life-time as essential to the good life. Indeed, other materialists have argued that no truly good life is possible so long as people must die. Marcuse, for example, distraught at the death of his wife, believed that "the idea that death is a part of life is false, and we should take much more seriously Horkheimer's notion that it is only with the elimination of death that humanity could be truly happy and free."[48] Thirty years after Marcuse's death, geneticists and allied scientists are actively seeking a "cure" for human death, so far, as obituary pages confirm, without much success.[49]

Perhaps paradoxically, life-grounded materialist ethics does not wish them success in this endeavour. Death is part of life, biologically and ethically. The ethical significance of death is two-fold. First, the temporal limitation of life-time is the most fundamental condition of human activities and experiences having life-value. The sorts of activity whose expression and enjoyment make a finite life valuable would become unbearable monotony if they were the content of an immortal life. As the undying protagonist of Karel Čapek's *The Makropulos Secret* warns the mortals who envy her, the price of immortality is the loss of the capacity to care about and value anything.[50] "You are so near everything! For you, everything has meaning. For you, everything has value because for the few years that you are here, you don't have time to live long enough." But for her, "everything is so pointless, so empty, so meaningless." Čapek's point is clear: anything valuable in finite life (love, social interaction, friendship, etc.)

---

48 Quoted in Habermas, "The Differing Rhythms of Philosophy and Politics: Herbert Marcuse at 100," in *The Postnational Constellation*, 157.

49 See Moody, "Who's Afraid of Life-Extension?"; Overall, *Aging, Death, and Human Longevity*, 124–82.

50 Čapek, *The Makropulos Secret*, in Kussi, 174.

loses its value once its finitude has been stripped away. The hard work of living, satisfying our life-requirements, and developing, expressing, and enjoying our capacities, is meaningful precisely because each experience, if judged from within the mortal frame of our existence, is rare in the sense that each moment is potentially our last.

Life-grounded materialist ethics thus agrees with Epicurus and not Camus. Time and death are not necessarily our enemies. Life-value depends on "a correct knowledge of the fact that death is nothing to us." This understanding "makes the mortality of life a matter of contentment ... by removing the longing for immortality."[51] Epicurus's essential argument is that we cannot properly value life until we have understood its finitude. Once we have accepted that life is necessarily finite, we can concentrate attention on the problem of how the finite life-time we have available may be structured so as to enable the maximum expression and enjoyment of life-valuable capacities within it. Then and only then can we live as well as it is possible for us to live because only then have we properly understood the necessary limitations to which all life is subject.

As I have emphasized in the preceding section, the comprehensive satisfaction of our socio-cultural life-requirements enables the development of our social self-conscious agency. As social, an individual self-consciousness understands the ways in which her individual life is entwined with the lives of other individuals and she cares about the quality of those lives. There is no reason why this care need be limited to the present moment. Someone who cares about others' well-being is capable of caring about the well-being of others who are not yet alive. Extending our care and concern into the future uncovers the second reason why life-grounded materialist ethics believes that finitude is ethically valuable. Were immortality to be achieved, humanity would have to cease producing new human beings since an ever-increasing population, each member of which enjoyed immortality, would soon exhaust the space and resources of the planet (and ultimately the universe, if the population expansion went on long enough). Immortality, then, would over time reduce the number of people able to be born, and thus also overall life-value, because fewer people than otherwise would exist in order to experience and enjoy it. The drive for immortality is, from the life-grounded materialist perspective, an exemplar of life-blind egocentrism rooted in fear and unwillingness to cede one's place to new life-bearers. In a less despondent frame of mind, it is once again Marcuse who best anticipated this argument. "The necessity of death does not refute the possibility of final liberation. Like the other necessities it can be made

---

51 Inwood and Gerson, *Hellenistic Philosophy*, 23.

rational ... men can die if they know that what they love is protected from misery and oblivion. After a fulfilled life, they may take it upon themselves to die – at a moment of their own choosing."[52] For human beings, the problem of a fulfilling life is thus less a problem of endlessly extending the quantity of life-time and more a problem of the structure of life-time within the societies they inhabit and the quality of the experience of those structures.

As I have argued, human life is harmed when the range of expressed activity is narrowed because certain essential life-requirements have not been met. It is also the case, I now contend, that people can be harmed even when their lives are rich in expressed capacities if those capacities are expressed within coercive routines imposed by the demands of the money-value system. Lives can be harmed not simply by gross failures of life-requirement satisfaction that constrict the actual content of life-activity but also by routinized forms of life-capacity expression. A life rich in capacity expression is better than a life impoverished in this dimension. A life in which a rich set of capacities is freely expressed is better than a life whose content is the result of compliance with prescribed routines. The free realization of life-capacities presupposes, in addition to the satisfaction of the first two sets of life-requirements, the experience of time as free.

In order to understand the experience of time as free it is best to consider the paradigmatic structure of unfree time – the time structure typical of capitalist society. In order to understand this structure we must turn again to Marx, who pioneered the materialist understanding of the ethical significance of the structure of time. His focus was on the contradictory relationship between capitalist productivity and the quantity of time outside wage labour that workers enjoyed. On the one hand, Marx argued, mechanized capitalist industry both extended the workday beyond its "natural" limits and produced a new experience of time as a reified power exerting coercive rule over human work-activity.[53] On the other hand, the transformation of the experience of time as a measurable quantity to be divided according to conditions of maximum productivity was the material condition for the ultimate liberation of free time from the routines of capitalist labour. In other words, as capitalism became more productive, less time was required for the production of necessities. As necessary labour time was reduced, potentially surplus time was created.[54] However, under capitalism, this potential surplus time cannot be realized. Instead, it is appropriated by the capitalist as surplus

---

52 Marcuse, *Eros and Civilization*, 236–7.
53 Marx, *Capital*, 1: 252–3.
54 Marx, *Outline of a Critique of Political Economy (Grundrisse)*, 109, 250.

labour and exploited to produce surplus value. The realization of this surplus time as free time depends, for Marx, on successful transformation of capitalist into socialist society. In the socialist future, free time would be made available as a social resource to be appropriated by individuals to do what they have a mind to do, as he famously said in *The German Ideology*.[55]

Marx's path-breaking critique of the structure of time in capitalist industry has been developed in the twentieth century, most notably by Georg Lukacs, Harry Braverman, Moishe Postone, Stanley Aronowitz, and Ursula Huws.[56] They demonstrate, in different ways, that twentieth-century capitalism has intensified rather than resolved the contradiction first disclosed by Marx. Objectively, capitalism has become more productive and thus has created more potentially surplus time. In social reality, workers have not experienced further shortening of the normal average work day beyond eight hours, at the same time as heightened competition between workers and new communication technologies have caused workers to internalize the demands of the workplace in such a manner as to indefinitely extend the feeling of being at work even when one is not physically present in the workplace. While Marx and subsequent Marxist analyses pioneered the understanding of free time as an essential social condition of free activity, it is not sufficient in itself as an explanation of the nature of the experience of time as free.

First, Marx and subsequent Marxists either ignored or failed to fully examine the independent role of the temporal constraints imposed upon women by the unpaid work they perform in the home.[57] More centrally for present purposes, Marx, subsequent Marxists, and liberal theorists who have recently come to understand the importance of free time for a free life treat time as a quantity and its free or unfree nature as a function of how that quantity is divided. The essential difference between free and unfree time for these thinkers is the amount of time outside paid or unpaid labour that one has available. This understanding tends to divorce the experience of free time from the experience of one's activity, and the experience of one's activity from the contribution

55 Marx, *The German Ideology*, 53.

56 Lukacs, *History and Class Consciousness*; Postone, *Time, Labour, and Social Domination*, 202, 212; Braverman, *Labour and Monopoly Capitalism*, 125; Aronowitz et al, "The Post-Work Manifesto," in *Post Work*; Huws, "The Making of a Cybertariat? Virtual Work in the Real World." For a non-Marxist but confirming analysis of how temporal experience is determined in contemporary high-technology industries, see Jeremy Rifkin, *The End of Work*, 181–97.

57 For the temporal impact of gender and family relations on the availability of what Marx calls "empty time" see Goodin et al., *Discretionary Time*, 153–96; 199–239.

it makes to others and one's own future. Free time is treated exclusively as a precondition of free activity and not an experience of time within activity, with the result that free time appears to be incompatible with any constraint on how individuals use that time. Liberals like Sen can thus concur with Marx's claim and conclude that freedom is engaging in any form of activity that one has "reasons to value," with no explication of the consequences of those activities on others or on one's own future. [58]

As will become clear, simply having a mind or a reason to value something is not identical to a good reason to use free time in pursuit of that goal. As socially self-conscious mortal beings, our sense of our own individual freedom must involve an understanding of "goals which embrace, protect, and unite life on earth," as Marcuse argued.[59] Otherwise, we may unwittingly contribute to patterns of social behaviour that shorten life-time, for ourselves or for others. Hence, life-valuable uses of free time must engage individuals in projects that contribute "in some active way to the well-being of the interrelated whole to which they belong to sustain their own functioning capacities and those of the larger bodies of which they are living members."[60] Free time thus cannot be simply time outside paid or unpaid work in which the individual is able to do whatever he or she feels like doing.

Of course, the life-grounded materialist interpretation agrees that free time, in one dimension, is time outside paid and unpaid work and as such a precondition for free choice of activity. It disagrees that free time as precondition of free choice of activity is the entire reality of the experience of time as free. Thus, for life-grounded materialism the problem of free time cannot be reduced to the problem of liberating surplus time from paid and unpaid labour. No one can experience time as free who must, as a matter of survival, work all one's waking life within prescribed routines. Creating the conditions in which work is freely chosen and not imposed is thus an essential condition of experiencing time as free. Since human freedom is a form of activity, and all activity takes place in time, the full experience of time as free depends not only on the quantity of time available for our own appropriation but on how we experience the time in which we act. The full experience of time as free is not given in the experience of not having to do one thing rather than another but of being able to do in the present what we decide is most life-valuable, unconstrained by temporal pressures generated by the ruling value system over our activity.

58 Sen, *Inequality Reexamined*, 26–34, 36–44, 56–7.
59 Marcuse, *An Essay on Liberation*, 46.
60 McMurtry. *The Cancer Stage of Capitalism*, 109.

Approached from the perspective of human life in general, time is the universal matrix of experience and activity. As an existential frame of experience and activity, time does not determine what anyone does or ought to do. The finite frame imposed on any particular life-time need not undermine our enjoyment; as I have argued, it emphasizes the rarity and thus potential life-value of each moment, motivating us to "use our time wisely." This aphorism assumes that there is time for us to use. Let us assume that there is. What then ought we to do with the time that we have at our disposal? Nothing? In present conditions, time outside work routines can sometimes be experienced as a burden and, as Adorno remarks, a cause of profound boredom.[61] Let us assume that Adorno is correct and that boredom is a function of alienated labour. Let us assume that labour is no longer alienated but freely chosen. What would the experience of time be like in this society? In such an experience, I believe, lies the answer to our question about the nature of time as free.

Abstracted from the social determination of time under capitalism, and conceived as a universal condition of human action and experience, time is an *open* matrix of possibilities for present action. By "open" I mean that time as free does not determine how we arrange our activity within it. Instead, people can, through imaginative reflection and projection, distinguish themselves from the social forces acting on them and decide as socially self-conscious agents what they will do. However, just because people can decide what to do with their time when they experience time as free, it does not follow, for a socially self-conscious agent aware of her own mortality, that any use of time she decides is good, is good. Free time as an open matrix of possibilities for present action is not identical to time available to waste by doing nothing of life-value. Life-valuable activity does not mean physical activity; contemplating, listening, meditating alone, in silence are all life-valuable modes of exercising our intellectual and sentient capacities. As free, time is an open matrix within which we decide which forms of action would be most valuable for us to pursue in the present moment. For mortal beings, the most life-valuable way of using one's present time is to act in ways whose intrinsic present value at the same time opens up possibilities for even richer activity in the future. If we learn something new by reading a book, we are able to read more books and deepen our knowledge. If we learn to play a sport, we can improve each time we play it. If we learn to listen, we become able to distinguish bird songs we had not noticed before, and then to hear more and more subtleties as our ear becomes attuned. All these are uses of time, but free and life-valuable uses, because it is our

61 Adorno, *Minima Moralia*, 175.

decisions and efforts that are determinative, and the consequences of those decisions are the extension and refinement of our capacities for experience, thought, and constructive action. Life-time thus becomes more intensely full as it approaches its necessary end point.

By contrast, time under capitalism is experienced as a *closed* matrix of routine. By "closed" I mean not only *determinate* as regards content but the *determining* power over life-activity. The core temporal principle of the capitalist value system is nicely expressed in the common aphorism that "time is money." The equation implies that time is a particularly scarce commodity which must be "spent" wisely. But what is a wise expenditure of time? We should spend time as we ought to spend our money, in "investments" that pay maximum returns in the future. Since we cannot be repaid with time, the sign of a wise temporal investment is more money. Note how the wise use of finite life-time is reduced on this understanding to service to the ruling value system. If we use our life-time to serve the growth of the money-value system, it follows, once again, that we are being used as tools of the growth of this system, and thus not acting freely as socially self-conscious agents. That is not to say that the instrumental relationship between past and future is a consequence of individual failures to appreciate the present moment. Instead, the causes are found in the structure of social power imposed on people by the ruling value-system. What damages our freedom is the structure that demands that we use our life-time so as to maximize the production of money-value. Such a use of life-time entails that the present moment is perpetually sacrificed to a future monetary reward. Present moments in a finite life eventually run out. The money-value system benefits by this sacrifice since more money is put into circulation. But the moment of conscious enjoyment of the present in which one acts (the present in which one *lives,* since all life is lived in the present moment) never arrives.

People speak of education as "an investment in their future," emotional effort put into relationships as "investments in the relationships;" parents speak of making "investments in their children's future," and so on. What is problematic with this understanding for life-grounded materialist ethics is that the moment of intrinsic life-value is absent. The maturation of the investment is always deferred. If all activities, experiences, and relationships are understood as investments in the future, it follows that nothing in the present is of any intrinsic value. If education is an investment, if our relationships are investments, if our life-projects are investments, it follows that they are not life-valuable expressions of who we are and what we are able to contribute to social well-being in the present; they are instrumental actions undertaken in order to return maximum money-value at some unspecified point in a future that never arrives.

For example, the latest fad for parents who can afford it is to hire tutors for their pre-school-age children.[62] Their aim, of course, is to give the children an "edge" in the subsequent competitive battles that will shape their lives. Viewed from the perspective of time as a human life-requirement, what these parents are doing is radically reducing the content of their children's present experiential field. This claim might seem simply wrong, given the apparent wealth of content to which such children are exposed: ballet lessons, swimming lessons, piano lessons, trips to museums, summer camps, and so forth. Are these not the very substance of what I have referred to as socio-cultural life requirements? In one sense they are. However, one must keep in mind the instrumental relationship between life-requirement satisfaction and life-capacity enablement. The goal of these various activities is not to enable the child to patiently and freely explore the life-value of the various courses he attends. Instead, the point of the different activities reduces to the ruling value of future monetary success. Rather than enjoy any of these activities as unique, intrinsic life-values, the child experiences them all as identical instruments of his future monetary well-being. The child is being taught that nothing matters save besting one's fellows, that nothing is interesting or worth doing in its own right, that the only valuable "expenditure" of time is one which serves the ruling money-value system. Time itself is not experienced as an open matrix of possibilities for different life-valuable projects but a series of discrete "modules" in which activity must conform to external standards of appropriateness, usefulness, and economic prudence.[63]

To be deprived of the experience of time as free is, for a mortal being, to be deprived of the final social condition of possibility for free life-activity. If time is experienced as nothing but a series of routines in which present activity is a tool for the sake of higher monetary rewards in the future, then the range of possible life-valuable activities is illegitimately reduced to those activities which serve money-value growth. Thus, the deprivation of the experience of time as free is a third form of harm to which all human beings are in principle liable. Once again we can point to a history of struggle as support for the claim that free time is an objective human life-requirement. The working class has for centuries fought to shorten the working day and, by shortening the working day, to create the material conditions for the experience of free time. As these struggles prove, the satisfaction of the life-requirement of free time is, like the

62 Kesterton, "Kindercramming."
63 For more on the "modularisation" of life-time see Van der Poel, "Leisure and the Modularisation of Daily Life."

satisfaction of the preceding two classes of human life-requirement, a social project and not a goal that can be realized simply through ego-adjustment to given circumstances.

To argue that there are objective requirements of life, human life, and free human life is to say that there are general natural, social, and temporal conditions without which the development of human life-capacities, whatever their particular content might be, is impossible. To argue that the primary ethical goal of human social organization is the growth of life-value is *not* to argue that any one culturally specific tradition has discovered the unique secret of how to fulfill this goal. Life-grounded materialist ethics seeks out the universal conditions for the growth of life-valuable forms of cultural and individual expression without chauvinistic attachment to any one form as ultimate.

The satisfaction of these three classes of life-requirement defines the universal enabling conditions for anyone anywhere being able to live, live as a human being, and live freely as a human being. Their mode of satisfaction can differ from culture to culture and person to person, relative to the sorts of resources available, the forms of institutionalization through which they are produced and distributed, and, where resources permit, individual choice between particular life-requirement satisfiers. There is necessary variety within the universality of our shared life-requirements, in terms of the actual life-requirement satisfiers available for people to appropriate, the institutions that mediate this appropriation, and the symbolic constructions through which life-requirement satisfaction and the capacities it enables are made meaningful. What does not vary – and this point is crucial – is the objective reality of the harm to people's lives, humanity, and freedom that ensues from systemic failures of life-requirement satisfaction. Starvation is starvation, dehydration is dehydration, political exclusion is political exclusion, drudgery is drudgery, routinization is routinization, instrumentalization is instrumentalization whatever its different contents and wherever and whenever it occurs. Hence the first significant ethical conclusion of the argument: there is a shared life-interest in the comprehensive satisfaction of these three classes of human life-requirement. People discover this shared life-interest not as a consequence of accommodating their thought to some alien and tendentious philosophical-political construction but by understanding themselves in relation to the life-ground of value. Nature and society are the permanent structures of life-support and development without which human beings cannot live, live as humans, or live freely. As soon as one thinks of nature and society as life-support and development systems (as soon as thought becomes life-grounded), it becomes apparent to anyone, whatever culture they might inhabit, whether nature and society are fulfilling that function.

In part two, the critical dimension of life-grounded materialist ethics is explicated. In its critical dimension life-grounded materialist ethics aims to expose the concrete ways in which life-requirement deprivation is caused by a systematic confusion between the reproductive requirements of a given social structure and its corresponding ruling value system and the life-ground of value. I treat this relationship as a contradiction between the reproductive requirements of the given society and its ruling value system and the life-requirements and life-values of its members. In the present historical context there is a pervasive contradiction between the full satisfaction of human life-requirements and the system-requirements of global capitalism. After explaining the general relationship between system-requirements and ruling value systems and life-requirements and life-value, the argument proceeds to examine the concrete manifestations of their contradiction, historically and today. I examine both the global structure of the contradiction (between wealthy Western societies and the rest of the world) and its manifestations within the advanced capitalist countries.

PART TWO

Life-Grounded Materialist Ethical Criticism

3

The Emergence of System-Requirements

CHAPTER TWO CONCLUDED that the requirements of system reproduction (system-requirements henceforth) and the ruling value system can be in contradiction with people's life-requirements and life-value. If that is the case, it might be objected at the outset that such a contradiction would destroy the society.[1] If people depend on their societies to satisfy their life-requirements, but the ruling value system prioritizes the satisfaction of system-requirements which are not life-valuable, then it would seem that such a society could not survive even two generations. The conclusion, however, is contrary to all historical evidence: a society that survived for only two generations would arguably not even be a society, and history knows no such catastrophes. Thus, it appears that the criticism to be developed in this chapter is, if anything, hyperbole and that no such contradiction between system-requirements and the ruling value system and life-requirements and life-values ever obtains in practice. If the objection is sound, it would further follow that whatever social problems may be observed to exist today, their solution would not require a fundamental transformation of existing capitalist system-requirements and values. This objection cuts to the heart of the practical goals of life-grounded materialist ethics. My argument in this chapter is framed with it in mind. The goal is to first provide a more precise explanation of the terms "system-requirement" and "ruling value system." This explanation is a presupposition of a clear explanation, in turn, of the meaning of the claim that existing capitalist society is contradictory when judged from

---

1 Absolute contradictions between ruling value systems and life-values are possible. (We in the capitalist world may be in such a situation.) Although he does not use the terms system-values and life-values, Jared Diamond explores instances of absolute contradiction between them and the civilizational collapse that ensues. See Diamond, *Collapse: How Societies Choose to Succeed or Fail.*

the life-grounded materialist perspective. A modified account of Marx's understanding of social development in *The German Ideology* will help to explain how system-requirements and ruling value systems emerge and how they can enter into contradiction with life-requirements and life-values.

3.1 SYSTEM-REQUIREMENTS, RULING VALUE SYSTEMS, AND THE COMMON LIFE-INTEREST

The term "system-requirements" refers to the institutional conditions a given social form must satisfy if it is to reproduce itself from generation to generation. Just as a human being must avoid starvation and other gross failures of life-requirement satisfaction, so too a given society must maintain an economic system that generates sufficient wealth for given social purposes, ensure political stability, avoid rebellions, and so forth. System-requirements are anchored in what Rawls calls "major social institutions." "Major social institutions" are those institutions in which the real life-horizons of the citizens of a given society are determined because individuals cannot avoid the effects these institutions have on their lives insofar as they are members of that society.[2] Major social institutions map the fundamental natural and social conditions for the maintenance and development of human life. Hence there are major social institutions concerned with the production and distribution of basic organic life-requirement satisfiers (economic institutions construed broadly to include forms of property, the division of labour, and the forces that emerge from and subsequently drive forward human productive activity). There are major social institutions that produce the legal principles required to fix and distribute social roles and establish the framework of allowable action required by social stability (political and legal institutions, again construed broadly to include all levels of government, the judiciary, and policy-generating institutions). There are, finally, cultural institutions (schools, the media, arts, sports organizations, and so on) through which the symbolic content of given forms of life is generated, disseminated, and normalized (those institutions through which what Habermas calls the "life-world" is produced).[3] The temporal requirements of free human life are not the object of any particular major social institution but rather depend on the overall pattern of human life-activity as structured by the major economic, political, and cultural institutions working together, under the steering role of the ruling value system.

2 Rawls, *A Theory of Justice*, 47–8.
3 Habermas, *Theory of Communicative Action*, 2: 138.

From the perspective of these institutions, their primary goal is to ensure the reproduction of their society from generation to generation with no major upheavals. From the perspective of life-grounded materialist ethics, the goal of major social institutions is to ensure the comprehensive satisfaction of life-requirements for the sake of the comprehensive and free development of life-capacities. Where systemic failures of life-requirement satisfaction are caused by the reproductive requirements of major social institutions, one finds a contradiction between system-requirements and life-requirements. All major social institutions have a fundamental life-supportive function as their underlying justifying ground. However, in their actual operation, this life-supportive function may be contradicted to a greater or lesser extent by the system-requirement to *not* satisfy, or not satisfy fully, one or more classes of human life-requirements for one or more groups of people in that society. As an example of the first form of the contradiction, expansionist societies may generate a system-requirement to eliminate indigenous populations in zones targeted for colonization. As examples of the second form, the labour of the majority of a society's citizens may be exploited for the sake of maximizing the monetary wealth of a minority and that society's political institutions used to pass laws that normalize and legitimate that exploitation. CAPITALISM

Human history has been dominated by system-requirements which prioritize the particular interests of ruling groups in consuming far beyond what their lives require at the expense of subordinate groups who, as a consequence, fail to comprehensively satisfy their life-requirements. These subordinate groups suffer failures of life-requirement satisfaction which impede the free realization and enjoyment of their capacities, which means that they live worse lives than their rulers. If people were simply functions of existing institutions without critical capacities, they could be bred to comply with the social roles prepared for them, as Plato proposed in *The Republic*.[4] However, people can perceive and think about and act against observable forms of deprivation, and *when they believe that these forms of deprivation are undeserved and corrigible*, they do take action. Social stability, the reproduction of society from generation to generation, thus also requires a ruling value system. By ruling value system I mean, following McMurtry, a systematic connection of "goods that are affirmed and bads that are repudiated as an integrated way of thinking and acting in the world."[5] The content will vary from society to society but will always express the underlying theme that those who have more and rule deserve to have more and rule, and those who have less and

4 Plato, *Republic*, Bk 3, 659.
5 McMurtry, *Unequal Freedoms*, 7.

serve deserve to have less and serve. The overall social good in every case is identified with the appropriateness of the place each group occupies, whether this appropriateness is decided by reference to natural hierarchies (as in Aristotle's justification of slavery) or differential effort and luck, as in the "free market" value system.[6] The underlying assumption of any ruling value system whose function is to justify systemic failures to comprehensively satisfy the life-requirements of subordinate groups is that it is *good* that such groups are unable to satisfy the life-requirements that they are unable to satisfy, either because they deserve the deprivation they receive or because they lack the capacity which the life-requirement enables or because it is necessary for the overall dynamism of the society. Hence the death of internal enemies in a civil war is called "good" because the enemy is demonized as inhuman. For centuries in Europe it was thought good that women were not educated because they were assumed to lack higher cognitive capacities. In periods of economic crisis, attacks on workers' benefits and wages are deemed "good" for the sake of returning firms to profitability. A ruling value system that is attempting to justify structural deprivations of life-requirements thus always legitimates radically different levels of life-requirement satisfaction for different groups. This legitimating function is based on the assumption that people can be morally ranked as more or less important.

When I say that the system-requirements and ruling value systems can enter into contradiction with life-requirements and life-values, I am not claiming that this contradiction must be life-catastrophic in all cases (although it can be, as I will explain in chapter 4. The contradiction does not usually affect the short- to medium-term ability of the society to reproduce itself. It affects, rather, the ability of subaltern groups to access the resources and institutions and relationships which are their due as human beings because the ruling value system determines that in some essential respect they are not human beings. Thus the contradiction is essentially ethical: a universal conception of the good justifies radically different life-conditions for *human* beings, thus denying in practice the common life-interest that ties all human beings together in the life-ground of value. This contradiction is therefore not always, as the initial objection worried, a structural contradiction affecting a society's ability to reproduce itself.

I have now explained why a contradiction between system requirements and life-requirements need not in every case cause the more or less immediate destruction of a society in which it exists. The critic may still rightly wonder how and why such contradictions can emerge. After

6 Aristotle, *Politics*, Bk 1, 1132–33.

all, if it is true, as I have said, that major social institutions map and serve, in some sense, the major requirements of life and human life, it seems a mystery that they could ever diverge from this function so as to generate ruling value systems that contradict the shared material conditions of everyone's leading a humanly good life. To an explanation of that emergence I now turn, drawing on, but also modifying, Marx's examination of this problem.

3.2 THE HISTORICAL EMERGENCE OF THE CONTRADICTION

While Marx is not explicitly concerned with the *ethical* critique of capitalism, his work can help to explain how system-requirements and ruling value systems emerge and come to appear as ultimate values. The analysis must begin with his conception of labour as the mediation between the natural field of life-support and the social field of life-development.

Read from the life-grounded perspective, labour is the primary form of interaction between human beings and the natural world. For Marx this relationship is expressed through the idea of metabolism. As John Bellamy Foster explains, "the concept of metabolism, with its attendant notions of material exchanges and regulatory action, allowed [Marx] to express the human relation to nature as one that encompassed both 'nature imposed conditions' and the capacity of human beings to affect this process."[7] Without constant interchange between human beings and nature, human life cannot persist. Thus every human society faces the same basic problem of how to produce life-goods in amounts sufficient for basic social reproduction. "The first premise of all human history is, of course, the existence of living human individuals. Thus the first fact to be established is the physical organization of these individuals and their consequent relation to the rest of nature."[8] Whatever else a society does, and no matter how exploitative its labour relations are, it must regularly produce and distribute sufficient quantities of basic life-requirement satisfiers if it is to persist from generation to generation.

In producing the means of subsistence, human labour at the same time produces new *social* conditions of life. In the words of McNally, social labour produces "new levels of determination" within the ready-to-hand natural world.[9] Improvements in productive techniques that define the new social conditions of life solve one problem – the regular production of sufficient life-resources to maintain life – at the same time

7 Foster, *Marx's Ecology*, 158.
8 Marx, *The German Ideology*, 37.
9 McNally, *Bodies of Meaning*, 85.

as they create novel problems that Marx associates with the production of new needs. "The satisfaction of the first [organic] need, the action of satisfying and the instrument of satisfaction which has been acquired, leads to the creation of new needs."[10] These new needs, viewed from the perspective of individuals, are the needs that I called in chapter 2 "instrumental" to particular projects. Viewed from the perspective of the social system as a whole, they are the "system-requirements" that I am examining here. For example, a newly emergent agricultural society will produce new needs for the implements required by agriculture. Society must now solve two problems. The first is the basic problem of producing enough food for the survival of its members. The second is to produce the implements its agricultural survival system requires.

As the example makes clear, the instrumental system-requirements are not necessarily alienated from the life-ground of value. They become alienated from the life-ground of value once social development has passed the point where economic surpluses are regularly generated. Once surpluses are regularly produced, class differentiation emerges, and class differentiation produces a third problem for society to solve – how to ensure that the ruling class is able to continue to appropriate the surplus product. Classes exist, according to Marx, because one group seizes control of the means of life-good production. As Joel Kovel argues, the first common life-good seized is the capability of women to reproduce life itself and maintain it through their care-giving labour as mothers to young infants. As Kovel argues, "this act was a profound mutation in human being ... First, the possibilities of exploiting another's labour are introduced, always in the direction of male over female. Second, the potentials for enduring social divisions are grounded in this, again male over female; these are to extend to the hunter band, the warrior band, and to the ruling class."[11] Once this control over the life-giving labour of women has been extended to the natural basis of life-support as a whole, the ruling class comes to control the material conditions on which all depend for their survival. The material basis of their social power thus enables them to appropriate the surplus product for themselves because the labouring class is now doubly dependent: on nature directly, and on the ruling class which controls access to nature indirectly. By ensuring compliance with its appropriation of the surplus product for itself, the ruling class is able to accumulate wealth at the expense of those whose labour they exploit and whose life-conditions they control. In this way, a system-interest in ensuring the reproduction of the dominant class

10 Marx, *The German Ideology*, 48.
11 Kovel, *The Enemy of Nature*, 127.

relations develops that is independent of both the life-supportive function of labour and social organization generally.

The structure of this system-interest is expressed through the social division of labour. "The division of labour ... simultaneously implies the *distribution*, indeed the *unequal* distribution, both quantitative and qualitative, of labour and its products, hence property."[12] Once inequality in the distribution of life-goods emerges, social reproduction is no longer simply a matter of producing the means of life and whatever instrumental conditions the production of the means of life requires. It must now also contend with the problem of justifying quantitative and qualitative inequalities in the distribution of life-requirement satisfiers and the expression and enjoyment of life-capacities. Once such basic social differences of access to life-goods exist between groups differently situated within the social division of labour, the ethical contradiction between the satisfaction of system-requirements and the satisfaction of life-requirements, the good according to the ruling value system and the good that follows from our common life-interest, becomes possible. Marx grasps this contradiction, at least in embryonic form. "The division of labour also implies the contradiction between the interest of the separate individuals or the individual family and the common interest of all individuals who have intercourse with one another. And, indeed, this common interest does not exist merely in the imagination, as the 'general interest' but first of all in reality, as the mutual interdependence of the individuals among whom the labour is divided."[13] Unpacked from the life-grounded materialist perspective, what Marx calls the general interest is the common life-interest of each and all in the comprehensive satisfaction of their life-requirements. The particular interest, by contrast, is now bifurcated along class lines into opposed instrumental requirements. Workers face the instrumental requirement to find remunerative work that will enable them to purchase more basic life-necessities. The ruling class, in contrast, is driven by the instrumental requirement to accumulate even more wealth through the more efficient exploitation of nature and workers' labour. Satisfying this interest depends on their ability to maintain the given structure of rule. In order to maintain the given structure of rule they must produce a convincing, universalized account of good human lives that identifies the good with those system-requirements that generate the inequality.

For Marx, the function of ideology is to convincingly identify the particular good of the ruling class with the universal good of all. With the

12 Marx, *The German Ideology*, 51–2.
13 Ibid., 52.

emergence of classes comes the emergence of the division of labour between those who produce and those who live on the surplus of what is produced. With the division of labour between producers and appropriators of the product of labour comes its further division into mental and manual labour, and thus also the differentiation of society into institutions in which mental labour proper can develop: parliaments, courts, universities, and so forth. The primary function of mental labourers is the production of justifications of the superiority of the given system-requirements. "The ruling ideas are nothing more than the ideal expression of the dominant material relations, the dominant material relations grasped as ideas; hence of the relations that make the one class the ruling one, therefore, the ideas of its dominance. The individuals composing the ruling class possess among other things consciousness, and therefore think. Insofar, therefore, as they rule as a class and determine the extent and compass of an historical epoch, it is self-evident that they do this in its whole range, hence among other things rule as thinkers ... and regulate the production and distribution of the ideas of their age; thus their ideas are the ruling ideas of every epoch."[14] In life-value terms, ideology functions by presenting the dominant system-values as life-values and the particular system-requirements as life-requirements.

The life-grounded materialist interpretation thus derives from, but is not fully explicated by, Marx's class-specific conception of ideology. Marx accounts for the success of ideology in terms of a process of reification by which a particular structure of social organization produced by human beings interacting in definite contexts comes to appear as "natural," i.e., fixed and given independently of human interaction. His critique of the "bourgeois" understanding of the "laws" of capitalist society provides a particularly clear example of this strategy. The problem with "bourgeois" political economy, he argues, is essentially that it treats a historically contingent set of tendencies as eternal natural laws: "Political economy starts with the fact of private property; it does not explain it to us. It expresses in general, abstract formulas the *material* process through which private property actually passes, and these formulas it then takes for laws. It does not *comprehend* these laws, i.e., it does not demonstrate how they arise from the very nature of private property."[15] Only by abstracting from the historical process by which particular social formations come to be can their particular system-requirements be presented as fixed laws to which all "normal" and "good" human behaviour must conform.

14 Ibid., 67.
15 Marx, "Economic and Philosophical Manuscripts of 1844," 270–1.

Life-grounded materialism deepens this analysis beneath the structure of class rule to focus on the more basic conflation of system-values and life-values. Because people are born into a society whose history and dynamics they do not understand, they find themselves dependent on its structures and processes for their survival and are educated so as to conform to its requirements. They normally internalize the dominant system-requirements and ruling value system as their own life-requirements and life-values. The process of reification through which "relationships between men" take on the appearance of a "relationship between things" is thus a complex process. Its success depends equally on the real dependence of people on the social mediations through which life-requirements are produced and distributed *and* the control of the institutions of intellectual production by the class whose particular interests are served by the given form of social organization.[16] The processes of socialization, enculturation, and education are neither forms of individual "brainwashing" nor a mere invention of tendentious Marxist critique. Every American school child begins the day by reciting the Pledge of Allegiance and Canadians begin by singing the national anthem. However, people are not simply programmed to accept these ideas. Their acceptance is conditioned by their real dependence on their society. For the most part, people have no option but to live where they are born, and most lack independent means of survival outside the forms of remunerative work their societies make available. Thus it appears to people that life outside of or in fundamentally different social institutions is impossible. While it is true that human life in general requires social organization, it does not follow that it requires forms of social organization determined by the contradictions between system-requirements and values on one side and life-requirements and life-values on the other. However, from within the hold of given ideologies, even concrete projects to resolve this contradiction in favour of the more comprehensive satisfaction of life-requirements can appear destructive. Think, for example, of the way in which environmental campaigns for cleaner energy can be derailed by government and business warnings that the economy will be destroyed if environmental activists succeed.

The contradiction at work here is thus deeper and more universal than that between ruling-class and working-class interests. Marx and the orthodox Marxist tradition have argued that the contradiction is between two contradictory forms of class interest, and that it would be resolved when the objective contradiction between the forces and relations of production created the social conditions for the maturation of the

16 Marx, *Capital,* 1: 77.

class consciousness of workers.[17] Once working-class consciousness has matured, the immediate contradiction between the forces and relations of production would be resolved and a total clarifying insight into all fundamental human problems would have thereby been achieved. This deeper point is pressed by Lukacs, who argues that only from the standpoint of the proletariat is it possible "to demonstrate that [social reality] is everywhere the product of man and of the development of society."[18] The life-grounded materialist standpoint is not identical to the standpoint of the proletariat. Rather, it is the standpoint in which the standpoint of the proletariat must be grounded if it is to be a force that successfully resolves the contradiction in favour of life-values. Historical developments themselves have demonstrated time and again that there is no necessary convergence between working-class consciousness and life-grounded values. Marcuse's analysis of one-dimensionality offers a sound starting point to the life-grounded understanding of this problem.

Marcuse's specific goal in formulating the thesis of one-dimensionality was to explain why the objective contradictions of capitalism had failed to produce the subjective conditions needed for revolution. Marcuse's answer was that economic growth improved wages, enabled higher levels of consumer spending, and integrated the working class by making them feel as if they had a stake in the ongoing health of the system. A social environment was created (especially in the context of the Cold War) in which the socially critical and politically explosive potential of universal concepts like freedom and equality could be contained. Freedom and equality no longer retained the reference to unrealized potential for human development and expanded ranges of activity that is essential in their function as concepts of social criticism.[19] Instead, their referent was restricted to existing institutions and this restriction supported by appeal to the reality of money-value growth and the comparative authoritarianism of the so-called "socialist" alternative in the Soviet Union.

While a historically specific theory, the conceptual structure of one-dimensionality has more general applicability. In a one-dimensional universe, "public discourse, speech moves in synonyms and tautologies, it never moves toward the qualitative difference. The analytic structure insulates the governing noun [the social value at issue] from those of its contents which would invalidate or at least disturb the accepted use of the noun in statements of policy and public opinion. The ritualized concept

---

17 Marx, *A Contribution to the Critique of Political Economy*, 20–1.

18 Lukacs, History and Class Consciousness, 159.

19 On the relationship between ethical and political universals, unrealized potential, and social criticism, see Marcuse, "The Concept of Essence."

is made immune against contradiction."[20] The tautological organization of conceptual justifications of given structures of rule describes not only the universe of public discourse in the America of 1964 but every universe of public discourse where system-requirements and system-values are at odds with life-requirements and life-values. The contradiction is "solved" by the ruling value system recoding life-requirements as system-requirements and system-values as universal life-values. People thus believe themselves to be acting in the common life-interest by complying with the reproductive demands of the system. Broadening Marcuse's argument, life-grounded materialist ethics claims that one-dimensional thought blocks socially self-conscious understanding of the real structure of life-requirements that underlies the ruling system-requirements and value system. The suppressed contradiction, therefore, is not between the forces and relations of production or between the immediate interests and true interests of the working class but between the prevailing system-requirements and values and life-requirements and values.

For life-grounded materialist ethics, the class-origin of ruling value systems is analogous to the natural history of human organic evolution. The development of classes explains how ruling system-values arise but, on its own, does not provide a complete account of their ethical structure, just as natural history explains how human organic capacities evolved but does not tell us what we ought to do with them. Just because one understands the fact that ruling value systems originate in the privatization of universally required means of life, it does not follow that one thereby understands the real ethical contradiction they can generate. Since these value systems structure society as a whole, they can function only if the subordinate classes and groups also see in them their own universal good. A really effective ruling value system will produce accounts of the good life that are universal, in the system-relative sense of embracing all legitimate forms of life in the given society. The problem of everyone's acting as these ruling value systems prescribe is thus not simply that the subordinate class acts so as to unwittingly advance the interests of the ruling class but rather that *everyone* acts in such a way as to reproduce and expand a set of system-requirements and values which contradicts everyone's common life-interests. In this way, socially pervasive forms of life-blind activity are able to reproduce themselves because all classes have come to accept the prescriptions of the value system as a "necessity to which there is no alternative" and to which "judgement [adjusts itself] in terms of its given principles of prescriptive organization."[21]

---

20 Marcuse, *One-Dimensional Man*, 88.
21 McMurtry, *The Cancer Stage of Capitalism*, 23.

An effective ruling value system will thus always involve an account of good lives that generate patterns of social activity that *all* classes and groups *feel* to be life-affirming. This effectiveness is best expressed in capitalist society, which is the only society wealthy enough to make luxury consumption a live option for working people. No plantation slave could aspire to be an owner of slaves, but many workers aspire to be the boss because in a capitalist society the ultimate value is maximizing monetary rewards for self, and most working people seek this goal as their own every bit as much as members of the ruling class. For example, if there are high-paying jobs in the forest industry, and the forest industry depends on clear-cutting forests, workers in that industry will have a real system-interest in maintaining their jobs where equally high-paying alternatives are lacking, even though the immediate and long-term consequences of that form of production are, overall, life-destructive of complex forest ecosystems with which the health of human society is ultimately entwined. Given the structure of dependence tying workers to the instrumental requirement of finding paid employment, the immediate class interests of workers coincide with the class interests of the owners of the logging firms. Both are mobilized to act so as to maximize monetary returns by destroying the forest ecosystem and thus both act contrary to the implications of life-grounded materialist ethics.

An orthodox Marxist will respond that the worker's consciousness is false and that what these workers need to grasp is their deeper historical mission to join in solidarity with all workers to build a socialist society. However, if socialism is understood simply as the universalization of the particular class interests of workers, with no deeper grounding in terms of socialism's better satisfying the common life-interests, socialism could simply replicate the essential contradiction between the satisfaction of system-requirements and values and life-requirements and values. As Michael Lebowitz has noted, the entire history of twentieth-century socialism has been riven by a contradiction between this "productivist" understanding of socialism, which focused on the narrow interest of workers in developing the productive forces, and an alternative vision with the universal life-interests of "real human development" at its ethical centre.[22] There is no guarantee that, if the good of the opposed system-value is understood simply in terms of narrow working-class interest, that system will solve the basic ethical contradiction under examination. Take for example Trotsky's account of revolution: "revolution is first and foremost a question of power – not of the state form ... but of the social

22 Lebowitz, *The Socialist Alternative*, 21.

content of government."[23] Trotsky implies that as long as the revolution-ary forces install a government with the correct "social content," all problems of social reorganization will be solved. Clearly, however, this functional conception of revolution fails to address the main ethical question: will the new society be better in terms of better enabling *everyone* to satisfy their real life-requirements for the sake of the more coherently inclusive and environmentally sustainable expression and enjoyment of life-capacities? If it is to be better, it must in a real sense be better for everyone who lives under this society. Yet, by questioning the express decisions of people who, in the current society, adhere to the given value system as legitimate, life-grounded materialist ethics seems to threaten the social basis for autonomous choice. If that is the case, then it would seem to lead to paternalistic and authoritarian institutions, which cannot be defended as "better" for everyone who lives under them. The chapter will conclude by considering a form of this objection.

3.3 THE PLACE OF HUMAN AGENCY IN THE REPRODUCTION OF CONTRADICTORY SOCIETIES

The analysis in 3.1 acknowledges that in all actual societies life-require-ments and life-values are re-coded as system-requirements and ruling value systems and this recoding shapes people's normal self-understanding as well as law and public policy. It might be objected that life-grounded materialist ethics thus treats human beings as automatons, even though, in its explanation of the function of ruling value systems, it invoked the power of human agency. Thus, to conclude this analysis of the contradic-tion between system-requirements and values and life-requirements and values, I will examine and respond to this sort of objection.

The argument developed thus far opens itself to this objection be-cause it maintains that people make decisions based on a conflation of system-values and life-values which, though affirmed by their own deci-sions, are, according to life-grounded materialism, contrary to their real life-interests. In this way, people can act on what they take to be their real life-interest and yet contribute to patterns of social activity that under-mine the satisfaction of life-requirements without anyone noticing the problem. McMurtry describes the problem as it pertains to contempo-rary capitalist society: "This structure of human life's reproduction and growth is, absurdly, assumed as 'allocation of society's resources for effi-cient production' ... yet the fatal disorder of assuming that only what

---

23 Trotsky, "Results and Prospects," in The Permanent Revolution and Results and Prospects, 122.

serves money sequences is of value, does not occur" to those who make the assumption.[24] Where system-requirements are not determined by the overriding goal of comprehensive life-requirement satisfaction, even the potential for contradiction cannot be understood from within the system's standards of self-evaluation. This seems tantamount to arguing that people do not understand what they are really doing, and thus that life-grounded materialist ethics expresses a superior form of knowledge to which people must accommodate themselves, *regardless of what they explicitly affirm as their life-interest.* It thus appears that life-grounded materialist ethics, far from uncovering the shared conditions for the free development, expression, and enjoyment of human capacities of people living as full human agents, contradicts those conditions insofar as it seems to reject freedom of choice and decisions as necessary goods.

However, while it is the case that life-grounded materialism does not accept the legitimacy of all individual choices just because they are choices, it does so for the sake of better securing the social conditions of individuality and free self-development. The point of disclosing the contradiction between system-requirements and the ruling value system, on the one hand, and life-requirements and life-value, on the other, is to disclose the life-destructive patterns of social action generated by *unthinking* compliance with the system-requirements and value system. It does not thereby call for equally unthinking compliance with life-grounded materialism treated as an alien ideology that will rescue people from themselves. Instead, it invites people to think about themselves as members of natural fields of life-support and social fields of life-development and to draw their own conclusions, confident that once the matter is approached from a life-grounded perspective, they will discover on their own the common life-interest. Life-grounded materialist ethics is thus not a moralizing demand for individuals to behave better but a call for individuals to think critically (and subsequently act politically) to bring about wider coherence between system-requirements and values and life-requirements and values.

This explication of these intentions notwithstanding, it could still be argued that since life-grounded materialist ethics contests the legitimacy of individual choices, it disregards Mill's caution that "with respect to his own feelings and circumstances, the most ordinary man or woman has means of knowledge immeasurably surpassing those that can be possessed by anyone else."[25] The link that Mill establishes between rationality, self-understanding, and the content of one's real interests as a human

24 McMurtry, *Value Wars*, 135.
25 Mill, *On Liberty*, 71.

being also informs Maeve Cooke's rereading of the epistemic authority of critical theory. Her main question is "how critical social theories are to avoid epistemological and ethical authoritarianism."[26] Her answer is that critical social theory can avoid epistemological authoritarianism only by anchoring its conception of the social good in people's autonomous self-understanding. In other words, it must avoid theoretical constructions of the good which are completely abstract from people's own reflective judgments. Since life-grounded materialist ethics is a critical social theory in its negative relationship to existing actuality, and since that criticism is expressed as criticism of the value system by which people choose, and thus by extension the legitimacy of the choices made, it would seem that it runs afoul of Cooke's concerns. Whether from the liberal or the contemporary critical theoretic perspective, it thus appears that life-grounded materialist ethics substitutes its own principles for people's mature judgment. Since both sides of this objection meet in the claim that to reject the legitimacy of people's considered judgments is authoritarian, I will target my response to their point of intersection.

The crucial point is that life-grounded materialist ethics values individual choice but demands that choices be understood in the material context in which they are made, and, perhaps more importantly, in the material implications they have for self, others, and natural and social worlds. Choices that are made under structural constraints imposed by system-requirements and system-values are not free precisely because the depth and breadth of reflection is constrained by the social pressure generated by those system-values. It can thus appear rational, in a capitalist society in which money-value is required to live, for a worker to choose to work in the oil sands. This choice is rational insofar as the person is a worker dependent on a money-wage. It is not rational insofar as the worker is an organism with physical-organic needs which would be harmed by catastrophic climate change, to the threat of which the oil sands contributes. Life-grounded materialist criticism does not paternalistically instruct this individual worker about what to do; it exposes the contradiction in which the individual lives but leaves the question of what is to be done up to the individual and others in his position. The hope is that by exposing the contradiction the individual is motivated to reflect more deeply on the general ethical contradiction of capitalist society, communicate with others about it, and generate novel collective response. At no point are people simply instructed about what to do from on high by life-grounded materialism as an alien system of thought.

26 Cooke, *Re-Presenting the Good Society*, 10. For a recent liberal restating of this argument, see Fairfield, *Why Democracy?* 103–6.

People themselves discover what is to be done – protect and develop the conditions of life and life-development – when they reflect as socially self-conscious members of natural fields of life-support and social fields of life-development.

Freedom of human thought, choice, and action is impossible if people, as organic-social beings, are deprived of the basic physical conditions of life and is impeded to the extent that the socio-cultural and temporal conditions of human life and free human life are instrumentalized in the service of reproducing the existing system. Contemporary liberal thought itself over the past thirty years has increasingly come to recognize that people require some degree of social support if their agency is to develop. [27] The most far-sighted liberals have speculated more deeply on the compatibility of liberal principles with the democratization of the workplace as well as on the essential role that free time plays in a free human life.[28] On the particular question of the relationship between ruling value systems and free choice, Nussbaum's work with women in the Global South has clearly disclosed the way in which ruling sexist value systems re-code women's choices to serve the prevailing structure of power.[29] Getting women to reflect critically on the causes of these choices is thus essential to enabling them to choose freely.

As will become apparent in chapters 6 and 7, there is disagreement between life-grounded materialist ethics and this liberal tradition about the social conditions required for the comprehensive development of human capacities. Here I am not focusing on the institutional structure of a life-grounded society but on the more general point that to critically scrutinize the content and implications of apparently free choices is not necessarily authoritarian. On this point, a large and influential group of liberal philosophers agrees with life-grounded materialist ethics that free choice is just a slogan unless the social conditions of free choice for each and all are known and satisfied.

Revealing the contradiction between the social conditions of free choice and the false freedom of individual choice in compliance with ruling system-values, therefore, does not constrain individual choice to some oppressively narrow range. Exposing the contradiction engages the

---

27 As evidence, consider not the liberals themselves but the openness of Marxists who maintain a commitment to the revolutionary overthrow of capitalism to incorporating the best insights of liberals like Rawls into a socialist conception of justice. The clearest example is Alex Callinicos's interpretation of Rawls. See Callinicos, *Equality*, 41–51, and Callinicos, *Resources of Critique*, 223–42.

28 See, for example, Gewirth, *The Community of Rights*, 257–87; Goodin, Rice, Parpo, Eriksson, *Discretionary Time*, 2008.

29 Nussbaum, *Sex and Social Justice*, 151–2.

intelligence of people, and by engaging the intelligence of people, life-grounded materialist ethics enables wider and deeper understanding of the social reality people inhabit. If people agree that the contradiction between life-value and system-value is real – and the experience of most people can confirm this reality on each of the three planes of being alive – people can begin to work together to change the social structures that determine typical patterns of action, as indeed they do, on local scales (the demand for locally grown organic food, for example), on national scales (the overthrow of the Egyptian dictatorship and the ongoing struggle for democratization), and international scales (anti-war movements). In each case people have decided to change themselves by changing the value system regulating their activity.

In all these cases, the individual mind becomes alive to something of which it was formerly unaware. The scope and depth of individual understanding grows, and new possibilities for social organization become apparent. Individual choice becomes all the more important since these new possibilities cannot be realized unless individuals choose to realize them and choose to work together to realize them. The philosophical contribution that life-grounded materialist ethics makes is to present *arguments, evidence, and reasons* which everyone is free to rationally evaluate and assess.

Authoritarianism is a structure of rule that dispenses with argument in favour of force. If life-grounded materialism contributes arguments that seek to awaken in people an understanding of the causes of the systemic social problems that everyone can easily observe today, it is not authoritarian, as the objection worried. Authoritarian philosophies support authoritarian structures of rule by lending their expertise to justifying the prevailing system-requirements and the ruling value system. In a society based on race slavery, philosophy can serve the interests of the slave owners by producing arguments about the "natural" inferiority of the slaves. Life-grounded philosophers could dispute that conclusion and in that way ally themselves with the oppressed. Life-grounded philosophers are not thereby substituting alien expertise for the experience and self-understanding of the oppressed. On the contrary, they stand in solidarity with them, marshalling their particular talents in resistance to the racist value system, participating in the struggle to maximize life-value *against* the given structure of rule. Thus, life-grounded materialist ethics is not authoritarian but a means of enabling critical thinking and transformative practice.

Since the life-ground of value is the total set of conditions necessary for natural life-support and social life-development and enjoyment, political arguments rooted in it can never be tendentious servants of authoritarianism. Where "feelings and circumstances" are detached from the underlying life-ground and enter into conflict with it, life-grounded materialist ethics seeks out the system-requirements served by this detachment. The aim of life-grounded materialist ethics is thus not to question individual motives in the abstract but rather to diagnose life-blind patterns of social action and participate in political movements that aim to replace life-blind with life-grounded system-requirements and ruling value systems. Because life-grounded arguments expose the sorts of social injustice involved in the operation of existing system-requirements, they will always be opposed by counter-arguments claiming that *any* questioning of people's "feelings and circumstances" is authoritarian. To acquiesce in the conclusion of those arguments is not to support people's freedom; it is simply to acquiesce to given structures of oppression and deprivation. Indeed, Mill's *On Liberty* itself is essentially an argument *against* people's feelings and circumstances insofar as it is a critique of the tyranny of custom. Where abstract individual choice is invoked today, it is typically not in defence of eccentric lifestyles but in defence of "consumer sovereignty" against critics who question its environmental consequences or psychological value. For example, Martin Wolf, in his defence of the globalization of the money-value system, attacks critics of globalization as enemies of free choice.[30] But what is globalization if not the forceful imposition of one definite way of life upon the myriad cultures of the world? To expose the tyranny of money-value rule is not to question people's choices; it is to illuminate the way in which the range of choice is violently contracted within a capitalist money-value social system.

This chapter has argued that all social organizations that persist for historically relevant periods of time do so by satisfying to some degree the real life-requirements of at least some people. Yet every social organization that we know of has also generated emergent system-requirements that contradict the life requirements of some classes of people. Since the satisfaction of life-requirements is the general material condition of people's lives being better rather than worse, a better society must better satisfy people's real life-requirements. The goal of life-grounded materialist ethics is thus a society whose system-requirements prioritize the satisfaction of the shared life-interest of each and all. All people share this common life-interest because they share a social-organic nature. Life-grounded materialist critique of life-blind system-requirements is rooted in this shared social-organic nature. Having explained the relationship between system-values, ruling value systems, and the underlying life-values anchored in our shared social-organic nature, the argument now shifts to consider the two dominant forms the contradictory relationship between ruling value systems and life-values has taken.

30 Wolf, *Why Globalization Works*, 194–5.

4

The Life-Blind Logic of Social Expansion

CHAPTER THREE EXPLAINED the emergence and structure of the general ethical contradiction between system-requirements and ruling value systems, on the one hand, and shared life-requirements and life-values, on the other. Wherever this contradiction develops, conflicts can arise between the group or groups whose life-interests are damaged and the group that benefits from the damage that prevailing system-requirements cause and the ruling value system justifies. These conflicts can arise either within or between societies. The history of colonialism and its contemporary analogues are paradigm cases of the latter. In what follows I use "colonialism" to refer to a general process by which less powerful societies have been reduced to being servants of the system-requirements of more powerful social forms, when the former has something that the latter wants, whether that be natural resources, land for settlement, or markets open to the more powerful country's advantage. As Aimé Césaire argues in his classic *Discours sur le colonialisme,* colonialism arises when "une forme de civilisation ... à un moment de son histoire, se constate obligée, de façon interne, d'étendre à l'échelle mondiale la concurrence de ses économies antagoniste."[1] The lives of colonized people are either eliminated as barriers to expansion or instrumentalized as servants of the colonial project. In either case, the project is legitimated by appeal to a ruling value system which denies the shared humanity, grounded in the common life-interest, linking colonizer to colonized.

In this chapter, I am not concerned with the political economy of colonialism or neo-colonialism. Instead, I focus on the structure of the contradiction between the colonial and neo-colonial ruling value

---

1 Césaire, *Discours sur le colonialisme,* 9. "A form of civilization ... at a certain moment in its history ... establishes itself, in an internal way, as bound to extend its competitive, antagonistic economy to the global level."

systems and the life-requirements and life-value that ultimately link colonizing and colonized peoples. While colonial regimes have tended to be based on systematic violence, they too require legitimating value systems. Indeed, since colonial projects have historically involved typically more direct, extensive, and brutal forms of life-destruction of both individual lives and collective life-ways, legitimating value systems are essential.

The argument contends that at the core of colonial and neo-colonial value systems is the principle that colonized people are not socially self-conscious human agents. As such, there is no harm either in physically liquidating them or in subordinating them to the tutelage of the superior culture. Humanity and social self-conscious agency are always conflated with the life-ways of the colonizing power, with the result that, by comparison, the life-ways of the colonized appear "barbaric" or "primitive" or "savage" and thus without any intrinsic life-value. The creation of instrumental and intrinsic life-value in the lives of colonized peoples thus appears to depend on the destruction of the indigenous life-ways and their replacement with the life-ways of the colonizing power. However, since different life-ways, to the extent that they satisfy life-requirements and enable the expression and enjoyment of life-capacities, have life-value, to destroy them just because they differ from some other set of life-ways is always life-destructive and not, as the colonial or neo-colonial value system contends, productive of greater life-value. Since the justification of colonial projects is always in terms of expanding life-value for the colonized, the justification of colonialism, historically and today, involves a contradiction between the particular ruling value system of the colonial society and life-value as such.

In section 4.1, I explicate this argument by examining the history of justification of British colonialism and contemporary justifications of the analogous but not identical "historical mission" of America to "bring democracy" to the Middle East. In section 4.2, I consider the objection that the life-grounded materialist critique of colonialism and neo-colonial domination is ethically self-undermining because it is rooted in a universal conception of human life-requirements and capacities. For critics of universal conceptions of humanity, the idea is either without practical effect (it cannot establish a meaningful ethical connection between people) or, if it can, it is via a pernicious *reduction* of the meaning of "humanity" to the particular interests of ruling powers. Hence, to critique colonial and neo-colonial value systems on the basis of a universal conception of life-requirements and capacities is to employ the language and concepts of the colonialists themselves.

4.1 THE CONTRADICTION BETWEEN RULING VALUE SYSTEMS AND LIFE-VALUE IN THE JUSTIFICATION OF COLONIAL DOMINATION

Colonial projects and their neo-colonial analogues always involve the active destruction of indigenous lives and life-ways. This active destruction raises the initial question, what is the basic condition that must be satisfied if the active destruction of lives and life-ways is to count as "good" to the colonial power? The short answer, which I unpack in the remainder of this section, is that the value-system according to which the colonizer judges colonial practice must deny that there are any common life-interests linking colonizer and colonized as human beings. This condition is terrifyingly but effectively illustrated by James Kelman's *Translated Accounts*, his fictional account of people living under military occupation. After witnessing the rape of a young girl, a character observes, "they do not think we are human beings. That is why, they do not think *what we are*. [emphasis added].[2] By not thinking "what we (the occupied people) *are*," it becomes possible for the perpetrator of the atrocity to deny the material harms the system of occupation and colonial domination generally cause. Chirot and McCauley, in their path-breaking study of the psychology of genocide, argue in the same vein that "turning frustration into killing requires a moral construction. Humans are moralizing animals who need to justify their acts. Poverty, disorder, political turmoil or other painful experiences may anger us, but we will not kill unless we have a specific target, and we may justify our anger towards that target by making its behaviour appear to us as morally repugnant."[3]

This explanation of the means of legitimating the most brutal forms of violence might seem obvious and uninteresting. The more difficult problem concerns the explanation and critique of what one might call "constructive" colonial projects. "Constructive" in this context refers to projects to build a new society *for* the colonized in contrast to projects like the Holocaust whose aim was simply to wipe out Jewish life altogether. Constructive colonialism is a more difficult problem for life-grounded materialism because its key value-metric – the more comprehensive satisfaction of life-requirements for the sake of more inclusively coherent expressions of life-capacities – is, in a sense, also claimed by constructive projects as their basis of legitimacy. "Progressive" colonialists, even if they do not use the term explicitly, have always claimed to have been guided by the goal of improving the lives of the colonized, even when they were tearing the heart out of the ancient life-ways they encountered. This

2 Kelman, *Translated Accounts*, 122.
3 Chirot and McCauley, *Why Not Kill Them All?* 67.

structure of argument poses a more difficult challenge to life-grounded materialist ethics. It appears that the progressive colonialist (or today's analogue, the human rights warrior), challenges my position by asserting that if life-grounded materialist ethics is serious about satisfying the common life-interest, then it must support the destruction of the oppressive structures of authority typical of non-liberal, non-capitalist, non-democratic societies. After all, life-grounded materialist ethics argues that cultural differences are neither good nor bad in themselves but must be judged by reference to their actual implications for the common life-interest. If that is the case, then what exactly is wrong with the colonial form of destroying those structures of authority in order to create new social conditions in which higher expressions of life-value might flourish?

Historically and still today, the destruction of ancient life-ways has been defended by the argument that, *ideally*, the members of progressive and backward cultures share life-interests, but the realization of those life-interests in the backward culture is impeded by their ancient life-ways and institutions. The structures of authority and the ruling value system that support these structures, defenders of colonialism or "Western intervention" claim, are so oppressive that they can only be overcome by force led by an external political agent. This belief links together people on opposite sides of the official political spectrum. Neo-conservatives like Lawrence Kaplan and William Kristol argue in defence of the Afghanistan and Iraq wars that "democracy is a political choice, an act of will. Someone, not something, must create it ... history suggests it comes most effectively from the United States."[4] Liberals like Hillary Clinton concur. Speaking during Human Rights Week at Georgetown University in 2009, Clinton argued that war is sometimes "right and necessary" when it is waged against a foe who "violently" denies the human rights of its citizens. Once again, the United States is positioned as the only force capable of protecting the human rights of these unfortunate, oppressed populations.[5] The point of intersection between these arguments is the underlying belief that the people who are the object of American intervention are *systematically incapable of solving their own political and social problems. They must be objects of external intervention because they are not yet capable of responsible political agency.*

The denial of responsible political agency to the objects of colonial or neo-colonial projects is not exclusive to contemporary American foreign policy but underlies the whole history of the encounter between expansionary Western societies and the indigenous life-ways of Africa, Asia,

HILLARY ✳ II

4 Quoted in Callinicos, *The New Mandarins of American Power*, 25.
5 Clinton, "Speech on the Human Rights Agenda for the Twenty-first Century."

and the Americas. Millions upon millions of indigenous peoples in these worlds have been sacrificed (and at least tens of thousands more Muslims have been sacrificed in today's "War on Terror") to the contradiction between the system-requirements and ruling value system of Western colonial and neo-colonial expansion and the life-requirements and life-values that at root link all people together.

The *locus classicus* of the justifying ethical logic of colonialism is J.S. Mill's *On Liberty*. Mill's political conclusions follow from an analogy between children and non-European cultures. He takes it as obvious that children cannot be allowed complete liberty because they are not capable of fully understanding the grounds and consequences of their actions. He then extends this reasoning to entire societies: "For the same reason, we may leave out of consideration those backward states of society in which the race itself may be considered as in its nonage. The early difficulties in the way of spontaneous progress are so great, that there is seldom any choice of means for overcoming them; that a ruler full of the spirit of improvement is warranted in the use of *any expedients* that will attain an end, perhaps otherwise unattainable. Despotism is a legitimate mode of government in dealing with barbarians, provided the end be their improvement, and the means justified by actually effecting that end. Liberty, as a principle, has no application to any state of things anterior to the time when mankind have become capable of being improved by free and equal discussion."[6] While Mill may not intend this defence of despotism as a defence of wholesale life-destruction, the crucial point for present purposes is his explicit denial that societies in their "nonage" are capable of changing themselves.

Perhaps curiously, one finds the identical structure of reasoning in Marx's evaluation of the results of British rule in India. This shared conclusion beneath differences of political goal demonstrates that one is here dealing with a pervasive structure of confusion between the spread of a particular value system and the growth of life-value. Marx differentiates himself from Mill only by beginning with a note of sympathy for the losses incurred by the colonized of India. However, his conclusions are the same: "Now, sickening as it must be to human feeling to witness those myriads of industrious patriarchal and inoffensive social organizations disorganized and dissolved into their units, thrown into a sea of woes, and their individual members losing at the same time their ancient form of civilization and their hereditary means of subsistence, we must not forget that these idyllic village communities ... had always been the solid foundation of Oriental despotism, that they restrained the human mind

6 Mill, *On Liberty*, 11.

within the smallest possible compass, making it the unresisting tool of superstition, enslaving it beneath traditional rules, depriving it of all grandeur and historical energies."[7]

In destroying this stultifying structure of rule, Marx claims, the British, though culpable of many a crime, are justified as the "unconscious tool of history" that will make possible the social revolution in Asia.[8] One can believe that it is justified to sacrifice millions of people's lives for the sake of the expansion of a particular value system only if one shifts attention away from the real and immediate life-consequences for the human objects of colonial domination toward an abstract theory of objective stages of social progress. This shift of focus, from concrete people to abstract principles, is the essence of the life-blind thinking that is always found wherever the contradiction between system-values and life-values must be justified.

In order to overcome this life-blindness it is necessary to listen to its sacrificial victims. Césaire is once again a most effective witness: "Et je dis que de la colonisation à la *civilisation* la distance est infinie; que, toutes les expéditions coloniales accumulés, de toutes les statuts coloniaux élaborés, de toutes les circulaires ministrielles expediées, on ne saurait réussir une seule valeur humaine."[9]

What both Marx and Mill share and what Césaire contests is the unsupported premise that it is impossible for human beings living in their so-called cultural "nonage" to emancipate themselves from the structure of rule that oppresses them, to the extent that they really are oppressed. Yet the history of Europe that Marx and Mill share tells completely against the truth of this premise. Both Mill and Marx judge ancient structures of social organization and the life-bearers who live within them as nothing more than impediments to a future of full life-value development. Both believe that life-value is contingent on the satisfaction of definite mechanical steps – freeing the mind from custom or the development of the forces of production. Marx's and Mill's theories, however, suffer from the very worship of reified system-values that they accuse Indians of worshipping. Insofar as both rank the forcible accomplishing of mechanical steps of social progress as of greater value than the present well-being of living individuals, they end by denying the humanity (the collective capacity to change themselves) of the Indian people.

---

7 Karl Marx, "The British Rule in India," in *On Colonialism,* 40.

8 Ibid., 41.

9 Césaire, *Discours sur le colonialism,* 10–11. "And I say that between colonialism and civilization the distance is infinite, because, within all the accumulated colonial expeditions, within all the elaborated colonial statutes, in all the ministerial circulars that have been sent off, one will not succeed in finding a single human value."

The issue here is not that all cultural differences are of equal value, or any romantic foolishness that ancient structures of life were free of domination, violence, and sacrifice of the well-being of the many for the sake of the few. For life-grounded materialist ethics, the value of any social system must be evaluated concretely, by reference to how well it satisfies its members' shared life-interests. The point is that human beings, whatever their cultural membership, are ultimately able to understand and solve their own problems. Asians and Europeans are not different species marked by qualitatively inferior and superior capacities; both have the same human potential for social criticism and life-grounded social change. It may be true historically that the activation in consciousness of life-grounded criticism is encouraged by some social conditions and impeded by others, but it does not follow that the conditions that support its emergence are identical to "modernization" along the lines suggested by the history of Europe exclusively. This claim can be supported by two arguments, one concerning the history of Europe, the other concerning resources of critique immanent to ancient life-ways.

First, Mill and Marx both agree that the "backwardness" of Indian society is expressed in the absolute hold of irrational superstition and custom over individual minds and practices. They infer from this premise that progress requires an external political agent willing to use violence to create the social and ethical space necessary for the development of critical intellect and democratic self-rule. Yet their entire critique of the Indian world would apply with precision to a medieval European village. Had Marx been a contemporary of Giordano Bruno, he would have shared a stake at the latter's burning. And yet no European thinkers of the nineteenth century, in looking back over their own history, regarded as miraculous the ability of Europe to free itself from religious domination without the intervention of an external political agent. Instead, the history of Europe is a history of the gradual emergence of self-reflective critical intellect. To be sure, this gradual emergence was punctuated by massive spasms of violence like the Thirty Years War, which did much to promote the necessity for religious tolerance. The issue here is not whether violence in history is necessary to the emergence of cultural learning processes, but whether people held in thrall by reified social values and superstitious beliefs can free themselves from them by their own power, whether through violence or otherwise.[10] The answer, I contend, is yes, because the crucial element that enables people to do so is the deep

10 The question of why the modern form of self and social criticism emerged most robustly in early modern Europe is still a live problem of historical sociological research. For the relevant debates see Goody, *Capitalism and Modernity*.

structure of our social self-consciousness, its ultimate ability to turn against given social structures by subjecting them to ethical *questioning*. Kant comes much closer to the truth than either Marx or Mill: "I cannot admit the expression, used by even intelligent men: A certain people ... is not yet ripe for freedom ... According to such a supposition, freedom will never arrive; for we cannot yet ripen to this freedom unless we are already free ... [and] we never ripen to freedom except through our own efforts."[11] To deny that people are incapable of ever ripening to freedom through their own efforts, Kant implies, is to deny that they are people.

This point leads directly to the second claim. Every human society, simply by its historical persistence as a *human society*, presents undeniable evidence of collective agency, and thus humanity. The complex societies of the Indian sub-continent were not built by Europeans; they were built by the actions and interactions of their members over millennia. This collective process produced a wealth of philosophical, artistic, scientific, and technological achievements. The same human energy and capacities that built Europe built India, but under different circumstances which gave rise to different structures of rule and different ruling value systems (and therefore different structures of internal contradiction between those value systems and system-requirements and life-values and life-requirements, e.g., the caste system). Every society is the collective product of its members' thoughts, actions, and interactions. Every known society has been structured by different forms of the contradiction between the ruling system-requirements and value system and the underlying human life-requirements and life-values. If the same capacities are necessarily activated in the ongoing construction of any society, the same general potential exists in all for ultimate recognition of the underlying life-ground of value, in its two-fold expression as the satisfaction of life-requirements and realized life-value. None, therefore, are in principled need of external political agents to intervene, as an adult rescuer must to save a drowning child.

Any society in principled need of an external political agent of change would be a society incapable of human action. But a *society* incapable of human action is a contradiction in terms. Societies are not animal hordes but systems of life-reproduction structured by institutions and ruled by value systems which are the collective product of human thought, action, and interaction. Hence, the very fact that a society exists and reproduces itself, whether "backward" by some external measure or not, demonstrates the humanity of its members, and thus their principled competence to *ultimately* change their society in accordance with life-values.

11 Quoted in Arendt, *Lectures on Kant's Political Philosophy*, 48.

Yet even the "backwardness" of societies targeted for colonization by the European powers may be contested. What *essential* difference is there between the Indian caste system, which condemned the untouchables to a life of absolute misery, and the class system of nineteenth-century England in which "all conceivable evils [were] heaped upon the heads of the poor?"[12] Is it only that internal resources of critique to which the untouchables might have in principle appealed were lacking? People who know Indian history better than Marx and Mill contest this claim. Amartya Sen, for example, explicates those elements of historical Indian culture that demonstrate that there were internal resources of criticism. He concludes that Indian society could in principle have overcome its internal contradictions by the exercise of its members' own capacities had the British not forcibly intervened.[13]

Further evidence of internal resources for reflective social criticism is provided in the history of the other "Indian" society, that of the indigenous peoples of North America. A shining example of the powers of human intellect at work in "backward" conditions is the Great Laws of Peace that established the Six Nations Confederacy. The 117 articles of the Great Laws of Peace make up perhaps the longest functioning constitution in the world, ruling uninterrupted from prior to the European invasions to the present day. The Great Laws of Peace are not only a constitution governing human interrelations; they also manifest a life-grounded consciousness of the integration of human society with the wider field of natural life-support systems, a consciousness completely absent in the "advanced" European countries of the day. "Whenever the statesmen of the League shall assemble for the purpose of holding a council, the Onandaga Rotiyaner shall open it by expressing their gratitude to their cousin statesmen and greeting them and ... offer thanks to the earth where men dwell, to the streams of water, the pools and lakes, to the maize and the fruits, to the medicinal herbs ... to the animals that serve as food and give their pelts, to the great winds ... to the Sun."[14]

The Confederacy knew a truth to which Europe was blind: humanity is one that expresses itself differently (the members of the different tribes are "cousins" within the family of human beings), and all together share natural conditions of life. Centuries later, in the midst of World War One, this was a truth still understood by First Nations people but not grasped by warring Europe. Diamond Jennes reported the following

---

12 Engels, *The Condition of the Working Class in England*, 128.
13 Sen, *Development as Freedom*, 227–48.
14 The complete text is reproduced in MacLaine and Baxendale, *This Land Is Our Land*, 100–21.

response from an Inuit hunter when informed of the war: "Ickpuk would not believe our western natives when they told him that the white men were killing each other like caribou ... He pondered the matter for some days ... Certainly, white men who deliberately used their extraordinary knowledge and powers for the wholesale massacre of each other were strangely unnatural and inhuman."[15] Ickpuk errs only in attributing the inhumanity to the *white men* – it is their actions, and the social structures that cause and legitimate such actions, that are inhuman. Humanity, by contrast, lies in our shared social-organic nature and the common life-interest rooted in it. Once that shared life-interest is recognized, it can no longer be denied that those who are slaughtered are fellow human beings. I will return to the practical implications of this recognition below. For the moment, the argument must shift from history to the present, to examine the analogous structure of thinking at work in the twenty-first century's great "civilizing" crusade, the War on Terror.

The political-economic critique of the agenda actually served by the policies undertaken by the American state since 11 September 2001 has been widely explored, and I do not repeat those analyses here.[16] Instead, I am interested in the structure of the ethical contradiction between the system-requirements and legitimating value system and the life-requirements and life-value that ultimately link people beneath political difference. In order to lay bear the contradiction, one must begin with the now well-known *Statement of Principles* of the Project for a New American Century. A detailed analysis of the entire set of documents published by the Project is not necessary here. The key principle for present purposes is derivable from the fourth and third "consequences" of the lessons that the authors believe the history of the twentieth century has taught the architects of American power. The fourth consequence states that "we need to accept responsibility for America's unique role preserving and extending an international order friendly to our security, our prosperity, and our principles."[17] An international order "friendly" to "our" security, the third consequence states, depends on "political and economic freedom abroad." Hence the principle to be abstracted from these two consequences is this: freedom abroad has no intrinsic value but is only an instrument for the advance of American

[handwritten in margin: NEO CONS]

15 Quoted in Ryerson, *The Founding of Canada*, 24.

16 For a more detailed political economic analysis and critique of the neo-conservative agenda see, for example, Ali, *Mr. Bush Goes to Baghdad*; Falk, *The Declining World Order;* Harvey, *The New Imperialism.*

17 Project for a New American Century, *Statement of Principles.* The main principles of the PNC were later reiterated and elaborated in the 2002 National Security Policy of the United States.

interests. In other words, America arrogates to itself the right to define for all what is and is not a free society. As evidence, consider the developments of March 2011. In Libya, a country ruled by a tyrant willing to slaughter his own people, America intervenes in support of the opposition. At the same time, in Bahrain, a country ruled by a tyrant who allows the United States' Fifth Fleet to dock in his country's main harbour, regime opponents may be killed with impunity.

Superficial differences between the previous two American governments notwithstanding, there is a shared commitment to an interventionist foreign policy rooted in the principle that only America can liberate people from their own oppressive customs. The practice of the Obama administration from 2009 to 2011 has not deviated from the principle first articulated by former president Bush as the National Security Strategy of the United States in 2002. In a much-discussed speech at the United States Army Academy at West Point, New York, where the strategy was introduced, Bush first invokes the classic values of nineteenth-century liberalism: "the twentieth century ended with a single model of human progress based on non-negotiable demands of human dignity, the rule of law, limits on the power of the state, respect for women and private property, and free speech and equal justice, and religious tolerance."[18] There is no disputing the real value of these principles if understood from a life-grounded materialist perspective. The problem is that these values are not understood as the social enabling conditions for the wider and deeper development of life-capacities of all human beings, but as system-values whose realization must serve the interests of the United States, as these interests are interpreted by the Americans with the institutional power to impose them. Bush makes this point abundantly clear later in his speech: "the United States National Security Strategy will be based on a distinctly American internationalism that reflects the union of our values and our national interests. The aim of this strategy is to help make the world not just safer but better."[19] These twin goals will be accomplished by American "military strengths beyond challenge."[20]

On one level the contradiction inherent in these arguments is clear. Freedom is meaningless politically if it is detached from practices of self-determination. Yet Bush defines freedom explicitly as compelled service to "American interests and American values." An *international* system of freedom cannot be at the same time free and determined in its structure

---

18 Falk, *The Declining World Order*, 196.
19 Ibid., 248.
20 Ibid.

and development by American military power "beyond challenge." In reality, democratic decisions will be disregarded if they do not align with American determinations of how people should govern themselves. Hence the national Iraqi resistance was denounced as "anti-Iraqi" and either liquidated or bought off. Hamas, the elected government of the Palestinian people, was marginalized and attacked beginning in 2006 and culminating in the American-abetted Israeli assault on Gaza in January 2009. The use of these movements as examples of the undermining of democratic decisions and power by the American military does not imply support for the strategies and tactics adopted by any of these groups. I will return to consider the life-grounded materialist understanding of legitimate resistance below. The point I want to emphasize here is that the life-value of practices like democracy and the rule of law is transformed into its opposite – tools of oppression and wholesale killing – when their life-value is reduced to the system-requirements and ruling value system of global capitalism as interpreted by the United States. Once that reduction has taken place, and service to principles replaces real consequences for the subjected population, then any degree of life-sacrifice appears to be justified.[21]

The life-value of democracy and the other political values cited by Bush or Clinton or anyone else in power cannot be realized if these "values" are mere instruments of the foreign policy of an external invading force. Instead, their realization as *life*-values can only succeed if the form of their institutionalization is determined by the collective power of the citizens reasoning in life-grounded ways about how to free themselves from the indigenous and external structures that undermine the shared life-interest. Otherwise, abstract political and ethical principles become justifications for rather than movements against life-destruction. The Bush administration is not alone in the contemporary world in committing the error of reducing life-value to its service to existing system-values. Even intellectuals, who have the luxury of time to deeply reflect on the structure of political problems, have fallen victim to collapsing universal life-values into service to the ruling value system. Michael Ignatieff, for example, went so far as to countenance pre-emptive invasion and even torture as legitimate, "lesser evils," if either could prevent

21 The situation in Iraq was still fluid as I was writing this section in January 2009. It is undeniable, however, that the living conditions of Iraqis have deteriorated terribly during the six years between 2003 and 2009. Estimates of the scale of civilian deaths vary widely but are at a minimum on the order of several tens of thousands of people. Public infrastructure remains in a state of near total collapse and many millions of Iraqis are refugees or internally displaced. See for a comprehensive overview of the collapse of life-conditions, Global Policy Forum, "Iraq's Humanitarian Crisis."

another terrorist attack on the scale of 9/11.[22] But human rights, much less human life, cannot be served by such thinking because once the lives of one group are treated as valuable only to the extent that they serve the ruling global power, their life-value is understood to lie solely in being sacrificial victims to the security of that value system, the "heavy price" that must be paid for political and ethical progress. Since all human life-bearers are unique and unrepeatable, it can never be in anyone's real life-interest to be *made into* a sacrificial victim of the ruling value system (to sacrifice oneself is a different matter, but not relevant here). To *be sacrificed* for the sake of an external ruling value system can never be legitimate because, through the sacrifice, all life-value for the life-bearer is destroyed without remainder. Those who remain live on in despair, mourning, and anger. The conditions for irrational and destructive cycles of revenge rather than overall life-security and life-development are thereby engendered.

To the extent that expansionary Western societies have treated the destruction of non-Western life as legitimate *because* such sacrifice served the ruling value system, it has created the conditions for the victims to feel justified in seeking their life-destructive revenge. One need look no further for confirmation of this claim than the self-justifying discourse of Osama bin Laden. Bin Laden argues that "it should not be hidden from you that the people of Islam had suffered aggression, iniquity, and injustice imposed on them by the Zionist Crusader alliance and their collaborators; to the extent that the Muslim blood became the cheapest and their wealth as loot in the hands of their enemies."[23] It would be difficult to deny the historical evidence that bin Laden marshals in support of his argument. One should not let disagreement with his tactics obscure the reality of the history that he invokes. In mirror image of the colonial violence he claims to resist, bin Laden concludes that the only solution to the problem is to destroy the forces that aim to destroy the Muslim world. All that he accomplished was to provide America with the pretext it needed for even more violence. Thus is engendered the irrational cycle of mutual life-destruction that continues to play out today.

One finds that whenever life has been treated as a fungible instrument of foreign policy the result has not been lasting peace at a higher level of civilization; it has been renewed grounds for warfare. The lasting achievements of civilization – the wider and deeper satisfaction of the life-requirements explained in chapter 2 – have not been the result of wholesale civilizational wars but of relatively peaceful mass struggle and

22 Ignatieff, *The Lesser Evil*, 160–7.
23 Osama bin Laden, *Fatwa of August 1996*.

patient construction over generations. War, the ultimate means of reducing and eliminating life-value, destroys the grounds for satisfying life-requirements; it never directly enables their expression at more coherently inclusive range and depth. War destroys the natural life-support systems on which life depends, it lays waste to social and family infrastructures, it cannot be conducted democratically, and it destroys not only free time but life-time as such for the tens of millions of lives it has consumed just in the twentieth and twenty-first centuries alone.

Might it not be objected that this argument depends on abstract moralizing that ignores historical necessity? Might the defender of colonialism or the War on Terror not respond that war between civilizations is sometimes necessary, if not always to spread the values of one civilization, then at least to defend them against threat? There are two problems with this position. First, defenders of "Western values" fail to account for the asserted superiority of the values they affirm. To the extent that individualism and liberal democracy are superior to alternative value systems, they must serve everyone's shared life-interest better than other possible values. At the very least, they must not be used as justifications for the type of life-sacrifice that I criticized above, since to affirm the value of individuality and at the same time to destroy the lives of real human individuals in the name of the abstract principle of individualism is materially irrational. Individuality as a life-value means that the ruling value system recognizes and prioritizes the satisfaction of the set of life-requirements that anyone must meet in order to differentiate him or herself through different forms of life-valuable self-realization. If the ruling value system treats some individuals as mere obstacles to be overcome, it contradicts the values it affirms in theory through its individual life-destroying practice.

However, perhaps this response misses the deeper point about historical necessity. There is no doubt that, from the perspective of the present in relation to the past, historical necessity exists. From the perspective of the present, history is the fixed reality of the human species. By "fixed" I mean given, absolutely determined, not any longer alterable by present or future human action. However, it is only in relation to the past that necessity has any real meaning as a limitation constraining human action. What has happened has happened, and there is nothing to be done in the present to change what has happened in the past. The Second World War, for example, can, from our vantage point today, appear necessary, given the confluence of events that led up to it. Still, that human beings are capable in principle of learning from the past is as undeniable as that the past has happened. Given our master capacity to learn and change ourselves in response to increased knowledge, it follows that the future is not determined in any strong sense. If this claim were not true, it would be impossible to explain historical change, since if change means anything it means differentiation over time, and differentiation over time implies that people have acted differently and, in acting differently, resisted the inertia of established practice. Therefore "necessity," in the strong sense (that any but one course of action is unthinkable, a contradiction in terms) does not apply to it. The future of the War on Terror, by contrast with past conflicts, is not necessary but depends on the policy options actually selected in the future by its main protagonists. There are life-grounded options available to end the War on Terror as surely as there is a human capacity to understand different perspectives, to admit mutual misunderstandings and failures, and to re-ground political practice, nationally and internationally, in policies that serve the construction of policy frameworks and social institutions that satisfy universal human life-interests.

Whenever necessity is invoked in the present to explain a future course of action, whenever this necessity involves "tough sacrifices" of other people's life-interests, it becomes ideological, an attempt to justify the ruined lives of the victims. Indeed, the invocation of historical necessity is one of the primary forms that denial of responsibility for life-destruction takes.[24] Any given social system, especially when it must be maintained *against* life-interests, will always invoke historical necessity as a means of justifying itself. At most, however, necessity in relation to the human future is a relative necessity, i.e., necessary only in relation to a particular system-goal assumed as unquestionable. For example, until a November 2007 United States National Intelligence Report asserted that Iran was most likely not trying to build a nuclear weapon, the Bush regime was working hard to convince the world that war with Iran was going to be necessary. The fluidity of policy proves that there is no absolute necessity binding present to future, but only past to present.

Still, one must avoid making the opposite mistake. Just as there is no strong necessity governing choices about the human political future, neither is there "free choice" in the abstract sense in which this term is understood in the liberal tradition. Freedom in foreign policy is real but constrained by the ruling value system according to which political powers judge the world and act within it. For example, in a world where military production is a system-requirement of the economy, "enemies" will be required to maintain support for the militarized sectors of the economy. The system-requirement that enemies be found will lead to higher incidences of open warfare. Political agents who act within this structure are thus more likely to find themselves in choice-contexts where

24 Cohen, *States of Denial*, 91–2.

the decision to go to war appears necessary. While the political agents considered as choosing individuals thus face real constraints on the range of choices in the given social context, it does not follow that the society as a whole must be determined by these immediate choice-contexts. Acting together on the basis of an ethical and political rejection of the system-requirements that generate these choice-contexts, people can, over time, reject the ruling value system and transform the system-requirements that generate the apparent necessities.

Whenever a ruling power invokes historical necessity to justify the violent destruction of an opponent in a colonial or neo-colonial context, its object of care and concern is never the people who are supposed to benefit from the strategy but the preservation and expansion of the system-requirements and values that make the project appear necessary. As a consequence, life that stands in the way of realizing the project appears as a disvalue, an obstacle to be overcome. When universal life-values determine action, by contrast, people will reject wholesale offensive violence and the destruction of others lives as necessary. Thus, millions of people marched against the looming war in Iraq on 15 February 2003, even though it was not their lives that were about to be destroyed. Millions more leant what support they could to the victims of the tsunami in South East Asia in 2005, even though they had lost nothing. In these and every other case one could mention, what occurs is an expansion of individual and local interests through recognition of common life-interests. Within the life-grounded frame of value, life cannot be sacrificed wholesale for the sake of a better future life because such wholesale sacrifice creates the conditions in which revenge will appear necessary to the objects of life-destruction, thus setting the stage not for social peace but for a new round of violence.

The widest possible expression of life-value presupposes social peace as a fundamental condition of life-security without which the satisfaction of life-requirements cannot be enjoyed. Social peace, in turn, presupposes an end to the cycles of revenge that structure so much of the history of human conflict. Overcoming these cycles of revenge requires that enemies be recognized as human beings and that problems are understood to be caused by corrigible ruling value systems and not unalterable ethnic or national identities or positions along some putatative developmental scheme of history. Non-mutually destructive forms of political struggle and change become possible only when the humanity of the enemy is recognized. Reconciliation and mutual adjustment of immediate political goals are in turn the fundamental conditions of the creation of political projects that have a chance of uncovering the common life-value shared between former enemies.

There are real-life examples of a conscious shift from a demonizing to a life-grounded frame of value. Perhaps the best example in recent history is the South African Truth Commission.[25] However, the most effective illustration of my meaning comes from literature. *God's Bits of Wood* is Ousmane Sembene's narrative of Senagalese resistance to French imperialism in the 1940s. In the midst of a railway strike, a number of union militants, along with a non-militant village elder, are jailed and tortured. Upon successful conclusion of the strike, some of the younger militants understandably want to track down and repay in kind their colonial jailer. At a union meeting they are confronted by the elder who challenges them: "if you want to kill him, you should also kill all the blacks who obey him, and the whites whom he obeys, and where would that lead? If a man like that is killed, there is always another to take his place. That is not the important thing. But to act so that no man dares strike you because he knows you speak the truth, to act so that you can no longer be arrested because you are asking for the right to live, to act so that all this will end, both here and elsewhere: that is what you must explain to others, so that you will never be forced to bow down before anyone, but also so that no one shall be forced to bow down before you. It was to tell you this that I asked you to come, because hatred must not dwell with you."[26] Once the demonizing ruling value system that encourages hatred is overcome by life-grounded recognition of common humanity beneath political differences, the driving force of revenge cycles can be arrested.

Hence, just as life-values form the ultimate basis of legitimacy of any particular value system, so too they function as the basis of legitimacy of resistance to life-destruction. No struggle of those who are the targets of colonial practices or its contemporary analogues is legitimate just because it is a struggle against a foreign entity. In certain cases, armed self-defence might be necessary, but a struggle waged in purely military terms without a political and ethical basis upon which mass, peaceful resistance can be built will not create the conditions for life-value development. The unfortunate degeneration of Libyan resistance to Gadhafi into yet another NATO-led adventure is a case in point. The legitimacy of struggles, like the legitimacy of social systems, can be decided only by reference to the life-ground of value. When either system-maintenance or system-change appears to require the wholesale destruction of the lives

25 The Truth Commission, of course, did not solve every problem of post-Apartheid South Africa, but to the extent that it checked the desire for revenge and thus helped to prevent a civil war, it must be supported by life-grounded materialist ethics.

26 Sembene, *God's Bits of Wood*, 350.

of the opponents, then either the system or the means of opposing it or both have become materially irrational from the life-grounded perspective. Since the justification of either regime defence or revolutionary struggle depends on demonstrating a superior ability to increase life-value, and life-value is always negated to the extent that the lives of some are treated as nothing more than obstacles to be removed for the sake of better lives for others, only mass democratic and not exclusively military struggle is able to ultimately prevail over life-blind system-requirements and ruling value systems.

Life-valuable struggle against colonial and neo-colonial projects, so perfectly articulated in its basic principles by Sembene, depends on a structure of thought and action that neither obeys simply because it is commanded nor commands simply because it has the power to do so. It is a structure of thought and action grounded in the recognition of what the colonizers have historically denied: the universal humanity that links them beneath the differences of culture to the colonized. When this shared humanity of life-interests is recognized, people can raise themselves out of the cycles of mutually assured damage and destruction that revenge cycles encourage. To be sure, to those conditioned to obey and command within the unquestioned circle of a given ruling value system, this argument will sound platitudinous or worse. We only have to look to our long and bloody history for a response. Human beings make actual life-grounded progress when they reject exclusionary value systems in favour of life-valuable systems which more comprehensively satisfy life-requirements and more inclusively enable life-capacities. Democracy developed where the exclusive privilege of landed property to control political institutions was overcome; material equality between people was advanced when the exclusive right of the wealthy to control life-sustaining and life-developing natural and social wealth was challenged; and in general all that may be called progressive in history is the more elaborate development of the social infrastructure of life-requirement satisfaction and life-capacity development.

Thus, the argument that colonialism and its contemporary analogues can be justified by appeal to the life-ground of value must be rejected. The results of colonial and neo-colonial projects have been destructive for the lives and life-ways of the colonized and have engendered violent revenge cycles in response. The creation of the social conditions for more coherently inclusive ranges of life-value, by contrast, must proceed on the basis of recognition of the shared life-interests materially anchored in our shared organic-social nature. Once this shared humanity is the object of care and concern revenge cycles can be broken and forms of life-grounded political struggle and social transformation can emerge. I will return to this concrete issue in part three. To conclude this chapter, the objection that the life-grounded argument is self-undermining must be explored.

4.2 SHARED HUMANITY AND CULTURAL DIFFERENCE

While it might sound banal to argue that colonialist life and life-way destruction is rooted in a ruling value system that actively denies the link of shared life-interests between colonizer and colonized, the claim is in fact controversial. The controversy generates an objection. The life-grounded critique of colonialism claims that recognition of shared humanity, grounded in shared life-interests in life-requirement satisfaction and life-capacity development, is the necessary ethical foundation for relations between societies that allow for more comprehensive development of life-value. In response, the objection asserts that the history of colonialism itself proves that such a conception of shared life-interests is either without motivating force or a tool of colonial and neo-colonial powers. Life-grounded materialist ethics thus undermines itself, either by relying on a useless abstraction which leaves its political conclusions ungrounded, or by directly repeating the universalist error of the colonial projects that it claims to critique. In reality, the objection concludes, there are only cultural and social differences. The political conditions for the comprehensive development of life-value require the recognition and affirmation of these differences. I will treat each form of the objection in turn.

The first argument, that the idea of universal humanity is an empty abstraction without ethical or political motivating force, derives from Hume. Hume argues that there is no such thing as "love of humanity" as such because all encounters between human beings are mediated by concrete identities, and all "love" is expressed through relationships between people with concrete identities. Hume claims that "humanity" is an abstraction which no one ever encounters in any concrete relationship. People have relationships not with "humans" but with brothers, aunts, bosses, Americans, Europeans, and so forth. The humanity of others is an abstraction that never appears in reality and thus cannot constitute grounds for any ethical relationship of care and concern. "In general, it may be affirm'd, that there is no such passion in human minds, as the love of mankind in general, merely as such, independent of particular qualities, of services, or of relation to oneself ... An Englishman in Italy is a friend, A European in China, and perhaps a man would be beloved as such were we to meet him in the moon."[27] For

27 Hume, *A Treatise of Human Nature*, 492.

Hume, a context in which one person might recognize another person simply as human was unthinkable, and thus he concludes that all human interactions and all relationships of care and concern will be based on some concrete identity. The fact that human beings can now walk on the moon has not been sufficient to undermine the attractiveness of Hume's argument. It persists in the postmodern valorization of differences as never resolvable into a truly shared humanity.

Hume's key assumptions are at the root of the "ethnocentric" liberalism of Richard Rorty. Rorty argues, like Hume, that one can have no concrete relationship with the humanity of others. As a consequence, the idea of humanity plays no role in establishing solidarity between people. Rorty claims that solidarity is rooted in more concrete identities like "Greek," "fellow Catholic," or "comrade in the struggle." He concludes that "I want to deny that 'one of us human beings' ... can have the same sort of force as any of the previous examples. I claim that the force of 'us' is, typically, contrastive in the sense that it contrasts with a 'they' which is also made up of human beings – the wrong sort of human beings."[28] Thus both Hume and Rorty claim that all real human relationships hold between concrete and particular identities and never between human beings as human beings. Since "humanity" never appears, it is never the object of social self-consciousness in encounters between concrete people, and if it is not a real object of social self-consciousness, it cannot form the basis of solidarity.

This argument has intuitive appeal as an explanation of the sorts of relationships people have, which are indeed typically structured around specific identities. Its conclusions are, nevertheless, ethically arbitrary, and this arbitrariness reveals a deeper problem concealed by the argument's surface appeal. Both Hume and Rorty allow that it is possible for human beings to construct very wide circles of affective identity. Rorty admits that it is possible, for example, for a Catholic to affectively identify with hundreds of millions of fellow Catholics around the world, but denies that it is similarly possible for people to construct an affective identity with all human beings. He fails to state what the relevant difference is between affective identity between hundreds of millions of people who share a faith but not a culture, and billions of people who belong to the same species, with the same requirements for physical resources, social relationships, and institutions, and an experience of time as free. Rorty's belief that as "humans" we share nothing at all ignores the shared material reality of human life-requirement, the shared sorts of harm to which this material reality makes us liable, and the shared natural and

28 Rorty, *Contingency, Irony, and Solidarity*, 190.

social conditions for the development of cultural differences. If Catholics lacked the ability to translate the liturgy into different languages, and the non-Catholic people they targeted lacked the capacity to learn it in any language, the faith could never have spread. So far as we know at present, only humans are capable of translating and learning languages. They cannot translate or learn languages if they have not been fed, educated, or had the time to do so. Thus Rorty and Hume simply assert an ethically arbitrary limit to the diameter of circles of affective identification without providing clear grounds for why such circles cannot be extended to all human beings as human beings.

This arbitrariness at the same time opens the door to more serious ethical problems. These potential problems are diagnosed by Norman Geras in his critique of Rorty. Geras begins by demonstrating that Rorty assumes a real capacity on the part of people to extend their range of concern beyond the self on the basis of identifications which can be more and more general, but at the same time refuses to extend this process of identification to humanity as a whole. Geras is interested in what causes the widening of the circle of identity to "stop short" of the widest possible identification with all human beings as members of humanity. When the circle "stops short" of identity with the humanity of human beings, Geras argues, the cause is always the elevation of some particular difference above the common elements that others share in as humans. Historically, the consequence of this elevation of difference over general human identity has been, more often than not, the sort of denial of humanity to others that, as I argued above, is the depth ethical cause of life-destructive relationships between cultures. "Starting, for instance, from fellow Americans, you might begin to extend your sense of 'we' ... But this process either stops short somewhere within humankind, or it does not. If it does, then some people, the people of Africa perhaps, or Hindus and atheists, get to be excluded from moral concern and they can go hungry or be massacred for all you care." Clearly, Rorty does not intend his argument as a licence for massacre. However, if he does not, then Rorty's own ethical concerns regarding the value of solidarity must be extended to the widest possible affective identification and moral concern, and that is identification with human beings as human. Geras continues: "On the other hand, if the process of extending your sense of 'we' does not stop short then you will get there after all: to a sense of 'we' capable of encompassing all of humanity."[29] Stopping the circle of identification short of the humanity of human beings does not deny that there is humanity, but only that whoever is left outside that circle does not count as human and thus is not a relevant object of ethical concern (i.e., the goodness or badness of their lives is of no consequence).

Perhaps the problem is not so easy to solve. The second form of the objection introduces an added complexity. This added complexity arises from considering the issue from the perspective of those who have found themselves outside the circle of "humanity" as constructed by colonialist discourse. If one looks at the problem of human identity from their perspective, the ethical consequences of positing universal human life-interests can appear to differ significantly from those posited by a life-grounded materialist perspective. The construction of universal human life-interests appears to be the primary cause of, rather than the solution to, their problems. Powerful groups have always legitimated their power by appeal to their being the true human beings, and thus their life-interests being the true life-interests. This conflation, it is argued, proves that the universalization of the idea of human being is always allied with the power to do so; the real life-consequence is the subordination of the life-value of those left outside "humanity" to the life-interests of the powerful. The solution does not depend on the excluded becoming included under this human identity but on their gaining an equal hearing for the differences that distinguish them as a particular group.

This argument is implied in the influential work of Iris Marion Young. While her object of analysis is the internal complexities of multiracial and multicultural societies rather than external relationships between colonial and colonized societies, Young provides a paradigm of the reasoning that underlies the second objection. Her essential point is that goods are always relative to particular groups. There is no shared good defined by human life-interests, and efforts to posit and promote such a good turn out to be illegitimate universalizations of a good particular to a given value system. "We only come to see ourselves mirrored in others. If we assume ... that communicative interaction means encountering differences of meaning, social position, or need that I do not share and identify with, then we can better describe how that interaction transforms my preferences. Different social positions encounter one another with the awareness of their differences. This does not mean that we have no similarities; difference is not total otherness. But it means that each position is aware that it does not comprehend the perspective of the others differently located, in the sense that it cannot be assimilated to one's own. There is thus something to be learned ... precisely because the perspectives are beyond one another and not reducible to a common good."[30] While I agree that differences are real and that communication across

---

30 Young, "Communication and the Other: Beyond Deliberative Democracy," 127.

differences is necessary to build understanding, Young's argument, like Hume's and Rorty's, tends toward being ethically self-undermining.

For Young, domination of all forms, whether within a particular society or between societies, would depend on the false universalization of a good that remains in itself particular. Hence the very idea of a common good would be at the root of domination because every common good is, in conditions of fundamental asymmetries of social power, really the dominant group's particular good forcibly imposed on the less powerful groups. If that is the case, then there is no real material basis for a common good grounded in our shared organic-social nature, but only differences of "need" that remain "beyond one another." But if the relevant differences remain beyond one another, then what is the motivation for *not* assimilating others' interests to one's own when they conflict and when one is in a powerful enough position to do so? Why should one want to learn from others if our identity is determined by our own interests, an implication that would only be encouraged and emphasized if we become conscious of ourselves through others who *differ* from us?

Young is forced to appeal to the *deus ex machina* of liberal tolerance of differences in order to provide ethical grounding for her ideal of constructive dialogue across differences. Her hopes notwithstanding, nothing in the idea of a conflict of interests, where each interest remains "beyond" the others and is never resolvable into a common human life-interest, provides grounds for concluding that, despite the opposition of interests, we can all learn from each other and deliberate together. It is only if we *respect* the differences of others as different expressions of a *common humanity* that we can account for any sense of ethical and political responsibility toward others. It is only when we learn how our differences are different ways of satisfying shared human life-requirements that meaningful co-operation and solidarity in their satisfaction is possible. When one recognizes that others, though culturally different, share the human life-requirements on which one's own life depends, one recognizes their equal liability to harm. Solidarity is possible only between people who recognize that they share an interest; universal solidarity is possible only on the basis of recognizing the universal life-interests that underlie cultural differences as the material conditions of the existence of the people who bear them and the socio-cultural and temporal conditions of their expression and enjoyment. The foundation of universal solidarity is thus the recognition of the universality of the requirements of human life because solidarity presupposes that one cares about the well-being of those with whom one stands in solidarity, and anyone's well-being depends in the first instance on the satisfaction of his or her human life-requirements.

If human beings recognize that, as humans, they share an equal liability to the harms of material deprivation, then it follows that they come to see that fundamental harms are a common threat. Whatever is required by our socio-organic nature is shared across differences as the life-ground basis of the conditions for the creation of good lives for each and all. If this argument is sound, then Young's understanding of cultural difference is both materially ungrounded (she ignores the natural and social conditions for the existence and reproduction of any cultural difference) and tends toward self-contradiction. The ethical horizon of her argument is agreement between different groups. She thus affirms by implication the extension of agreement between different groups that ultimately generates recognition of a common good. Yet she denies both the possibility and the ethical value of a common good. This tendency toward self-contradiction is a consequence of her failure to distinguish between system-requirements and ruling value systems which may be forcibly imposed on others, and the universal life-requirements and life-capacities whose satisfaction and free expression define in general terms the good life for any human being. It is precisely the satisfaction of these life-requirements for which all oppressed groups struggle. The differences in the struggles derive not from differences in their mode of being human but from differences in the social and historical systems that have structured their oppression.

The essential point is that two distinct and opposed conceptions of "humanity" are possible. The first, which reduces humanity to service to one particular set of system-requirements and ruling value system, is the fundamental justification of all forms of social domination. The second, anchored in our shared life-requirements, is the basis of the shared life-interests of all members of all groups and cultures, no matter how different the symbolic content of their lives. Recognition of common humanity in this sense is not the basis of oppression but rather the basis of care and concern for the life-conditions of others out of which solidarity with the oppressed is built. To recognize others as fellow humans is thus to affirm a common interest in comprehensive life-requirement satisfaction. It entails, therefore, a rejection of any and all social conditions in which some groups are forced to suffer deprivation of those life-requirements for the sake of others' luxurious accumulation.

The two forms of the objection to the life-grounded materialist idea of common humanity in shared life-interests are thus ultimately unsound. They are unsound not because cultural differences are not real or of potential life-value but because the objections take cultures to be self-contained wholes whose value is *assumed* rather than *explained*. Like the classical liberal conception of self-interest criticized in chapter 2, the understanding of culture implicit in these objections is developed in abstraction from the life-ground of the very existence of cultural differences. Just as the classical liberals simply assumed the existence of adult egos with different preferences and interests, so too Hume, Rorty, and Young assume the existence of different cultures structured by different conceptions of the good. Before an ego can form preferences that differ from other egos' preferences, the underlying requirements of its developing into an adult with the minimal intelligence necessary to form preferences must be satisfied. An analogous argument holds with regard to different cultures. Unless its members' life-requirements are minimally satisfied, a culture will not persist for a historically relevant length of time. The material conditions for the persistence and reproduction of all cultures are the same because their members' life-requirements are the same. The ethical problem at the root of colonialism is thus the denial of humanity to colonized or analogously dominated others. It is only because colonized others' humanity is denied that their life-ways can be forcibly destroyed or instrumentalized as mere tools to be exploited in the service of the expansionary society's system-requirements and ruling value system.

However, life-grounded materialist ethics must also take care to avoid the opposite and equally damaging understanding of difference. The opposite understanding of differences treats them as completely irrelevant to the structure and content of ethical care and concern. This problem is manifested clearly in Alain Badiou's attempt to reduce cultural differences to ethical irrelevance by demonstrating their ontological banality. Like the postmodernists whose arguments he otherwise rejects, Badiou recognizes differences as all-pervasive realities. But unlike postmodernists, he concludes that, just because differences are basic features of the universe as a whole, they are normatively irrelevant. He argues that "contemporary ethics kicks up a big fuss about 'cultural differences' ... but what we must recognize is that these differences hold no interest for thought, that they amount to nothing more than the infinite and self-evident multiplicity of humankind, as obvious in the difference between me and my cousin from Lyon as it is between the Shi'ite community of Iraq and the fat cowboys of Texas."[31] The problem with this argument is that the attempt to reduce cultural differences to ethical irrelevance by demonstrating their ontological banality is constructed in abstraction from the life-ground of value. It is of course true that, viewed as an abstract assertion, "a is different from b" tells us nothing of ethical interest about the terms of the relation. However, an understanding of human

31 Badiou, *Ethics*, 26.

differences cannot be achieved in abstraction from the real-life implications that follow for the human individuals or groups who differ from each other. Ontologically, there is no difference between the differences between Badiou and his cousin and between Texan cowboys and the Shi'ites. All differences are identical insofar as they are comprehended under the category "difference." Considered from the standpoint of the life-ground of value, however, there are ethically significant differences between differences when these differences are deployed as justifications for the domination and oppression of others. In order to comprehend the ethical significance of differences, they must be comprehended not in an abstract ontological register (the identity of all differences insofar as they are differences) but in a concrete life-grounded ethical register (differences as justifications for dominating others versus differences as the concrete expression of life-valuable human capacities).

Life-grounded materialist ethics understands cultural differences neither as absolute barriers between human beings nor as ethically irrelevant ontological categories. Instead, it understands cultural differences as the expression of human capacities in definite natural and social contexts. If the life-grounded form of institutional organization prioritizes the satisfaction of life-requirements for the sake of more coherently inclusive ranges of capability realization, then there is a common life-standard for the evaluation of changes to any established pattern of institutional life. When the changes introduced by an external political agent are rooted in the drive to expand that agent's domestic social system to a foreign context, it will be justified by reference to the absence of political agency on the part of those being assimilated to the colonial or neo-colonial project. In all such cases, one finds the ethically illegitimate universalization of culturally particular system-requirements and ruling value system as the justifying ground of the practices. It does not follow that every conception of the good and its material presuppositions is a cultural particular. If that were the case, then genuine solidarity would be impossible.

The concept of the good life for human beings does not make sense if it is abstracted from the natural and social life-requirements that human life as such presupposes. To the extent that the good refers to life as it can be lived on earth, it must be grounded in access to human life-requirement satisfiers and to the social institutions that produce and distribute them. These resources and institutions are the shared conditions of being alive and developing the capacities that make human life worth living. Cultural differences are valuable to the extent that these differences constitute different ways of satisfying life-requirements and engendering more coherently inclusive ranges of life-capacity realization on the planet as a whole. Different ways of actually satisfying life-requirements are unified by their instrumental life-value. At the same time, they can serve as sources of learning for other societies whose institutional structure might be deficient in the provision of resources required for the satisfaction of life-requirements in one or more dimensions. Changes that rectify such deficiencies without imposing new life-costs on anyone else are thus life-valuable to the extent that the political power to make those changes is generated by the people affected by the deficiencies and actually leads to their successful correction. Where changes are initiated by an external power and are designed to increase the instrumental value of others as servants to the expansionary society, those changes are illegitimate and disvaluable from the life-grounded materialist perspective.

The reality of shared life-requirements is the material foundation for the idea of a shared humanity in common life-interests. The idea of a shared humanity, in turn, highlights the reality of the inhumanity of treatment that the colonized have suffered at the hands of expansionary societies. Our shared life-requirements form the foundation of solidarity with the oppressed. Insofar as people who struggle to continue to live prove by their struggles that they value life, it must be assumed that they value that which human life requires. Since human life has shared life-requirements, it follows that all who struggle to satisfy those life-requirements demonstrate thereby a common life-interest in the natural, socio-cultural, and temporal requirements of free human life. Human social self-consciousness, when it opens itself to the shared life-requirements and capacities of others, is always capable in principle of recognizing the common life-interest denied by the justifying discourses of colonial domination. Once this common humanity is recognized, a "universal human response" of "wanting to do something" about the suffering of others is engendered.[32]

This universal human response mobilizes people in "advanced" countries against the politics and policies of their own government. These movements thus prove that the ethical contradiction between system-requirements and values and life-requirements and values can emerge within societies as well as between them. In the next chapter, I examine the structure of this contradiction within liberal-capitalist societies as it affects their ability to recognize and satisfy their members' life-requirements in each of the three classes examined in chapter 3.

32 Cohen, *States of Denial*, 195.

5

The Instrumentalization of Life-Value:
The Material Irrationality
of Global Capitalism

AS I ARGUED IN CHAPTER TWO, no society can persist for a historically relevant length of time if it does not regularly satisfy at least the physical-organic life-requirements of the majority of its members. However, it does not follow that in satisfying these requirements the human good of its members is intended. Oppressive and exploitative societies can satisfy life-requirements not because it is life-valuable to do so but because the reproduction of the system requires that there be sufficient numbers of people healthy enough to perform the socially necessary labour. Slave economies are the extreme expression of this form of instrumentalization of human life. Since contemporary liberal-democratic capitalist societies are not slave economies, since they are structured by constitutions that assert inviolable individual rights, and since they allow for periodic changes of government, it might be thought that these societies have solved the contradiction between system-requirements and values and life-requirements and values. In this chapter I argue that, real advances notwithstanding, the contradiction has not been solved by liberal-democratic capitalism.

To argue that this contradiction has not been solved is not to argue that liberal-democratic capitalism does not do a better a job of satisfying its members' life-requirements and coherently enabling their life-capacities than the slave societies of the past. I do not dispute that liberal-democratic capitalist society is capable of materially and legally including under the protections of citizenship groups formerly excluded as congenital inferiors. The ability of liberal-democratic capitalism to change in response to struggles of the marginalized, exploited, and oppressed is evidence that it is a more consciously life-grounded form of social organization than others premised on invidious moral hierarchies of sex or race or caste. At the same time, the real gains in life-coherent satisfaction of subaltern members' life-requirements have not been achieved without struggle and, as neo-liberal attacks on social security and public institutions from the 1980s to the present prove, are always fragile.

Indeed, the systematic attempt to roll back the life-valuable gains of past struggle is the primary evidence that the ruling value system of liberal-democratic capitalism is not life-grounded. Instead, as I have already observed, money-value rules liberal-democratic capitalist society. Thus, the ethical contradiction between liberal-democratic capitalism's system-requirements and ruling value system and life-requirements and values takes the form of the instrumentalization of people's life-requirements and life-capacities by the money-value system. This instrumentalization is not noticeable from within the money-value system because the system conflates life-value with money-value, with the consequence that where money-value is expanding, it is assumed that life-value is expanding as well. Yet, not only is there no material identity between the growth of money-value and the growth of life-value; the history of struggles against capitalism suggests that life-value can develop only when the money-value system is subordinated to it.

These struggles are directed against the social structures of dependence that define liberal-democratic capitalism. Social dependence on money-value follows from the commodification of life-necessities. Since people must pay for that which their lives require, they find themselves bound to labour markets to earn the wages they need to pay for necessities made available for sale in commodity markets. This constitutes a structure of oppressive dependence because people have no real choice but to work for a wage if they are to survive and flourish under capitalism. The life-requirement satisfiers which people must access in order to live and live well are available only as commodities. Commodities are produced and distributed not because people's lives require them but when it is profitable to do so. Instead of depending on nature and collective labour to directly satisfy their life-requirements, human beings living in a capitalist society depend on finding a job that pays enough to enable them to purchase the commodified forms of life-requirement satisfiers. This dependence on labour *markets*, rather than *labour*, has the further effect of instrumentalizing human life-requirements and capacities as tools of money-value growth.

The development of human life-capacities, rather than occurring in ever more inclusively coherent ranges of life-valuable expression and enjoyment, is dependent on what labour markets are willing to purchase. Concretely, this means that humans living in a capitalist economy must instrumentalize their own possibilities for life-valuable activity, conforming their interests and talents to what they gamble labour-markets will be willing to buy. Thus, capitalism makes possible the development, expression, and enjoyment of life-capacities, but only those which prove money-valuable. The capacities which are of greatest value to capitalism are those whose development will return most money, both to those who employ labour and to the workers. Whether these life-capacities have life-value is not considered independently of their money-value.

For life-grounded materialist ethics, comprehensive life-requirement satisfaction is instrumentally valuable as the necessary condition for the expression and enjoyment of the intrinsic life-value of our sentient, cognitive, imaginative, and creative capacities. Under capitalism's money-value system, the satisfaction of our life-requirements and the expression and enjoyment of our life-capacities are both reduced to instrumental values of the expansion and accumulation of money-value. For life-grounded materialist critique, this instrumentalization of life-requirements and the life-capacities their satisfaction enables constitutes the primary problem of liberal-democratic capitalism. Although this critique has roots within and maintains a conceptual connection to the Marxist criticism of capitalist exploitation and alienation, its aims are not reducible to a universalized conception of working-class interests or an understanding of socialism as a more productive society than capitalism. Its concerns are more general – diagnosing the systematic ways is which money-value instrumentalizes the totality of human life-requirements and life-capacities, not only the productive labour of the working class; and its goals more universal – limiting economic activity to the scale necessary to achieve the goal of comprehensive satisfaction of life-requirements. In order to understand both the critique of the instrumentalization of life-value by money-value and the differences between life-grounded materialist ethics and the Marxist critique of capitalism, the argument must begin with a more complete explication of the nature of the money-value system.

5.1 THE CONFLATION OF LIFE-VALUE AND MONEY-VALUE IN CAPITALISM

Recognition of the conflation between life-value and money-value as a material ethical problem is as old as recorded human thought. In the Book of Isaiah the prophet writes, "woe to men who add house to house, who join one field to another, 'till there is room for none but them in all the land."[1] Isaiah's point is clear: the real value of homes and fields is that they satisfy human life-requirements; it is not their money-value to those who would accumulate them without limit. He thus uncovers the general

---

1 Isaiah 5: 8–10, in Moffat, *The Bible: A New Translation.*

conflict between life-value and money-value central to the present argument. Capitalist society is a historically specific form of this conflict. What is unique about the capitalist form of this conflict is that its ruling value-system denies the very possibility of a conflict. Judging from within the ruling value system of capitalism, there cannot be a conflict between the life-value and money-value of natural resources and the social products of labour because life-value and money-value are conflated.

One of the earliest and clearest expressions of this conflation is found in Hobbes. He is perhaps the first to openly equate the value of human beings with their price. With characteristic bluntness he declares that "the *value*, or Worth of a man is, as of all other things, his price, that is to say, so much as would be given for the use of his power and therefore is not absolute."[2] While Hobbes is writing in a pre-industrial economy, the social changes out of which industrial capitalism would emerge were already well advanced by the time of the English Civil War.[3] Hobbes makes clear that by this time it was possible to think of the value of anything, including human life, as identical to its price. It follows that if human life is valued only by its price, it becomes, like any other thing with a price, a fungible good, valuable to the extent that it is exchangeable. A person who has no price has no value.

Initially, it was the reduction of human beings to exchangeable commodities that motivated Marx's critique of capitalist society. What concerns Marx about this reduction is first, that it destroys the bonds of solidarity between people, and second, that it threatens the satisfaction of human life-requirements and the development of life-capacities. While not nostalgic for pre-capitalist societies, Marx is nevertheless clear that social solidarity must be weakened where people relate to each other primarily as buyer and seller. "If money is the bond binding me to *human* life, binding society to me, connecting me with nature and man, is not money the bond of all bonds? Can it not dissolve and bind all ties? Is it not, therefore, also the universal agent of separation? It is the coin that really separates as well as the real binding agent."[4] Recast in life-grounded materialist terms, Marx asserts that the specific ethical difference of a capitalist society is that money, as the universal medium of valuation and exchange, becomes at the same time, and for that reason,

COMMUNITY

---

2 Hobbes, *Leviathan*, 68.

3 The problem of the emergence and consolidation of agrarian capitalism is far too complex to enter into here. See Brenner, "Agrarian Class Structure and Economic Development in Pre-Industrial Europe" and "The Agrarian Roots of European Capitalism," 10–63, 213–328; Wood, *The Origins of Capitalism*; McNally, *Political Economy and the Rise of Capitalism*; Moores, *The Making of Bourgeois Europe*, 155–86.

4 Marx, "Economic and Philosophical Manuscripts of 1844," 324.

the basis of all social relationships. Human exchange relationships, which, as I argued in chapter 2, developed as a series of networks and interactions whose purpose was to support and maintain life, become alienated from their life-ground. Instead of production and exchange supporting life-maintenance and development, life-maintenance and development now serve the growth of money-value. Those who have no money have no legitimate claim on the assistance of others or on social wealth to satisfy their life-requirements.

Under the capitalist money-value system, the existence of life-requirements as necessities without which life cannot survive or develop does not constitute the basis for legitimate demands on other individual members of society or social institutions such as governments. Under the money-value system, there is no binding legal obligation to fulfill others' life-requirements just because they will suffer harm if they are not met. There is only an economic opportunity to make them pay for the things they require. As Smith says of food in *The Wealth of Nations*, "It is not from the benevolence of the butcher ... that we expect our dinner, but from [his] regard to his own interest. We address ourselves, not to [his] humanity, but to [his] self-interest, and never talk to them of our own necessities but of their advantages."[5]

Once money has become the universal basis of valuation and exchange, it interposes itself between people, nature, and collective labour as a system-requirement of their survival. While nature and collective nature always remain the ultimate foundations of life-support, money appears as the immediate requirement without which life cannot survive or develop. Once money has become a system-requirement in this way, it forces a revaluation of human capacities in money-value terms. If people's lives depend on the possession of money, and money can be gained only in exchange for labour, then people experience their own life-capacities only as potential commodities for sale on labour markets. "You must make everything that is yours *saleable*, i.e., useful," says Marx. Making yourself an object for sale is necessary precisely because the money-value system is incapable of grasping the intrinsic value of life-capacity expression.[6] Thus, unless a buyer can be found for one's talents then, no matter how exquisite the creations of those talents, they will be regarded as worthless. The internalization of the culturally approved markers of success, authorized by the ruling value system, results in an internal alienation from the life-ground of value. This internal alienation is produced in people by the external alienation of the ruling

5 Smith, *The Wealth of Nations*, 119.
6 Marx, "Economic and Philosophical Manuscripts of 1844," 310.

money-value system from the life-ground of value on which the institutional environment in which they live is based.

The social structure that has developed in liberal-democratic capitalist societies cannot reproduce itself unless the external alienation between the ruling value system and the life-ground of value is accepted as normal and legitimate. The transition from a system-value externally alienated from the life-ground of value to a norm guiding individuals' actions is not a mechanical reflex of economic forces; it is strategically cultivated in people by the education system, the corporate media, and government policy; is reinforced by peer pressure and what Fromm calls "automaton conformity" (the desire to not stand out born of feelings of isolation and helplessness); and finally undergirded by everyone's real dependence on capitalist economic growth for their life and livelihood.[7] Horkheimer and Adorno capture this strategic cultivation of normative compliance in *Dialectic of Enlightenment:* "everyone is enclosed at an early age in a system of churches, professional associations, and other such concerns, which constitute the most sensitive instrument of social control. Anyone who wants to avoid ruin must see that he is not found wanting when weighed in the scales of this apparatus. Otherwise, he will lag behind in life and ultimately perish."[8] Internal alienation from the life-ground of value thus appears as the conscious valuation of an individual's own life as good to the extent to which it conforms to the patterns of activity required by the money-value system.

In illustration of this argument consider the following – admittedly extreme – example. The content of the example was drawn from the court records of a civil lawsuit filed in Utah and reported in *Harper's* magazine. The case concerned a sales manager who decided that his staff needed extra motivation. He organized a hike and asked for a volunteer to undergo an undisclosed ordeal that would illustrate the sort of commitment to the job expected of everyone. The events that ensued express perfectly the consequences of the internal alienation from the life-ground of value that the internalization of the money-value system produces. "In an effort to prove his loyalty and determination to Christopher [the manager] and the company, Chad Hudgens volunteered. Christopher told Hudgens to lie down ... and ordered other team members to hold Hudgens by the arms and legs. Christopher then slowly poured a gallon jug of water over Hudgens' mouth and nostrils in an exercise ... known as waterboarding. At the end of the demonstration, Christopher told the team to work as hard at making sales as Hudgens

7 Fromm, *Escape from Freedom,* 183.
8 Horkheimer and Adorno, *Dialectic of Enlightenment,* 150.

J

had worked to breathe."[9] Hudgens and Christopher manifest different forms of internal alienation between themselves and the life-ground of value. Hudgens did not know what to expect when he volunteered. The evidence suggests that he did not care, motivated as he was by the desire to curry favour and advance his career. In Hudgens, the money-value system compromised his care and concern for his own well-being. In Christopher, by contrast, the money-value system compromised his ability to care and concern himself with the well-being of others as fragile organic-social beings. Christopher's actions are best understood as a distorted form of care for his team, rather than an absence of care altogether. The way he expressed this care ignored the physical and psychological harm his treatment of Hudgens would cause because he was treating Hudgens not as a fragile organic-social being but as a potential maximizer of money-value. Christopher's confusion of financial well-being with life-value is a particular example of the general conflation between money- and life-value that rules capitalist society.

The conflation of life-value and money-value is not confined to the pricing of life-requirements and life-capacities but extends as well to the totality of objects of the human senses. In this dimension, the conflation between money-value and life-value occludes the qualitative distinctiveness of these objects. All things are reduced to the different quantities of money for which they may be exchanged. "The dealer in minerals," says Marx, "sees only the commercial value but not the beauty and specific character of the mineral."[10] It would be more accurate to say that the mineral dealer sees the beauty *as* the money-value of the mineral, but the fundamental point is not altered: people who depend on money tend to internalize it as the value-system that governs their valuations of themselves, other people, and the things of the world. There is thus a pervasive conflation between life-value and money-value, a conflation which not only impoverishes our experience of ourselves, other people, social relationships, and the natural and social worlds but generates materially irrational policies. It blinds people to the dangerous reality that the growth of money-value depends on the unsustainable exploitation of natural life-support and social life-development systems.

Capitalist economies depend for their "health" on the steady growth of profitable investment opportunities. As Marx argues in the *Grundrisse,* money is incapable of any form of movement other than a quantitative one; it can only increase itself. According to its concept, it is the essence of all use values; yet as always being a definite quantity of money (hence

9 "Breathing Is for Closers," *Harper's* (June 2008), 28.
10 Ibid., 302.

capital), its quantitative limitation contradicts its quality. Hence it lies in its nature to exceed its own limits.[11] Money is the essence of all use-values because use-values can be acquired only though monetary exchange. But if monetary exchange did nothing more than return to the investor exactly what was advanced, no one would invest because the whole point of investment in a capitalist economy is profitable return. Thus money must not only circulate, it must circulate as capital, i.e., as money-value that produces more money-value. Ultimately, the process through which money-value grows traces back to the conversion of natural resources into saleable commodities. Money-value cannot expand unless nature is exploited more and more intensively. Human beings find themselves trapped between the system-requirement of paid employment imposed on them and their more fundamental life-requirement for a natural environment that can sustain life.

At this point, the concept of life-value, implied but never explicitly developed in Marx and the Marxist humanist tradition, comes to play a necessary role. While Marx systematically exposed both the form of dependence on money-value peculiar to capitalism and the way in which money-value, by implication, appears as the measure of life-value, he did not develop his arguments in a systematically life-grounded direction. This lack of explicit life-grounded development is most evident in his straightforward adoption of "bourgeois" political economy's conception of use-value. For Marx, as for Adam Smith, a use-value is anything that any person requires or simply demands for any reason at all. It makes no difference, Marx argues on the first page of *Capital*, whether a demand stems from the "stomach or the fancy."[12] If use-values are not themselves grounded in an explicit concept of life-value, and if socialism is understood as a society that prioritizes the production of use-values over exchange values, then there is no internal brake on the possibility that socialism too becomes driven to materially irrational scales of production. I will return to this problem in the final chapter. Here I want to concentrate on the specifically capitalist money-value system.

The deepest problem generated by the capitalist money-value system is that it is systematically life-blind in its development. That money-value is not identical to life-value is proven by the fact that there are many forms of profitable investment that, as a direct consequence of the productive methods they employ and the products they produce, destroy life. The way in which the ruling money-value system understands the problem of carbon emissions illustrates this key claim.

11 Marx, *Outlines of the Critique of Political Economy*, 200.
12 Marx, *Capital*, 1: 43.

From the money-value perspective, increased productivity and energy consumption mean that the economy is growing. If the economy is growing, there is more money-value in circulation, which the ruling value-system counts as good. If money-value growth registers as good, then anything that might disrupt it registers as bad. Placing limits on the consumption of fossil fuels would check money-value growth, and it is thus counted as a bad, even though, from the life-value perspective, the limits are necessary. The claim advanced in the introduction to a 2007 report by then Canadian Environment Minister John Baird illustrates this point. He wrote that "Canadians want balanced solutions to environmental protection and economic growth. Balance means making sure that economic decisions are environmentally responsible. But balance also requires that environmental decisions be economically responsible."[13] If balance must be established between two factors, then it follows that those two factors are independent of each other (otherwise there would be nothing to balance). Instead of understanding the economy as the hinge between the natural field of life-support and the social field of life-development with life-value the connecting term between them, the report treats the environment and the economy as external to each other.

This externality is overcome by establishing money-value as the basis on which "responsible" decisions can be made. The minister urges that environmental decisions be responsible to "economic growth." But what does economic growth mean in the context of the report? It means growth of the Canadian GDP as measured by the money-value of the goods and services produced in the country each year. "Gross Domestic Product is the best available indicator of the overall health of the Canadian economy, as it measures the market value of the goods and services produced in the Canadian economy."[14]

The life-blind nature of this construction is immediately evident. As a growing body of ecological economics research has demonstrated, money-value growth as measured by GDP masks the environmental costs of economic growth in a materially irrational manner.[15] Human life and life-activity, including economic activity, is always activity that occurs within and depends on the natural field of life-support. Where economic health is understood as money-value growth, this real structure of dependence is obscured behind materially irrational demands for endless economic growth. As George W. Bush once said, strategies to combat climate

---

13 Drummond, "The Cost of Bill C-288 to Canadian Families and Business," 2.
14 Ibid., 18.
15 See, for example, Brown and Garver, *Right Relationship*, 9–12; Victor, *Managing without Growth*, 129–31.

change must be developed "that [do] not undermine economic growth or prevent nations from delivering greater prosperity to their people."[16] Since human life is compatible with many forms of economic activity, but cannot survive in environments that fail to satisfy its organic conditions of existence, it is obvious, if one begins from the life-requirements of human beings, that the natural field of life-support is necessarily prior in importance to any other value the economy might serve. Therefore, it is materially irrational to construct the economy as an independent system of value which has interests equal and opposed to the shared human life-interest in a life-supportive environment. Yet, that is exactly what the report proceeds to do.

To elaborate on this problem, consider the main driver of Canadian economic growth since 2003 – oil sands extraction in northern Alberta. The high price of oil has made this extraction process profitable, and therefore good from the money-value perspective. From the life-value perspective, on the other hand, this industry is destructive. Oil sands extraction requires almost as much energy input (in the form of natural gas which is burned to produce the heat necessary to separate the oil from the sand) as it yields in refineable crude oil. Second, it requires massive amounts of water to produce the steam used in the separation process. As a result, the Athabasca River, its watershed, and the people of the First Nations who still depend directly on the health of the river system for their livelihood are threatened. Finally, oil sands extraction is a massive producer of greenhouse gases.[17] Nevertheless, successive Canadian and Albertan governments continue to insist that so long as the oil sands are profitable they will be developed, regardless of the environmental life-costs.

The life-blind nature of money-value growth under capitalism is paradigmatically expressed in the many cases where the economic "health" of corporations is secured by profits on the sale of life-destructive commodities.[18] The life-destructive effects of such forms of investment can appear only when money-value and life-value are distinguished, and the former made subservient to the latter. Where money-value and life-value are conflated such that the growth of money-value appears as the growth of life-value, life-value can be destroyed without anyone noticing the problem. As McMurtry concludes, "the [money]-value system does not calculate

16 Biello, "Bush Administration Pushes Climate Change Action into the Future."

17 Polaris Institute, "Controversial Oil Substitutes Increase Emissions, Devour Landscapes." See also, Environmental Defence, *Canada's Toxic Tar Sands: The Most Destructive Project on Earth.*

18 Adpated from McMurtry, *Unequal Freedoms,* 299.

into its judgment [about investment strategies] whether life has been gained or lost ... its objective is to net more money ... Money is not used for life. Life is used for money. The final measure of the Good is increase or decrease of money sums."[19] The almost magical productivity of capitalism, a productivity which could be used to ensure that no one suffer the harms of life-requirement deprivation, is squandered in a ceaseless quest for more money-value growth, even to the point at which long-term environmental health is threatened. Instead of comprehensive satisfaction of life-requirements in a materially rational, sustainable life-economy, one finds despoliation of the natural life-support system alongside human deprivation on all planes of being alive: homelessness; lack of access to water; mass starvation or malnutrition; lack of access to health care; political, educational, and cultural systems reduced to servants of the growth of money-value; and loss of the experience of free time.

In summary, the money-value system is the ruling value-system of liberal-democratic capitalist society. As the ruling value-system it is the ultimate basis of legitimacy of both public policy and individual choice. In liberal-democratic capitalist society, life-value is ultimately measured by money-value, with the result that good and bad policy, law, and individual choice are determined relative to the expansion or contraction of money-value. Life-value is, at the level of principle, conflated with money-value, with the result that, at the level of practice, life-value is instrumentalized by money-value. Life-requirements and life-capacities are reduced to instrumental factors in the reproduction and growth of the money-value system. This instrumentalization of life-requirements and capacities is the basic structure of ethical harm in liberal-democratic capitalist societies. Where policy and people mistake the growth of life-value for the growth of money-value, they can support policies or make decisions in their own lives which reduce life-value but increase money-value without noticing the loss of life-value. Materially irrational patterns of social behaviour are generated which systematically damage the natural field of life-support and the social field of life-development. People can unwittingly contribute to patterns of life-activity whose long-term consequences threaten the collapse of the life-sustaining and life-enabling fields of natural and social organization. It is now time to consider in more detail the structure of ethical harm in liberal-democratic capitalist society. In section 5.2, I clarify the philosophical principles underlying this conception of harm. In section 5.3, I examine the manifold ways in which people are harmed by the instrumentalization of the three classes of human life-requirements.

19 Ibid.

5.2 LIFE-VALUE AS END IN ITSELF

There is a close connection between the life-grounded materialist critique of the instrumentalization of human life-requirements and life-capacities and Kant's famous formulation of the categorical imperative: "act so that you treat humanity, whether in your own person or in that of another, always as an end and never as a means only."[20] The aim of this section is to explore this connection and indicate the ways in which life-grounded materialist ethics goes beyond Kant's understanding of this principle.

For Kant, persons are ends in themselves because they are rational beings capable of autonomous goal determination. Kant's concern is not simply with mundane interpersonal interactions in which individuals might violate one another's rights but equally with the implications for individuals of the institutional organization of society. Forms of social organization that violate the rights that follow from our being persons are as unethical as the intentional actions of individuals. As Harry van der Linden argues, "heteronomy is not merely being conditioned by the laws of the inclinations, but also by being subject to the arbitrary will of others. Thus we can characterize existing social and political institutions as heteronomous [to the extent that their ruling value system treats the people subject to it as mere means]."[21] Thus, Kant is not concerned exclusively with personal ethical rules of individual conduct but at least implies a properly social ethics with implications for the institutional structure of society. Since Kant is concerned with the effects of actions on others, and actions are always institutionally mediated, it follows that his claim that "this principle of humanity and of every rational creature as an end in itself is the supreme limiting condition on freedom of the actions of each man" must have implications for the institutions within which action takes place.[22] The categorical imperative makes sense only when we consider human action in a social context. In such a context, the crucial questions are: what forms of activity does the given institutional structure valorize and enable, and what forms does it ignore and disable? Moreover, the full ethical value of Kant's understanding of human beings as ends in themselves unfolds if his argument is modified along life-grounded materialist lines. Two modifications are needed.

First, for life-grounded materialist ethics, humans are ends in themselves as organic-social beings expressing ourselves through "thought,

---

20 Kant, *Foundations of the Metaphysics of Morals*, 54.
21 Van der Linden, *Kantian Ethics and Socialism*, 32.
22 Kant, *Foundations of the Metaphysics of Morals*, 55.

felt being and action." [23] This materialist understanding of the ground of intrinsic value contrasts with Kant's abstraction of rationality from the embodied human whole. Life-grounded materialist ethics stresses the unity of body and reason, of instrumental and intrinsic life-value. The social self-conscious agency through which we make our lives intrinsically valuable expressions of our life-capacities can develop if and only if our life-requirements are satisfied. For Kant, by contrast, only rational selves have intrinsic value; everything else, even those things that satisfy a life-requirement without which that rational self cannot continue to live, has a price. "In the realm of ends everything has either a price or a dignity. Whatever has a price can be replaced by something else as its equivalent; on the other hand, whatever is above all price, and therefore admits of no equivalent, has a dignity. That which is related to general human inclinations and needs has a market price."[24] The problem that Kant fails to note is that the life of human beings as rational selves depends on the satisfaction of the body's life-requirements. When those life-requirements are priced commodities, the dignity of human beings is compromised when, for reasons that are social and beyond their power as individuals to control, they lack the money to purchase the commodity they require. The objects that satisfy our life-requirements are non-substitutable goods without which our lives are necessarily harmed. Since the exercise of autonomous determination of goals presupposes organic life, there can be no real separation of rationality from its embodied foundation. Consequently, if market prices are driven above what a person is able to pay, her dignity will inevitably be undermined because the life-capacities that must develop in order for her to live as a rational, self-determining being will be disabled or destroyed.

Kant does not see this problem for his own conception of ethical value for three interrelated reasons. First, as Lucien Goldman argues, Kant's historical context presented no progressive alternatives to capitalism. Thus, his social and political imagination was limited to the triumph of liberal-capitalism over archaic structures of paternalistic and authoritarian law.[25]

Second, the metaphysics of the person that Kant treats as a necessary presupposition of the metaphysics of morals depend on ethically prioritizing the rational over the material elements of human being. Hence Kant's conception of the person as a rational mind, on one side,

23 McMurtry, "What is Good, What is Bad: The Value of All Values Across Times, Places, and Theories," 96.
24 Kant, *Foundations of the Metaphysics of Morals*, 60.
25 Goldman, *Immanuel Kant*, 170.

and a material body, on the other leads him (despite the deeper implications of his conception of persons as ends in themselves) toward a dualistic conception of value. Only our rational nature has intrinsic value; our life-requirements and inclinations are of relative value. Nevertheless, this rigid distinction in value is unsustainable. While it is true that life-requirements are instrumental to the realization of intrinsic life-value, they are not of secondary ethical importance. For socially self-conscious embodied agents, failure to satisfy life-requirements necessarily reduces or destroys the ability to express and enjoy intrinsically life-valuable capacities, while satisfying them in free interaction with others is itself a form of intrinsically life-valuable realization of our social nature.

Third, Kant's argument lacks the conceptual resources needed to make the essential distinction between objective life-requirements and subjective consumer demands. For Kant, both fall under the more general category of heteronomous drives. These drives are so lacking in dignity that Kant believes it must be "the wish of every rational being ... to free himself completely from them."[26] This claim can apply only to those subjective inclinations which impel us toward life-indifferent or life-destructive ends. Our humanity, by contrast, is defined by the structure of our species' life-requirements and the development of the life-capacities that their satisfaction makes possible. To wish to be free of our human life-requirements is to wish to be free from our human nature, and therefore the material basis of our humanity, and therefore from the very basis of ethical value (treating *humanity* as an end in itself), which it was the great philosophical achievement of Kant to identify. The wish of every human being who understands her real conditions of life is to live in a society which satisfies those requirements for each and all as the necessary material condition of each and all achieving the widest and deepest development, realization, and enjoyment of life-valuable capacities consistent with the health of the natural field of life-support and the social field of life-development. This goal leads to the second necessary modification.

The second life-grounded materialist modification concerns Kant's understanding of the relationships between individuals in a legally well-ordered society. Unlike Hobbes, who assumes that individuals are essentially threats to each other, Kant understands human beings as linked together in positive relationships of mutual affirmation of each others' goals. The ends of any person, who is an end in himself, must as far as possible also be my end if the conception of an end in itself is to have its full effect on me.[27] The limitations in Kant's view concern once again its

26 Kant, *Foundations of the Metaphysics of Morals*, 53.
27 Ibid., 55.

abstract and one-sided character. If the goal of mutual affirmation of each other's ends is to realize its full ethical value as the organizing principle of human social life, the content of the ends must themselves be examined for consistency with the natural and social conditions of life and life-development. If one pays attention only to the abstract universality of the ends, it is possible to ethically affirm individual actions which cumulatively destroy the natural conditions of life. In a sense, just this sort of tacit agreement exists among people who "agree" to continue to consume energy at unsustainable levels in order to maintain their "standard of living." To ensure that mutual agreement is materially and not only formally rational, individuals must ground their individual purposes in a prior shared commitment to maintaining and enhancing the life-supportive capacity of nature and the life-developing capacity of society. If our individual ends contradict the shared conditions of life and life-development, the formal universality of our projects can undermine the shared material universality of conditions of life-support and development. Life-grounded materialism thus points beyond the antithesis between individual ends and social regulations by disclosing the material irrationality of ignoring the potential incoherence between individual projects and their natural and social conditions of possibility. As McMurtry argues, "the individual is not reducible to, but grounded on, this social life host for self-articulation to be possible. The individual achieves individuality by expressing this social life-ground in some way particular to personal capacity and choice."[28] Thus, the intrinsic value of individuals is not an a priori abstraction but an achievement of natural and social life-organization. The life-value of the instituted structures of organization is determined by the degree to which they enable free life-valuable activity through the comprehensive satisfaction of people's life-requirements. As I will now argue in detail, the liberal-democratic capitalist world does not realize this value.

The ruling value system of liberal-democratic capitalism does not treat human life-requirements as the instrumental conditions of life-capacity realization but as structures of dependence to be exploited in the service of the growth of money-value. Instead of understanding human life-requirements as instrumental to the development, realization, and enjoyment of the life-value of our defining capacities, the money-value system treats these life-requirements simply as sources of consumer demands whose satisfaction is instrumental to the realization of profit on investment. To have the material basis of one's humanity treated as an instrument of the reproduction of the system is to suffer harm, not only

28 McMurtry, *The Cancer Stage of Capitalism*, 89.

because for billions of people even the basic requirements of life are priced beyond their means but also because one's life-value is subordinated to the non-living system-value of profitable investment. It is the instrumentalization of life-requirements and life-capacities by the ruling money value-system that constitutes the most pervasive form of harm in liberal-democratic capitalist societies. I now turn to the more detailed examination of the different manifestations of this structure of harm.

5.3 THE INSTRUMENTALIZATION OF HUMAN LIFE-REQUIREMENTS AND CAPACITIES

In order to avoid misunderstanding, it is important to emphasize at the outset that the forms of harm to be explicated here have been abstracted from the more ethically and politically complex social context in which they affect peoples' lives. These forms exist in tension and conflict with struggles to maintain varying degrees of life-grounded institutional structure. I have abstracted them from this more complex background for purposes of clarity, not political hyperbole. That said, these harms are real and their reality is subject to empirical confirmation.

5.3.1 The Instrumentalization of Physical-Organic Life-Requirements

The life-value of the natural world lies in its being the ultimate source of all physical-organic life-requirement satisfiers. Under the ruling money-value system, this life-value is systematically conflated with the money-value that can be realized as a result of the commodification of nature. The harm this conflation between the money-value and life-value of nature causes is rooted in the pricing of non-substitutable physical-organic life-requirement satisfiers without regard for people's ability to pay for them. In a society ruled by the money-value system, these life-requirements, because they are non-voluntary requirements of human life, constitute a structure of dependence between human beings and the commodity circuits of the capitalist market. As Lebowitz notes, it is true that workers in a capitalist society can in principle choose to whom they sell their labour "but they cannot choose whether or not to sell their power to perform labour (if they are to survive)."[29] Instead of our shared physical-organic life-requirements being seen as an opportunity for a co-operative social project, they are understood as opportunities to be exploited for money. This social dependence on money is harmful to

---

29 Lebowitz, *Build It Now*, 15.

human beings in a way that natural dependence on physical-organic resources in general is not.

To be dependent on nature for the resources that our organic being
requires is not to be instrumentalized by nature. Nature is not a conscious entity and thus cannot exploit the living things which have evolved
within it. Natural dependence is thus not a source of ethical harm but
simply the basic material framework outside of which life is impossible.
Were society organized on the basis of explicit recognition of our shared
life-interests, our dependence on nature would be the basis for a co-
operative social project. Where the money-value system rules, our shared
life-interest in satisfying physical-organic requirements of life appears as
a private interest in maximizing money-value by exploiting natural resources and the labour of others. The necessity of regularly satisfying
these life-requirements is thus treated as a source of power over the materially dispossessed. To be subject to the arbitrary power of others is to
be reduced to a mere means to others' ends. The commodification of
basic life-requirement satisfiers turns the shared life-value of their satisfaction into money-value accumulating in private hands.

What applies to human life-requirements applies also to the natural basis of their satisfaction. Capitalism originates in the privatization
of the natural field of life-support. Over the past three hundred years,
this process of privatizing enclosure has become more extensive and intensive. The enclosure movement which expropriated the commons
from the English peasantry has spread across the world through a process that David Harvey calls "accumulation by dispossession."[30] However,
enclosure is no longer confined to natural spaces and resources; increasingly, the privatizing drive is extending into the molecular structure of
life itself. The new enclosure movement, to use Pat Roy Mooney's apt
term, is a struggle to control the most basic chemical processes of life
through obtaining patents on the "products" of genetic engineering.[31]
As with the original enclosure movement, it is small-scale farmers, especially in the Global South, whose lives are most negatively affected. As
Vandana Shiva argues, "the corporate demand for the conversion of a
common heritage into a commodity, and for profits generated through
this transformation to be treated as property rights, will have serious political and economic repercussions for Third World farmers ... patent
protection...makes them totally dependent on industrial supplies for vital inputs such as seeds."[32]

30 Harvey, *The New Imperialism,* 137–82.
31 Mooney, "The ETC Century: Concentration in Corporate Power."
32 Shiva, *Biopiracy: The Plunder of Nature and Knowledge,* 54.

The heart of this new enclosure movement is the corporate project of instrumentalizing the evolved system of life to programmed service to the accumulation of money. Shiva grasps clearly the threat this project poses to the natural bases of life-value. In the era of genetic engineering and patents, she warns, "life itself is being colonized. Ecological action in the biotechnology era involves keeping the self-organization of living systems free – free of the technological manipulations that destroy the self-healing and self-organizational capacities of organisms, and free of legal manipulations that destroy the capacities of communities to search for their own solutions to human problems from within the rich biodiversity that we have been endowed with."[33] Thus, not only means of life but life itself is reduced to a mere instrumental value of money-value circuits.

The instrumentalization of means of life and life itself has dire consequences for humanity as a whole. For life-grounded materialism, the most basic condition of social rationality is a system of food production which is sustainable and which produces and distributes food in sufficient quantities and of appropriate quality necessary to satisfy the human life-requirements involved with food consumption. A sustainable food system is defined as "an interdependent web of activities generated by a set of structures and processes that build the civil commons with respect to the production, processing, distribution, wholesaling, retailing, consumption, and disposal of food ... [such that] universal access to the life-good of food [is ensured]."[34] The money-value food production system is concerned neither with sustainability nor with universal access to healthy foods.

The corporate food system is driven by the goal of maximizing profits, and it achieves this end through the industrial-scale production of unhealthy food commodities. "The food system is the largest contributor of greenhouse gas through its reliance on fossil fuels, so there is a connection to climate change. There is also a direct connection to pollution on land and in water through the use of agricultural chemicals and run off ... Five of the ten leading causes of death in the United States are diet related."[35] If the problem in the United States is over-consumption of unhealthy food, the problem in the Global South is under-consumption, a problem exacerbated recently by growing demand for ethanol. Arable land is increasingly being used to grow crops to produce vehicle fuel, which has created the conditions for the spiraling food prices that

33 Ibid., 39.

34 Sumner, "Serving Social Justice: The Role of the Commons in Sustainable Food Systems," 69.

35 Pearson, "The Future of Food," 22.

created global shortages of staples, first in 2008 and again in 2010. As Joseph Stiglitz remarked just before the onset of the first crisis, "with the rise of biofuels, the food and energy markets have become integrated. Combined with increasing demand from those with higher incomes and lower supplies due to weather related problems associated with climate change, this means high food prices – a lethal threat to developing countries."[36] Yet, in the inverted ethical world which is the money-value system, lethal threats to some create the conditions for super-profits for others. As a report in *The Independent* noted, "Giant agribusinesses are enjoying soaring profits out of the world food crisis … The prices of wheat, corn, and rice have soared over the past year, driving the world's poor – who already spend about eighty per cent of their income on food – into destitution."[37] A recent study commissioned by the British government warns that the trends toward higher food prices are systemic and that without concerted action by world governments the world's poor will face increasing difficulty accessing the food their lives require.[38] The real basis of the problem is not the day-to-day market price of food but the structural way in which its commodification makes people generally dependent on the market forces that govern its production and distribution. This social dependence is exploited as the means by which money-value grows. Humans without sufficient money are left vulnerable to starvation even though there is no ecological reason why sufficient food cannot be produced and distributed.[39]

The same colonizing drive of global capital to control life and life's most essential conditions is evident, too, in the struggle over water. Across the poorest regions of the globe, the world's dispossessed find themselves in conflict with the corporate attempt to privatize water. As a non-profit study of the current state of access to water concludes, "Transnational corporations see this water scarcity crisis as a huge profit-making opportunity." They have successfully exploited this opportunity – profits of corporations which controlled formerly public water supplies reached 1 trillion dollars in 2001.[40] Seeing a natural structure of dependence connecting people and a life-resource that, from the perspective of the ruling value system, is "underpriced," multinational capital colludes with pliable national governments to privatize the water system. That the new

NOTE

36 Stiglitz, "Stagflation Waiting in the Wings."
37 Lean, "Multinationals Make Billions in Profit out of Growing Global Food Crisis."
38 Foresight, *The Future of Food and Farming*, 64.
39 The longer-term threat posed by the corporate control of the world's food supply is explored in Roberts, *The End of Food*, 208–36.
40 Public Citizen, "Democratic vs. Corporate Control of Water: A Fight for Survival."

"market price" is beyond the means of most to pay does not factor into the calculations driving the appropriation of the life-resource. As a consequence, access to safe drinking water has declined across the Global South and the ill-health affects of lack of access have increased.[41] Once again, people's basic organic life-requirements appear as exploitable instruments of profit-seeking commodity producers. The proof of the reality of the harm lies in the resistance privatization generates. The case of the peasants of Cochabamba, Bolivia, who successfully wrested back life-grounded control of their water from the Bechtel Corporation, is only the most famous of a number of struggles against water privatization.[42]

Food and water are absolutely basic to life, but as I argued in chapter 2, fundamental life-requirements extend beyond physical inputs to include institutions like health care. For life-grounded materialist ethics, our shared liability to organic system failure and disease constitutes the basis for legitimate claims on health care resources. From the money-value perspective, by contrast, our susceptibility to disease is a weakness to be exploited by sellers of medical commodities. For money-valuable medical industries, what counts is not the degree of health achieved by a society but people's ability to pay to consume medical commodities, whether they are required to maintain or restore health or not. Privatized medicine thus targets community and publically funded health care as a barrier to its profitability, despite the fact that publically funded health care does a demonstrably better job at ensuring that health care needs are met.[43] In Canada, where maintaining the public health care system regularly tops the list of citizens' political priorities, successive governments have followed the neo-liberal strategy of attack on public goods by systematically underfunding the health care system. The subsequent crisis of access and quality is then portrayed as endemic to the public system itself. The privatization of this life-requirement is then presented as the only solution to the crisis of public health care. As Maude Barlow argues, "ideologically driven governments have used the funding crisis to prove that the public system doesn't work and that the 'more efficient' private sector can do the job better."[44] That the evidence does not support the neo-liberal argument has proven no impediment to the efforts of those

41 Labonte and Schresker, "Globalization and the Social Determinants of Health: Promoting Health Equity in Global Governance," 21.

42 For discussion of this crucial struggle see McNally, *Another World Is Possible*, 206–7, 239.

43 Armstrong et al., "Market Principles, Business Practices, and Health Care: Comparing the U.S. and Canadian Experiences."

44 Barlow, *Profit Is Not the Cure*, 90.

who would privatize health care, not only in Canada but wherever publicly funded health care exists.

Analogous arguments could be made in relation to the remaining physical-organic requirements of life. The ruling money-value system regards them all as structures of dependence tying people's lives to their ability to pay for commodities. However, the three examples given provide sufficient evidence for the core ethical argument: the ruling money-value system treats our basic life-requirements as instruments of its own growth. Not only does this mean that people's life-requirements are met only if they can pay. It also means that if money is being made by selling food, water, and medical care, then it will be assumed, for that reason, that the society is doing a good job of ensuring universal access to nutritious food, potable water, and health-maintaining medical care. As we have seen, there is no necessary connection between this assumption and reality.

5.3.2 The Instrumentalization of the Socio-Cultural Requirements of Human Life

In the previous section, I argued that the conflation of money-value and life-value masks the causes of pervasive failures of physical-organic life-requirement satisfaction observable across the world. The structure of private control over universally required resources on which the rule of money-value depends confers on the people who control these resources as private property the social power to exploit others. In this way, shared dependence on nature is converted into particular dependence on the appropriating class. As I will now argue, this structure of power generates cascade effects that alter the way in which people understand and try to satisfy the socio-cultural requirements of human life. I trace these effects following the order in which I explicated the socio-cultural requirements of human life in chapter 2.

Recall that any life-valuable economic system has two dimensions. It must be instrumentally life-valuable insofar as it must produce and distribute life-requirement satisfiers in a sustainable way, and it must generate opportunities for intrinsically life-valuable labour for all who require it. For life-grounded materialist ethics, economic systems are good to the extent that they are instrumentally and intrinsically life-valuable and bad to the extent that their measure of value tends to reduce life-value in either or both dimensions.

The complexity of even the smallest capitalist economy today rules out the possibility of any detailed, case-by-case study of the instrumental and intrinsic life-value of every particular type of work made available. I therefore confine my concern to the general principles that govern the distribution of work and the patterns of action to which these principles give rise. I aim to expose the harms generated for workers by the conflation of the money-value and the life-value of work. Since there are real opportunities for the expression and enjoyment of life-valuable capacities in a capitalist economy, the experience of this form of harm is not invariant or universal. Nevertheless, since capitalism does not prioritize the instrumental and intrinsic value of labour, but only its money-value, the opportunities for life-valuable labour are few, making this structure of harm pervasive, even if not universal.

The money-value system employs only as much labour as is profitable. Profitability presupposes competition over relatively scarce jobs. Since people require paid labour in order to satisfy their physical-organic life-requirements, most have no choice but to engage in this competition. In order to "succeed," workers must instrumentalize their own lives, seeking in their life-capacities those "skill sets" that can best be marketed to potential employers. People must regard themselves and their own capacities as commodities for sale to the highest bidder and be willing to limit their own horizons to what prospective employers are willing to purchase. The content of work life is therefore not a function of workers' own decisions about which of their capacities are most life-valuable but of which of their life-capacities are most likely to find a purchaser.

As I argued in chapter 1, the social field of life-development is an institutionally mediated network of interactions between interdependent individuals. This interdependence follows directly from our evolved organic nature. Human beings reproduce sexually, we require extended periods of care while young, we cannot produce the total set of life-requirement satisfiers by separate individual effort, and the expression and enjoyment of capacities presupposes the existence of others for whom and with whom one expresses and enjoys them. The fact of human interdependence gives rise to two opposed ethical possibilities. For the majority of human history, the fact of interdependence has been treated by the powerful as a source of exploitable advantage over less powerful groups. On the other hand, from the life-grounded materialist perspective, the fact of interdependence is the material basis for solidarity, human unity, and mutual care and concern. From this perspective, the basic conditions of human life, being the same for all, generate social self-consciousness of a shared life-interest in working together to meet the basic challenges of satisfying our life-requirements. Where the former principle rules, work life will be exploitative and alienating to different degrees. Where the latter principle rules, work life can be mutually rewarding as a shared space in which each can express and enjoy their capacities in a way that is life-valuable for all. Where both principles operate in tension, one should expect to find a contradictory structure of work life in which the life-value of activity is subordinated to the ruling value system. It is the latter scenario that plays out in capitalist labour markets.

The categorical imperative of labour markets is to purchase only so much labour as can be profitably employed. This categorical imperative appears economically rational only to the extent that labour markets are incapable of recognizing the instrumental and intrinsic life-value of labour. The most obvious sign of the life-blindness caused by this alienation from the life-ground is the fact that not all who require work, both as a means of obtaining the money necessary to live and as an opportunity to contribute to the development of life-value in other lives, can find it. Beyond this obvious expression of life-blindness is the more insidious determination of the content of work activity by the overriding goal of profitable production. This governing money-value principle means that even where work is not de-skilled in Braverman's sense, it can still lack instrumental and intrinsic life-value, or set these two dimensions of life-value at odds.[45] Where work is challenging and meaningful to individuals, but produces products or services that lack life-value, the individual meaning of that work activity for the particular worker is contradicted by the lack of instrumental life-value of the products or services produced by the industry within which he or she works.

Consider the example of a highly skilled, highly educated worker in the arms industry. The American economy is by far the most dependent on arms production. For the fiscal year 2008–2009, including the costs for the wars in Iraq and Afghanistan, and the defence-related spending of Departments of Energy, Justice, Veteran's Affairs, and Homeland Security, the total defence-related expenditure of the American economy approached one trillion dollars.[46] More than 5 million American jobs are dependent on this spending.[47] The scientific and technological demands of military production mean that "a good proportion of the jobs created by the military budget will be high paying and professionally challenging."[48] From the abstract perspective of the individual so challenged, work in this field could express intrinsic life-value. Since the

45 Braverman, *Labour and Monopoly Capitalism*, 107–26.
46 Johnson, "Going Bankrupt: Why the Debt Crisis is now the Greatest Threat to the American Republic."
47 Pollin and Garrett-Peltier, *The U.S. Employment Effects of Military and Domestic Spending Priorities*, 2.
48 Ibid.

Second World War, some of the greatest scientific intellects have been employed by the American military. The precision demands of military production can be satisfied only by highly skilled technicians and production-line workers, and these latter must be motivated if they are to successfully meet the challenges that the work poses to them. Herein lies the contradiction.

The over-development of the American arms industry is not simply a consequence of the geo-political ambitions of successive American governments. There are "sound" economic reasons for any firm to attempt to gain entry into this field of production. "A money-sequenced economy," McMurtry argues, "selects *for* weapons commodities as highly advantageous" for four interrelated reasons: 1) their high value-added price for the manufacturer combined with guarantee of sale and profit; 2) a high rate of obsolescence and thus the guarantee of ever new capital investment; 3) the semi-monopoly conditions of production, guaranteed by state secrecy laws and the high entry costs to so capital intensive a branch of industry; and 4) guaranteed, ongoing, massive state subsidies.[49] Production of the means of life-destruction is thus a highly profitable investment. For the workers in these industries, the production of intrinsic life-value is dependent on participation in an industry whose instrumental life-value is, at best, zero (when the weapons are not used) and at worst negative relative to the number of lives destroyed by their use.

This example is not meant as an abstract criticism of people who work in the arms industry but as an illustration of the pervasive contradictions forced on workers living in a money-value economy. It is not that such economies cannot create opportunities for challenging, interesting, and individually meaningful forms of work but rather that individuals are forced to find meaning in their individual work-activity in industries whose development is governed by the imperative of maximizing money-profit without regard to instrumental life-value. Workers, dependent on finding remunerative employment in order to live, and challenging work in order to live well as human beings, become internally alienated from the life-ground of value because of the external alienation of the money-value economy from the life-ground of value. Since there is no "outside" to the capitalist economy, those who lack independent means of subsistence must find meaningful work within the money-value economy. Individuals are therefore forced to instrumentalize their own potentially life-valuable capacities (scientific understanding, technical expertise, etc.), becoming in the process the servants of patterns of activity that either lack instrumental life-value or actively destroy it.

49 McMurtry, *The Cancer Stage of Capitalism*, 172.

The structure of harm to which individuals are thus subject when they instrumentalize their life-capacities in this way is not a consequence of their own abstract choices. Hence it is not a sound objection to the life-grounded materialist argument to respond that people can simply choose only those lines of work that combine, in coherent synthesis, intrinsic and instrumental life-value. Not only does this objection ignore the primary role of labour markets in the distribution of available jobs, it also ignores the entire socialization process to which adults who eventually must choose a job have been subjected. As I have emphasized throughout, choices are not made by abstract egos but by living, embodied beings who have grown up, learned to think and choose, and to evaluate the good and bad of their own lives in social contexts dominated by the money-value system. The impact of this ruling value system is felt in all major social institutions – the family and the educational system as much as the economic system. One cannot understand the life-blind choices that individuals make unless one studies the institutions in which their emotional, cognitive, and creative capacities are developed. Thus the argument must now move to an examination of the ethical contradictions of adult care and concern for children and educational institutions in a society where the money-value system rules.

Because human beings are socially interdependent, the life-value of their capacities depends on their expressed content considered in itself and on the contribution that content makes to the life-value of others' lives. Human beings are not born with knowledge of social interdependence; it must, like everything else in human life, be learned. As I argued in chapter 2, the primary social institution responsible for teaching the young about social interdependence is the family. The family is a social and not abstractly natural institution. As such it is subject to determination by the ruling money-value system. Families can cause all manner of harms to their members. Here I am not concerned with the life-destructive abuse to which so many children are subjected. Nor am I concerned with the real harm that patriarchal domination in "traditional" nuclear families can cause by constricting the ego development of children to conformity with existing gender norms. This form of harm has been exhaustively studied in contemporary feminist critiques of the family.[50] In line with the plan of this chapter, I am interested in the way in which the life-value of the family (providing structured care and love to children) is conflated with its service to the money-value system (socializing the young as passive replicators of its rule).

---

50 See, for example, Barrett and McIntosh, *The Anti-Social Family*; Fraser, "What's Critical about Critical Theory"; Hartmann, "The Family as the Locus of Class, Gender, and Political Struggle"; Hartsock, "The Feminist Standpoint.".

The instrumentalization of the family institution and its individual members by the money-value system manifests itself as an overweening realism which even responsible adult care-givers find themselves pressured to transmit to their children. I use "realism" in its common sense signification of an attitude of unquestioning acceptance of the social world and its ruling value-system as fixed realities which cannot be changed. Love and concern for children is thus expressed as preparing children for the real world, i.e., teaching them to abandon all hope for realizing any dream or goal that does not conform to the money-value-system.

For life-grounded materialist ethics, this mode of expressing care and love for children is contradictory precisely because it is a genuine expression of care and love. It would be irresponsible not to teach children that the "real world" is often a destroyer of dreams. At the same time, when adult caregivers transmit this message to their children, they are equally transmitting the code according to which the money-value system successfully reproduces itself: obey and succeed, challenge and be destroyed. By becoming programmers for the money-value system, adult caregivers express their love by confining their children's horizons to those shores visible from the established society. As Erich Fromm argues, families "transmit to the child what we may call the psychological atmosphere or the spirit of the society just by being what they are – namely representatives of this very spirit. *The family thus may be considered the psychological agent of society.*"[51] What Fromm calls "spirit" I call "ruling value system," but the point is the same: responsible parents, trying honestly to prepare children for the demands of adulthood, act as value programmers who, in effect if not intent, confine children's life-horizons to attaining the best possible returns from the socially prevalent reward system. The depth message of this socialization strategy is that a good life demands self-subordination to the prevailing social reality. It thus appears that the responsible expression of adult care and concern is to encourage children to make themselves instruments of the prevailing social order, and especially the labour markets that will inevitably determine one's future income.

As with the choices that people make about their work lives, life-grounded materialist ethics does not make abstract objections to how parents choose to raise their children but instead exposes the contradictions that structure the social context in which choices are made. At the same time, materialist ethics is opposed to any functionalist fatalism according to which, since a single individual choice cannot change the social choice situation, what individuals choose to do is irrelevant. By exposing the ethical contradictions of the situation of choice, life-grounded materialist

---

51 Fromm, *Escape from Freedom*, 285.

ethics intends to enable individuals to work together to change them. But collective action is not a reified process separate from the actions of individuals whose interrelation produces it. In the present example, this claim means that parents need to teach children that the "real" world is not a fixed reality to which they must conform but the cumulative outcome of interrelated human actions in whose development they can participate as socially self-conscious individual agents, guided by the deeper life-interest they bear in unity with others. Teaching children that the world as it is, is not the world as it once was, and that the world that could be depends in part on what they do now, is teaching them that the full value of their lives depends on their assuming the responsibility to not accept as legitimate any structure or institution simply because it exists and demands their compliance, but only those which are comprehensively life-valuable.

Nevertheless, adult caregivers are rightly fearful that if they teach their children to be independently minded and suspicious of the ruling money-value system, they will undermine the possibility of their children's future happiness. While this fear is entirely reasonable in light of evidence that those who refuse to conform as automatons will be punished (with mockery, unemployment, and in harsher political environments with imprisonment or even death), there is evidence that the opposite result from the one intended occurs. Tim Kasser reports that children who were socialized to accept the accumulation of money as the highest good of social life were more anxious; less able to form lasting, mutually supportive relationships; less able to care for others and the wider natural world; and were overall more unhappy than others who had been raised to value social relationships and non-monetary achievements.[52] If the socialization of children were more life-grounded, and more young adults were thus willing to assume the risks of independent thought and action, new patterns of collective action could emerge that would transform major social institutions, thus ending the risks associated with refusing to be treated as a mere instrument of the ruling value system.

The most important social institution for the development of the capacities for thought and imagination is the educational system. Here again, the education system, instead of serving the intrinsically and instrumentally life-valuable growth of these capacities, tends toward treating them as instruments of money-value growth. By way of initial orientation to the problem, consider the attempts of economists to develop investment models for early childhood education. On the one hand, these attempts recognize that, because children require education, some amount of social wealth should be invested in it. On the other

---

52 Kasser, *The High Price of Materialism*, 29–33, 88–9.

hand, the goal of these strategies is not the free and comprehensive development of their life-capacities but enhancing their future employability.[53] To fully understand why and to what extent the education system has become a servant of money-value, we need to set its development in historical context.

In his examination of the development of the English welfare state, T.H Marshall demonstrates that by the early twentieth century the industrial economy and universal suffrage generated a system-requirement for a literate and numerate public. In response, new institutions for the education of classes and groups formerly excluded from all formal education had to be created.[54] Although designed to meet this system-requirement, once these institutions began to operate, they could not avoid being influenced by the older liberal-philosophical ideal of education as the transmitter of human culture and the basis of all-round personal development. The history of mass schooling in North America and Western Europe has been shaped by the contradictory demands that it produce at one and the same time workers able to comply with the functional demands of life in the modern world *and* cultivated individuals capable of autonomously appropriating the wealth of human artistic and scientific culture.

Unfortunately, these two demands cannot be coherently realized at the same time because their outcomes are opposite types of people. Consistently realized, the system-demand for compliant workers would produce people willing to assume whatever role society as it presently exists makes available for them. By contrast, the consistent realization of the life-valuable development of cognitive and imaginative capacities would produce students unwilling to simply adapt to prevailing conditions and motivated to think and act for themselves, to question and challenge established reality. To the extent that the mass schooling system succeeds in developing the life-valuable capacities of independent thought and action, it can expect to face opposition from those who recognize that success in that dimension means potential failure in the dimension of meeting the system-requirement that education is also expected to serve. Today this opposition takes the form of historically unprecedented levels of direct corporate involvement in schools.

Just as in the case of public health care, the context for the neo-liberal invasion of the school system is created by systematic underfunding. With less money available from governments, schools are forced to turn to private donations in order to procure needed resources. Funding

53 Heckman, "The Economics, Technology, and Neuroscience of Human Capability Formation."

54 Marshall, "Citizenship and Social Class," 82.

from individual donors like parents and community members is insufficient to meet key institutional requirements. The only non-governmental source of significant funding is the corporate world. Corporations do not make donations for the sake of increasing the life-value of education but in order to convert the educational system, its teachers and students, into instruments of the growth of money-value. At its pedagogically mildest, this influence takes the form of advertising and sales of the donor's product. At its most severe, it can take the form of the privatization of curriculum content or even entire public schools. A Canadian study correctly concludes that "the application of business practices and business-speak is constructed as part and parcel of helping public education compete and evolve ... students are 'clients,' parents are 'customers,' and teachers are 'front-line service providers'... required to measure 'inputs and outputs' to ensure that, upon graduation, students are prepared to take their place as workers and consumers in the New Global Order."[55]

Fully realized, the privatization agenda would eliminate anything that is actually *educational* from the education system. The distinctive nature of the human capacities to think and imagine is that they are *not* determined by external stimuli in the way instinctual behaviour is. This fact is easily demonstrated. Two students who study exactly the same content will arrive at completely different conclusions. Without this freedom of thought in relation to content there would be no history of human scientific and artistic change and development. The corporate education agenda aims exclusively and entirely at shaping the development of human cognitive capacities in entirely predictable ways. Not only is it harmful to the individuals whose cognitive and imaginative capacities it instrumentalizes, it would be fatal, if ever brought to fruition, to the humanity of the species as a whole. Understood from the standpoint of its ideal goal, the money-value system's education agenda would result in absolute scientific and artistic stasis since the self-differentiating power of thought would be arrested by the system-requirement of absolute compliance with the given structure of social reality. This is not politically tendentious fear-mongering but a measurable result of the corporatization of schools.

Research conducted by Alexander Astin and reported by Tim Kasser has tracked the changing attitudes of first-year college students in the United States (the country with the deepest penetration of corporate interests into primary and secondary schools) from the 1960s to the 1990s. Students who went through the first phase of the corporate invasion of the public school system in the 1980s and early 1990s expressed completely different expectations than their older counterparts. "The percentage of students who believe that it is very important or essential to 'develop a meaningful philosophy of life,'" Kasser reports, "decreased from over 80 per cent in the late 1960s to around 40 per cent in the late 1990s. At the same time, the percentage that believes that it is very important or essential to 'be very well off financially' has risen from just over 40 per cent to over 70 per cent. Society's value-making machine is an effective one."[56] As this research proves, changes at the elementary and secondary levels of education will force changes at the post-secondary level by altering the expectation structure of incoming students.

Given the fact that universities are research institutions as well as educational institutions, the instrumentalization of the universities by the money-value system is more globally pervasive. The United States is a leader in this global phenomenon, as it is in the privatization of public education, so much so that critics worry that public university education is in danger of being completely subsumed by "academic capitalism." The means of privatizing public university education are the same as in health care and primary and secondary education: first defund, then declare a crisis, then allow the corporate sector to take over funding. "The slow and continued decrease in state block grants as a share of annual operating revenues at public universities, marked by periodic, intense fiscal crises, has played an important part in legitimating academic capitalism," write Slaughter and Rhoades in their path-breaking empirical study of academic capitalism's gradual emergence.[57]

Even before state funding cuts began to undermine the public nature of public education, military funding had diverted it away from exclusive service to the growth of instrumental and intrinsic life-value. While military funding of universities extends back to the Civil War era, it was not until the Manhattan Project that military funding began to directly program scientific research in the universities. The Cold War provided the context needed to normalize the extraordinary demands placed on scientists during the Second World War . Increased links between the military and universities means, at the same time, increased links with the corporations that produce American armaments, and thus once again with the ruling money-value system. As the historian Richard M. Abrams concludes in his study of the history of military funding of university research, "nothing has had the overall force of the military establishment in redirecting basic and applied research, in putting limits on the free exchange of intelligence, in dampening discussion of the merits of research

---

56 Kasser, *The High Price of Materialism*, 104.
57 Slaughter and Rhoades, *Academic Capitalism and the New Economy*, 14.

that has policy implications, or in converting scientists into policy advocates or scholars into entrepreneurs."[58] Limits on the free development and exchange of intelligence do not result exclusively from military funding. Across the entire range of academic disciplines and in countries other than the United States, there is a growing denigration of research that has no immediate commercial results or, worse, questions the very normative foundations of existing system-requirements.

The most pervasive sign of corporate reprogramming of the universities is the ever increasing pressure across academic disciplines for expert research to be consciously tailored to the production of marketable commodities. As Martha Nussbaum warns, "the pressure for economic growth has led many political leaders ... to recast the entirety of university education – both teaching and research – along growth-oriented lines, asking about the contribution of each discipline and each researcher to the economy."[59] As a result, scholarship that produces novel insights into human life – its organization, its creations, its depth existential and social problems – and poses novel but not immediately realizable solutions to those problems, is increasingly marginalized and targeted for elimination. Academics face heightened pressures to engage only in such research as government and corporate funding agencies are willing to finance, and those agencies rarely fund research that is essentially critical of the prevailing institutional order and its ruling value system. Frank Furedi, a sociologist at the University of Kent at Canterbury, notes the consequences for scholarship of the changes that have beset universities in the United Kingdom over the past two decades: "[some] scholars ... obsessively pursue intellectual goals that are of no concern to research councils or other funding bodies. Consequently, they are less passionate about applying for grants tied to agendas not their own. They are barely tolerated in British higher education."[60] It does not follow from the individualistic nature of scholarship that its results lack general instrumental life-value. On the contrary, by freeing research from the content control exercised by funding bodies, the results of scholarship are more rather than less likely to produce insights that have no commercial value but that expose the loss of life-value invariably caused by the total commercialization of research.

This transformation of university scholarship into externally funded commodity production is aided and abetted by university administrators. Despite their vocation, some unthinkingly instrumentalize themselves as

58 Abrams, "The U.S. Military and Higher Education," 28.
59 Nussbaum, *Not for Profit*, 127.
60 Furedi, "Is There No Room Left for Reflection?" 2.

servants of corporate and government funding agencies who prescribe the restructuring of academia. Instead of using the mental capacities cultivated in their own education to question what is demanded, they repeat the claim that the demanded changes are natural, inevitable, and essential to carrying on the intellectual mission of the university. For example, in an editorial written by the current president of the University of Alberta, the central claim is that the only way to become "world class" is to abandon institutional independence in favour of partnerships with the private sector. "Canadians have great expectations for the future. We want to be active players in the international arena, spearheading solutions to global problems, achieving breakthroughs in every field, creating and retaining ownership of international businesses, and winning Nobel prizes. The future could ... be ours. But in today's ruthless global marketplace, where our competitors are leaping ahead of us ... we must quickly and strategically increase our competitiveness."[61] Ordinarily, ruthlessness is recognized as a vice, as condemnable, as a deranged way of treating others. Applied as an epithet to the "marketplace," however, it becomes a reality to be accepted, regardless of the costs its acceptance imposes on the institution, those who work and study there, and society more generally.

The general social consequence is that a perfect of circle of closed dogma substitutes itself for the open horizon of critical engagement with natural and social reality. If educational systems do not produce citizens capable of questioning the normative structure of the given reality, it is unlikely that any other system can. The ideal-typical result projected by this dogmatic closure is machine-like reproduction of the given with no social ability for recognizing or arresting the life-destructive consequences engendered by the normal operation of this social reality. Research becomes a form of paid service to business clients who recognize no life-value in scientific, social, philosophical research or in artistic creation, but only potential money-value. Teaching becomes a form of paid service to the ruling money-value system, its intended goal no longer to enable the comprehensive development of our cognitive and imaginative capacities but the assembly-line production of silent and compliant drones who execute the program of the ruling value-system.

The instrumentalization of education by the ruling money-value system is potentially the most serious harm to which young people especially can be subjected. To the extent that students treat themselves as clients of a service industry, they instrumentalize their own cognitive and imaginative capacities in the hope of finding work that will produce maximum

---

61 Samarasekera, "Partnerships Are the Order of the Day."

monetary value in the future. In so doing, they radically restrict the life-valuable development of the capacities latent in their brains. The human brain is unique in the field of known evolved life in its capacity to compre-hend the entire universe of being, seen and unseen, and to create new universes in imagination without specifiable limit of development. By treating these capacities as "skill sets" to be auctioned off to employers, the young person never becomes aware of the unbounded reach of her human intelligence. From the beginning, she is encouraged and pres-sured to discover her niche, to brand and market herself.

As with the preceding arguments in this chapter, I am describing and criticizing a structural transformation in the institutional vocation of uni-versities and not making abstract, moralizing claims against individual students. Students themselves often recognize the problem of instru-mentalization but feel powerless to solve it given the fact that within the ruling money-value system they will be forced to find jobs, and thus must "make themselves saleable," as Marx said everyone must. The long-term tendency of this structural change in education is, however, materially irrational, insofar as, if allowed to completely determine the educational system, it would result in a society unable to think critically or under-stand systematic problems that cannot be resolved within the ruling val-ue system. Problems are reduced to engineering problems, i.e., problems of the application of existing techniques. But if the existing techniques are themselves the cause of the problem, this sort of "problem solving" is materially irrational.

While the same degree of material irrationality might not be generat-ed by the instrumentalization of the human life-requirements for the institutional protection of beautiful natural spaces and the production of human artistic creations, this instrumentalization is still a source of harm for the individuals who suffer it. Recall that human aesthetic life-requirements derive from the expanded range of sentient and emotion-al relationships that human social self-consciousness can establish with the natural and built environment. A society that allows the money-value system to instrumentalize the requirement for the conditions for these non-utilitarian relationships might not threaten its long-term prospects of survival or the freedom of its citizens, but it will lose the capacity for aesthetic experience which is, as I argued in chapter 2, perhaps our most human. Unlike our other emotional and sentient relationships to the world, the aesthetic relationship to both the natural and built world must, by its nature, rest content with that which presents itself in the form in which it presents itself. It is when human beings find beauty in an object that they are most able to let that object be in the form in which it presents itself.

As with the instrumentalization of the preceding life-requirements, the instrumentalization of the aesthetic requirements of human life by the commodity cycles of the money-value system allows only those modes of satisfaction which serve its growth. It is not that the money-value system necessarily negates beauty as such but rather that it puts a price on access to the objects of beauty. By pricing access to beauty, the money-value system alters the human relationship to it. Beauty is conflated with price such that the value of beautiful things is no longer seen to lie in their free appropriation by aesthetic consciousness but in their possession and sale. Our most human sensory relationship to the world is reduced to an instrumental hunt for objects and spaces saleable because of their beauty. In this way natural beauty and artistic creation become forms of market advantage. Real estate becomes more economically valuable if it occupies an awe-inspiring natural space. The natural beauty of the place makes it a target for forms of development which inevitably remove it from the common wealth of human experience and make it a preserve of the rich. The beauty is not thereby destroyed, but it can no longer be freely appreciated by all in virtue of their capacity to see, hear, smell, etc. The human capacity to experience beauty is thus transformed into the instrumental capacity to discover spaces not yet privatized by the money-value system and buy them up before someone else does. As a potential commodity, the same space becomes yet another zone of capitalist competition and conflict.

The human life-requirement to experience the beauty of human creations is analogously instrumentalized by the money-value system. Beautiful works of art can still be produced in a money-value system, but the ability of artists to create (and therefore the ability of others to experience their creations) depends on the ability of artists to make a living by their work. Artistic work, like work in general, becomes subject to market forces, in this case the forces generated by the art market. Not every artist conforms, of course, but as with the other life-requirements, the focus here is not on individuals but on social dynamics generally. Just as the ability of workers to make a living is dependent on the state of labour markets, so too the ability of artists to make a living is dependent in general on the state of art markets. The production of art thus becomes bound up with the system of commerical art galleries, dealers, and wealthy purchasers. Not only does this absorption of art by the art market erect money and status barriers in the way of the free experience of human creations, it reduces the social life-value of artistic creation as free manifestations of the highest human creative power to the money-value that art can generate.

The clearest expression of the reduction of the social life-value of art to commercial value is found in the influential work of Richard Florida.

Florida reconceives artistic capacities as "creative capital" and has worked out a theory of urban development which uses creative capital as a measure of economic health. While Florida's intention is to vindicate the value of artistic creativity against the more philistine-utilitarian faction of the capitalist class, his intention is undermined by his failure to distinguish between the life-value of art and its money-value. Instead, he follows the neo-classical economics he believes that he is arguing against insofar as he treats the value of creative capital as nothing more than its money-value. "The creative capital theory ... says that regional economic growth is driven by the location choices of creative people – the holders of creative capital – who prefer places that are diverse, tolerant, and open to new ideas. It thus identifies a type of human capital, creative people, as being a key to economic growth."[62] No better example of the systematic confusion between life-value and money-value is possible. What Florida ought to say is that openness, tolerance, diversity, and creativity are expressions of life-value, and money-value ought to serve life-value growth. Instead, because his argument lacks the category of life-value, he instrumentalizes creativity as a condition for the production of money-value. Without intending to, Florida exposes the problem: creativity and the life-value of creations are negated by the mono-value of money-wealth which serves as the only measure of value. From the standpoint of the creative capital theory, there is no difference between fashion, design, advertising, and art. These quite different forms of activity collapse into the general category of "creative capital" and their value is not judged by distinct aesthetic criteria but by the master value of money-value growth.

The long-term tendency of the reduction of the life-value of the experience of beauty to the money-value of "creative capital" is thus toward the elimination of all life-valuable creativity. If creativity is in essence creative capital, then it too, like all forms of capital, must be governed in its development by market forces. Since people are the bearers of creative capital, to be governed by market forces is to be governed by standards of production that are extrinsic to the uniquely emergent standards of singular acts of creative activity. That is, to treat oneself as a bearer of creative capital is in essence to *conform* to the mono-value of the money-value system, and therefore not to *create* anything novel at all. Again, the life-grounded materialist argument does not single out individual artists for approbation for failing to assume some existential duty of the artist. The "blame," if such a word must be used, lies in the social forces that artists, like everyone else who lacks independent means of subsistence, must serve in order to live. Unless those social forces can be subordinated to a

62 Florida, *The Rise of the Creative Class*, 223.

ruling set of life-grounded principles, individual artists no less than individual workers remain subordinated to a ruling value system that is driven onward by the system-requirement of producing what is profitable. Unless that system-requirement can be controlled and altered by democratic politics, individuals will always find themselves more or less trapped by the real power of these life-blind-system requirements.

I argued in chapter 2 that the most fundamental socio-cultural requirement of human life is the need to effectively participate in the governance of collective life. Liberal-democratic institutions of politics and civil society partially satisfy this requirement. Institutions like freedom of speech and assembly enable citizens of liberal-democratic societies to determine which issues of public concern are not being adequately addressed by official political parties and institutions. Official parties and institutions allow individuals to choose their political representatives and give some democratic legitimacy to the laws that all are expected to obey. At the same time, given the formal separation of liberal-democratic capitalist society into a political public sphere, on the one hand, and a private economic sphere, on the other, and the fact that people's lives and livelihoods depend directly on the economic sphere, this supposedly private sphere exerts tremendous power over the political public sphere. Because "capital has gained private control over matters that were once in the public domain," Ellen Meiksins Wood argues, "even all those areas of social life that lie outside the immediate sphere of production and appropriation, and outside the direct control of the capitalist, are subjected to the imperatives of the market and the commodification of extra-economic goods."[63] These areas of life include the political sphere, which tends to function as an instrument of money-value growth while representing its service to the money-value system as in the common life-interest. These institutions thus become the instrument of private economic power. To the extent that the legitimacy of the institutions depends on people's continuing to participate in them, people's political activities become instrumentalized by the money-value system.

Democratic institutions are instrumentally life-valuable because they allow for the non-violent, non-mutually destructive solution to fundamental social conflicts. In principle, they allow groups to publically articulate the deprivations to which they are subject and to build movements in support of change. This instrumental life-value is a concrete expression of the intrinsic life-value of democratic institutions: they are the highest form the life-ground of value takes in human life. In a fully democratic society, neither the law nor reified social forces rule over human

---

63 Wood, *Democracy against Capitalism*, 280.

beings as external coercive forces, but all obligatory rules are the result of explicit agreement on the part of citizens working together to ensure the best possible conditions of life for all.

Yet when we examine the actual ends served by existing liberal-democratic institutions, we discover that the human life-requirement to participate as social self-conscious agents in the determination of the rules that govern social life are once again instrumentalized by the ruling money-value system.[64] People's beliefs in the reality of democracy are exploited as commitment to one or another political party as representative of the common good, when the evidence suggests that all political parties obey capitalist market forces regardless of the expressed demands of the people whose interests they claim to represent. A recent example is the wave of protests sweeping Europe since 2010 in response to "austerity budgets" imposed by parties of the right or social-democratic left alike. The reason governments have passed these budgets has nothing to do with any democratic mandate given by real majorities to cut back life-supportive public institutions, and everything to do with the private power of money-value driven bond holders over purportedly public policy.

This power is not an accident but itself the product of systematic changes to global capitalism over the past forty years. As Hugo Radice argues, "as a result of the combined processes of deregulation, financialization, and globalization ... governments no longer have this degree of control over finance."[65] That is, they do not have the power to resist the demands of bond markets because they depend too strongly on them for income. At the same time, policies adopted by these states enabled these changes to global capitalism, and these policies were adopted precisely because they were supposed to secure growth and overcome economic crisis. States are thus "enveloped in capitalism's irrationalities" to the precise extent that they employ public power to enable the growth of money-value in whatever form private market agents see fit.[66] The life-value of democratic participation is thus instrumentalized in the service of the materially irrational dynamics and consequences of the capitalist economy.

A *society* is democratic in the life-valuable sense to the extent that none of its major social institutions is the preserve of private power whose

64 I have examined the historical and systematic contradictions of existing liberal-democracy and its normative foundation in systems of rights in detail in *Democratic Society and Human Needs*. I do not repeat those arguments here but instead limit my focus to the way in which the human life-requirement for political participation as an agent is instrumentalized by the money-value system. I will provide a framework for a life-valuable alternative in the concluding chapter.

65 Radice, "Cutting Government Budgets: Economic Science or Class War," 95.

66 Panitch and Gindin, "Capitalist Crisis and the Crisis This Time," 17.

interests contradict the shared life-interest. Yet this is exactly the structure of liberal-democratic capitalism, with formally democratic and life-valuable political institutions on one side and private economic power on the other. The formal means exist to determine the policies necessary to serve the common life-interest, but the interests of the appropriating class militate against the realization of this life-value because it threatens their power to maximize money-value for themselves. The outcomes of economic decisions made in response to market signals are a primary material determinant of people's lives in a liberal-democratic society and they are not normally subject to democratic veto. Even Habermas, whose interpretation of liberalism is among the most sophisticated and democratic available, and who once argued that the capitalist economy always threatens to colonize the life-world, accepts a free market economy as a condition of any possible democracy.[67]

When the "necessity" of the link between democracy and the free market is challenged in the name of the life-valuable democratic principle of collective control over universally required life-resources, the movement *against* unaccountable private economic power will be attacked as undemocratic. An examination of the structure of these attacks shows even more clearly the way in which the instrumentalization of democracy by the money-value system is an existential threat to it.

The struggle to build "twenty-first century socialism" in Venezuela serves as a case study of this problem.[68] Hugo Chavez has now won three elections, (the most recent in 2006 with 62.7 per cent of the popular vote), defeated an American-influenced coup attempt and a general strike in the oil industry designed to topple his government, and won a recall referendum organized by the opposition and supported by the United States. Despite these formally democratic successes, Chavez is still regularly denounced as an anti-democratic tyrant by both the United States and its supporters within the Venezuelan opposition. This apparent contradiction can be understood only by examining the life-valuable

---

67 Habermas, "What Does Socialism Mean Today?" 40.

68 Chavez's Bolivarian movement for "twenty-first century socialism" is not without its contradictions and manifests anti-democratic tendencies that are in tension with the democratic social forces that it has cultivated. In what follows, I consciously set aside these contradictions in order to make clear the generally unexamined alienation of liberal-democracy from the life-ground of value. That the reaction to Chavez reveals this structure of alienation clearly does not at the same time prove that the Bolivarian movement's approach to systematic life-crisis is a model that should be mindlessly copied elsewhere. A detailed, balanced, and incisive examination of the democratic strengths and weaknesses of Chavez's policies can be found in Wilpert, *Changing Venezuela by Taking Power*.

democratic reforms that the Chavez government has undertaken and their implications for the domestic and international appropriating class.

What substantive changes have been made in Venezuela to invoke domestic and American opposition? Social rights have been recognized as of equal democratic importance to civil and political rights. These social rights in turn have been actualized in community-based experiments in democratic means of satisfying the life-requirements for housing, health care, and education. These democratic economic experiments are integrated with new neighbourhood-level participatory-democratic political institutions which together not only give the poor a voice in political power but put the material means of solving the problem of life-requirement deprivation in their hands. Finally, there has been a systematic effort to create the conditions in which society-wide, democratic economic institutions and practices can progressively supplant the money-value economy. The life-value linking these developments together is clearly expressed in the government's 2001 Economic and Social Development Plan. It defines the social economy as a complementary alternative to the private economy which serves the "common social interests," and is governed by the "participation of citizens and workers [in] ... alternative enterprises, such as associative enterprises and self-managed micro-enterprises."[69]

The "social" economy that together these reforms are developing is life-grounded because the ruling principle of production and distribution within it is not the maximization of money-value profit but the comprehensive satisfaction of human life-requirements. The contrast between money-value maximization and life-value creation is clearly implied in the Chavez government's critique of the proposed Free Trade Area of the Americas (FTAA). "Public services [all of which would be subject to privatization under the FTAA] are for satisfying the needs of the people, not for commerce and economic profit. Therefore its benefits cannot be governed by the criteria of profit but by social interests."[70] From this perspective, democracy requires, in addition to the formal mechanisms and guarantees central to the liberal-democratic interpretation, the actual satisfaction of these social interests.

From the perspective of the ruling money-value system, this society-wide mobilization of political power is not democratic but constitutes "interference" in the "free" market. Even when these developments have been formally legitimated by the mechanisms of free elections and constitutional change, and even when they demonstrably enable more

69 Wilpert, *Changing Venezuela by Taking Power*, 76. For the details of the other reforms see Wilpert, 35-6, 53-67, 120-49.

70 Ibid.,156.

coherently inclusive ranges of expression and enjoyment of political agency, they will be attacked. In the case of Venezuela, this was the argument employed by the opposition in building support for its recall referendum in 2004. The recall referendum was funded in part by a private American company, Development Alternatives, set up by the main development agency of the American government, USAID. Development Alternatives describes its role as providing support for "democratic institutions and processes to ease social tensions and maintain democratic balance. The grants support projects that emphasize conflict mitigation, civic education, confidence building, dialogue, and efforts to bring people together around common goals for the future of Venezuela."[71] Had the recall referendum been successful, the new participatory neighborhood-level political organizations would have been eliminated, the use of natural resources and social wealth to improve access to health care and education at all levels would have been stopped, public investment in worker-controlled co-operatives and microenterprises would have ceased, and the collective social effort to gradually free the lives of Venezuelans from the life-blind dynamics of global money-circuits would have been replaced by the return of the neo-liberal policies whose failure enabled Chavez to win election in the first place. In other words, had Development Alternatives achieved its goal of helping the opposition to win, the result would not have been conflict mitigation, democratic balance, confidence building, or dialogue, but the return of the unchallenged rule of socio-economic forces that widen class inequalities, intensify social conflict, and ignore the shared life-interests of Venezuelans.

When the state actually acts in the collective life-interest to use natural and social wealth to satisfy life-requirements and enable life-capacities, especially of those who have been historically deprived and oppressed, it is denounced as tyrannical. Yet, the policies pursued in Venezuela, or anywhere else where the legitimacy of the money-value system is systematically contested, are not accidental, but contemporary forms of response to centuries of struggle. What else have the dispossessed and impoverished been fighting for in widely different cultural contexts, if not to establish the satisfaction of their unmet life-requirements as the basis of political legitimacy? The risks assumed by groups in the ongoing struggle for democracy, where it does not exist, and deeper democratization, where it is only partially realized, would be incomprehensible were one to assume that people are struggling for little more than the right to stamp public legitimacy on the private interests of the appropriating class.

71 Ibid., 171.

As with the preceding cases of instrumentalization of life-requirements and life-capacities, the ultimate outcome of this contradiction in existing democratic practice is materially irrational. Thought through to its ultimate implications, the subordination of democratic institutions to the ruling money-value system tends toward the destruction of democracy itself. One does not have to be tendentiously "economistic" in the Marxist sense of the term to understand that politics ultimately depends on the dynamics of the economic system. For human beings living in a capitalist economy, access to even basic life-requirement satisfiers is mediated by money, and access to money depends on participation in labour markets. As I have argued above, the social requirement for access to money entails a structural dependence of all on the economic system, while the money-value economic system is not similarly dependent on any *democratic* participation of people in its institutions. Given this one-sided structure of social dependence, the money-value economic system is able to extract compliance from both governments and individual citizens alike, especially in contemporary conditions of a true global market in which capital is mobile and workers are not.

The result is a political system that serves the goals of the money-value system. People's life-requirement for participation in the collective determination of the organization and governance of society as a whole, and their life-capacity to do so, are instrumentalized. Private power trumps collective life-interest; but it is the collective life-interest that must rule in democracy, if anything does. Viewed collectively, these various forms of instrumentalization of the socio-cultural requirements of human life work against the free realization and enjoyment of life-valuable capacities. They do not eliminate the expression of capacities entirely, but tend to constrict them to predictable functions exercised in conformity to the interests of the ruling money-value system. In this way the social self-conscious, creative life-activity of human beings is reduced to the programmed behaviour of machines. I argued in the first chapter that self-organization distinguishes life at its most basic level and that social self-conscious world-building activity distinguishes human life from life in general. Machines produce, but they do not create meaningful worlds. Their production is programmed by their designers, and breakdowns in their functioning are corrected by changing a part or replacing the machine. Is this not how people and their life-requirements and capacities are treated by the ruling money-value system? Life-requirements are fully satisfied only if it is profitable to do so, and capacities can be developed only if there is a market for them. If markets for a given capacity dry up, then the person whose life expressed that capacity is simply thrown out, in the same way that obsolete machines are thrown out. Just as the machine feels no sorrow over its obsolescence, so too people rendered redundant are expected to simply accept their fate, adjust to the "new reality," and find a new way of conforming to the structure that rendered them useless.

If we view societies in life-grounded terms, they are forms of meaningful interaction through which human life reproduces and develops itself. Yet we know that human life-*re*production is at the same time human life-value *pro*duction since the forms through which human life reproduces itself are not simply natural but involve, from the initial moment they emerge as human, ethical consciousness expressed as care and concern for the quality of life. Thus every society, as a society of human beings, must be evaluated not only from the functional standpoint of its process of reproduction but from the life-grounded materialist ethical standpoint of the quality of life of its citizens. The more coherently inclusive the range of life-valuable capacities any society enables, the better it is from the life-grounded materialist perspective. In order to widen the range of expressed and enjoyed capacities, everyone's life-requirements must be comprehensively satisfied, and if they are to be comprehensively satisfied, the natural resources and social wealth required to satisfy them must be democratically controlled.

Liberal-democratic capitalist society claims pride of place in human history as *the* solution to the problem of a freedom-enabling structure of rule. Individual rights guaranteed by a constitution, the principle of democratic participation in the formation of collectively binding law, an open and tolerant civil society in which a variety of "experiments in living" (Mill) are possible, the bold assertion of human equality, and an economic system of such productivity that no one need suffer life-requirement deprivation are indeed forms of social life that enable more coherently inclusive ranges of life-value expression and enjoyment. These are achievements to be preserved, not targets to be smashed. The full realization of the life-value of these achievements, however, is impeded by the rule of money-value over major social institutions.

From the perspective of this ruling value-system, the growth of money-value is the growth of life-value. The long-term tendency of this conflation of life-value with money-value is, as I have argued, materially irrational. The material irrationality is not only expressed in the possible collapse of natural life-support systems but equally in the reduction of human life to a machine function. The untrammeled operation of the processes ruled by the money-value system is justified in life-grounded terms as freedom, liberty, equality. However, these values are alienated from their life-grounded meaning. As so alienated, they refer not to wider and deeper ranges of human life-capacity realization and enjoyment but to more profitable circuits of money-value investment to which people's life-activity must conform. Yet, to conform to circuits of a life-blind value-system as the condition of having a meaningful and valuable life is necessarily to surrender freedom to that reified system value. Hence the material irrationality of the money-grounded system; acting in conformity with its demands in order to secure one's freedom is, in life-grounded reality, to make one's life an instrument of social dynamics which value people only to the extent that they serve the hypertrophied growth of money-value. The depth of the ethical problem these forms of instrumentalization pose for human beings becomes fully apparent when approached in the context of a finite human life. To conclude this examination, I thus turn to the problem of the instrumentalization of life-time by the money-value system.

5.3.3 The Instrumentalization of the Temporal Requirement of Free Human Life

I argued in chapter 2 that time is both an existential framework within which life must be lived and a social structure. The quality of our experience of the existential framework – whether it is experienced as an open matrix of possibilities for life-valuable activity or a closed structure of routine – depends on the social forces determining the structure and experience of time. The experience of time under the rule of money-value typically takes the form, whether at work or not, of what Moishe Postone calls "abstract time." The structure of abstract time is indifferent to the quality of the activities that occur within it.[72] It is the basis of possibility for measuring the duration of any activity. Under the money-value system, abstract time is structured as a coercive force ruling over human activity in the interest of money-value efficiency: maximum output for minimum temporal input. Whether at work or at leisure, people experience time as determined by the imperatives of productive labour or productive consumption of the commodities of labour which together drive the money-value system and ensure its reproduction. Work activity is reduced to carrying out instructions under the imperatives of capitalist efficiency; leisure activity is reduced to the passive consumption of pre-packaged entertainment commodities and temporally delimited experiences. Thus, life-time as a whole is instrumentalized by the money-value system insofar as every life-activity is subjected to the temporal structure of abstract time upon which capitalist productivity depends. In general, the less time an activity takes, whether it be welding a fender,

---

72 Postone, *Time, Labour, and Social Domination*, 202.

writing a song, or getting a university degree, the more money-valuable it is. In this way, the whole of life-time appears as a unified instrument of money-value production (work) and realization (spending).

The productivity gains which Marx hoped would liberate people's life-time from its coercive determination by abstract time have been achieved. Yet, people have not gained more empty time. Despite continued increases in productivity, the actual experience of people in the liberal-democratic capitalist world is toward less rather than more empty time.[73] Recent trends indicate working weeks in the advanced capitalist world are lengthening after long periods of decline. In Canada, the average workday has increased from 506 minutes in 1986 to 536 minutes in 2005, and in the United States the average annual hours of work for middle-income families have risen from 2150 hours per year in 1979 to 2181 hours per year in 2002 for men and from 919 hours per year to 1385 hours per year for women.[74] The lower the family income, the smaller the amount of empty time and the greater the experience of time pressure. The group most deprived of empty time in the Western world is single women with children, the group which also ranks lowest in terms of household income.[75]

It is not only the poorest members of society who suffer from lack of empty time. As Goodin et al. note, "people's subjective sense of time pressure has become increasingly urgent. Americans complain ever more stridently that they are 'overworked,' the 'leisure' class that it is 'harried,' working wives about their second shift at home, and the 'time bind' that they suffer in consequence."[76] However, these experiences are not merely subjective; they are a response to changes in the dynamics of labour markets affecting workers across the division of labour, from the most menial of jobs to well-paying professional work. The phenomenon of internalizing the demands of the work world and feeling as if one must always be working is not a pathology – "workaholism" – but, as Ursula Huws argues, a consequence of tight labour markets. "Another factor ... to use Rajan's phrase, is to insist on 'mindset flexibility.' Practices such as management by results, performance-related pay, and contracts in which working hours are not specified combine with intensified pressures of work and fear of redundancy to produce a situation in

73 Aronowitz, *Post-Work*, 59–64.
74 Turcotte, "Time Spent with Family during a Typical Workday, 1986–2005"; Economic Policy Institute, "Annual Median Hours Worked for Middle Income Husbands and Wives with Children, 1975–2002."
75 Goodin, Rice, Parpo, and Eriksson, *Discretionary Time*, 64–5, 264–5.
76 Ibid., 69.

which the coercive power of the manager is internalized. The pace of work is therefore driven by a self-generated compulsive drive rather than the explicit external authority of the boss."[77] This internalization of the drive of capital to expand affects the bosses too. They are, after all, also human beings with but one lifetime to live. For example, a thirty-one-year-old self-employed entrepreneur testified concerning his experience of life-time, "I only have three years left … three years before I burn out … It's a race; things are moving five, ten times faster than they used to … you have only a very short window, if you are going to brand yourself."[78] Whether one is boss or worker, once one's life-time becomes an instrument of money-value, it becomes increasingly impossible to *enjoy* the exercise of one's capacities because it becomes impossible to concentrate on the moment of their expression. This inability to focus on the moment of expression expresses a deeper dimension of life-time instrumentalization: the instrumentalization of the present moment by a future moment which never arrives.

A number of years ago a major Canadian bank ran a television advertisement that reconstructed the entire human life-cycle as a series of necessary interactions with the bank. The commercial began with a young couple recently married. Things are going well. They are about to start new careers and have begun to start planning for their future. From the perspective of the bank, planning for the future means coming to an understanding of it as a set of new financial obligations and opportunities. The new jobs open up access to the bank's money in the form of a mortgage. Getting the mortgage means they can buy a house. Having new jobs and buying a house mean that they can now plan to have a child. But having a baby immediately resolves itself into a series of further banking transactions. The child's education must eventually be paid for, which means a registered education savings plan must be set up. Furthermore, work life ends, so the problem of saving for the couple's own retirement must be solved. In a one minute ad, the entire course of life from birth to death is summed up as a series of banking transactions. Lest anyone misinterpret the images, the narration is sung to the tune of the old song "Shin Bone." Instead of the anatomy of the body, the song explains the unity of life as a sequence of money-access problems: "the new job's connected to the *mort*-gage," and so on.

Each moment of the human life-cycle thus loses the intrinsic life-value of being a moment of *enjoyment.* Even the wide-eyed freedom of childhood is instrumentalized by the system-requirement imposed on the parents to

---

77 Huws, "The Making of a Cybertariat? Virtual Work in the Real World," 14.
78 Quoted in Kovel, *The Enemy of Nature,* 65.

prepare the child for the harsh realities of life under contemporary capitalism. If the child does not succeed in primary and secondary school, he or she will not get into a good university. If the young adult has the vocation for higher-level studies but no money, the vocation cannot be pursued. Even having the vocation and the money for higher education is not enough. The student has to choose the right program because he or she must think of his or her future career. So the horizon-expanding function of education is negated by its reduction to career planning. The life-value of the moment of education is lost in the system-requirement of having to think past the present to the future career moment to which education is instrumentally linked. The content of the career moment, in turn, is not determined by what is most life-valuable as one's life's work but by which of the available opportunities pay the most. Thus the life-value of adult work life – the potential to express and enjoy one's cognitive and creative capacities in life-serving ways – is reduced to service to labour markets. Even if a person does not care about money, the world in which that person lives is organized according to its imperatives. Thus, possessing money is a social imperative that no one can ignore. But even if one does find a career that pays well and has some life-value to it, one cannot enjoy the contribution that one's life's work makes to the world. The life-value of the career is negated by the system-requirement that one save enough money for retirement. Thus the life-value of old age – continuing to act according to your capabilities while also gathering together the disparate moments of your life into a coherent whole, i.e., evaluating the contributions that you have made to your world – once again becomes a money-value. A "good" old age is any old age that is supported by sufficient retirement income. Every moment of present enjoyment from birth to death is thus attacked by the money-value system.

The deprivation of an experience of time as free is a consequence of, and ties together into a coherent unity, the deprivations of our more basic natural and socio-cultural life-requirements. Because capitalism depends on the alienation of human beings from the natural life-support system, people are dependent on a wage in order to live. Because people are dependent on their wages, labour markets exert coercive effects across the spectrum of human socio-cultural life, commodifying anything that can be commodified and compelling governments to always be cognizant of and serve "economic realities." Because the natural and social moments of life exert coercive power over individual human beings, their own motivations and goals tend to be reduced to programmed functions of system-requirements rather than free choices about how best to express and enjoy intrinsic life-value. This result means, concretely, that the experience of one's life-time takes the form of a sequence of compelled behaviours in reaction to external pressures. In other words, life-time is not experienced as an open matrix of possibilities for life-valuable activities but as behaviours within closed structures of routine. Unlike, say, a vitamin deficiency which can be made good through taking a supplement, there is no supplement that can restore to a mortal being time lost in the execution of coerced routine. Any damage to life-time is permanent damage, making the deprivation of the temporal life-requirements of human beings arguably the worst form of harm to which we are liable.

The examples of the causes of damage to humanity's shared life-interests presented here are ideal-typical cases. The aim is not to tendentiously distort reality but to bring into clear light the operation of the money-value system that governs liberal-democratic capitalist society today. The goal is to enable understanding of the harmful effects of this value system, effects which grow to the extent that its actuality approaches its ideal-typical presentation. There are always competing tendencies and struggles that contest the legitimacy of the untrammeled operation of the money-value system and resist its life-harmful implications. Those harmful implications are, nevertheless, real across the spectrum of human life-interests.

The concrete presentation of these forms of life-harm is not intended simply as abstract criticism but as a foil against which people might begin to think together in a positive way about a society that prioritized the satisfaction of our life-requirements. What would be the principles of such a society? The most fundamental would be that social institutions be organized such that our life-requirements are comprehensively satisfied for the sake of the free development, expression, and enjoyment of our life-capacities, and not as instruments of the money-value system. The free development, expression, and enjoyment of human life-capacities describe in general terms the life-grounded materialist conception of the good. To a more complete explanation of its meaning and social conditions I now turn.

PART THREE

Life-Grounded Materialist Ethics and the Human Good

6

The Human Good as Free Life-Capacity Expression and Enjoyment

IN PART ONE I BEGAN the construction of a life-grounded materialist ethics by arguing in favour of a complex materialist ontology. In contrast to reductionism, a complex materialist ontology understands the universe as a continuum of nested levels of organization and complexity. The continuum ranges from the fundamental forces and elements of physical reality to the self-conscious symbolic constructions of human social life. These levels are mediated by emergent properties and properly form a continuum since no transcendent ideal power or entity is posited as an explanation for higher-level structures of organization or the capacities appropriate to them. Simpler levels of physical organization function both as the material basis out of which higher levels of complexity evolve or are created and as constraints or frames limiting the powers of the higher levels of organization. Each level of reality must ultimately be grasped through concepts appropriate to the emergent properties that distinguish higher levels of organization from lower. This point is especially important when examining the evolutionary emergence of life from its non-living molecular elements. With the evolutionary emergence of life a new and unique possibility developed: a universe that is meaningful and valuable.

The existence, expression, and enjoyment of life-value presupposes the existence of living things capable of caring and concerning themselves with the conditions and quality of their own and others' existence. Life-grounded materialist ethics points to the struggles of living things to avoid and overcome limitations of their range of activity as the natural soil out of which social self-conscious conceptions of the good life develop. The content of these struggles also tells us something important about the content of the good life for humans. What do animals always struggle against? They struggle against externally imposed limitations which appear to threaten their ability to access the things their lives require. Higher and lower qualities of life are not arbitrary theoretical posits but are grounded in the ability of any living thing to access what its life requires. If it is successful, its vital activity is maintained or enhanced. If it fails, that vital activity is diminished or destroyed. As the history of ethical philosophy attests, human beings are capable of constructing diverse theories of the good life. To be coherent as theories of good *life*, they had to comprehend at the very least the conditions of existence of the philosophers who articulated them. This fact tells us something of essential philosophical importance when thinking about the human good: whatever its content turns out to be, it must be grounded in the life-requirements and life-capacities that define human beings for, if it were not, there would be no one alive to defend any particular idea.

While anchored in nature as the universal system of life-support, the good life for human beings is ultimately social in nature. As I emphasized in chapter 1, our nature is integrally organic and social. As such, our life-activity is not confined to satisfying physical-organic life-requirements but extends beyond that rudimentary form to the conscious creative labour involved in the construction of societies. Societies are not reducible to the physical processes that underlie them; they are structured by institutions and governed by value-systems. Life-grounded materialist ethics is thus not primarily concerned with species or social reproduction as ends in themselves. Instead, it presupposes the sustainable reproduction of society as a material precondition of good human lives. The key ethical question is not, does the society enable people to reproduce, but rather, does the ruling value system enable people to freely develop their life-capacities as instrumentally and intrinsically life-valuable expressions of themselves?

As ethical thought throughout history has stressed, the good is the highest of which human beings are capable. Since from a life-grounded materialist perspective life is essentially activity, the good life for human beings in general must be the highest form of activity of which we are capable. The highest form of activity of which human beings are capable, both collectively and individually, is free, self-determining activity. The essential problem of this chapter is to explain how free self-determination is compatible with two seemingly opposed claims: 1) that the free realization of intrinsically valuable life-capacities must also make instrumentally valuable contributions to the natural and social worlds of which one is a member; and 2) that freedom is compatible with the limitations on the content of expressed life-activity imposed by the life-ground of value. The general argument will be that if freedom means nothing more than doing what one wants to do, without regard to the natural conditions of life or the life-requirements of other people, it undermines rather than coheres with the life-ground of value, and thus tends toward material irrationality.

The arguments in chapter 6 unpack this general argument. I begin my account in section 6.1 by examining the complex relationship between the individual good and the social good, arguing that there is no necessary opposition between them. Individual and social good stand in tension, I will argue, only where the ruling value system fails to understand the ethical implications of natural dependence and social interdependence. Still, even if the opposition between the individual and social good can be resolved, it seems contradictory to maintain that free capacity realization is the good life for human beings, and yet at the same time insist that the life-ground of value imposes limitations on the content of the capacities it regards as free and good to express and enjoy. In section 6.2, I examine this deeper contradiction and contend that it can be resolved by differentiating between external limitations on activity (like systemic life-requirement deprivation) and internal limitations (like the belief that it is not good to do something, even though one has the power to do so). Only external limitations count as coercive restrictions on freedom, while internal limits are in fact exercises of freedom insofar as they are acts of *self*-limitation. Consciousness of the life-ground of value takes the latter form. Finally, in section 6.3, I bring the philosophical argument to a close by contrasting life-grounded materialist ethics with the "capabilities approach" to social justice developed in different ways by Sen and Nussbaum. By explicating the systematic differences between life-grounded materialism and the capabilities approach, the unity and distinctiveness of life-grounded materialism will be emphasized.

6.1 GOOD FOR SELF AND GOOD FOR WORLD

Life-grounded materialist ethics distinguishes itself from egocentric traditions in philosophy by rejecting the claim that there must always be a contradiction between the good for individuals and the good for society. Life-grounded materialism rejects any *necessary* opposition between individual and social good because it follows Marx in the belief that individuals are social beings. This claim does not mean that individuals are mere functions of social systems but rather that human individuals develop their social self-consciousness capacities for individuated modes of action through the appropriation of natural resources and social institutions and symbolic systems which they did not create. The point is not to mechanically reduce the individual to the natural field of life-support and the social field of life-development out of which they emerge, but to emphasize that *unless nature and society satisfy the three classes of life-requirement, social self-conscious agency cannot develop.* As McMurtry argues, "the social level of life-organization in its full life-protective evolution [is] the basis and guardian of individual life from which the individual person differentiates as a unique and unrepeatable bearer of life-value."[1] Life-grounded materialism extends this reasoning to assert that ruling value systems which mandate the use of natural resources and social wealth to ensure the comprehensive satisfaction of the three classes of life-requirement are *not* coercively imposing a reified conception of the good upon individuals. They are satisfying the shared material conditions without which no truly individual conception of the good is possible. If the natural dependence and social interdependence of human individual life is properly understood, then people themselves willingly assume a duty to contribute to the health of the natural field of life-support and the social field of life-development, *as the enjoyed substance of their individual good life.*

It is not surprising that doctrines like Von Hayek's, which reject any strong conception of life-requirements, would argue that the life-grounded materialist conception of the essential connection between the social and individual good must rely on coercive measures. I will not reiterate the criticisms of this classical liberal argument that I made in chapter 2. Instead, I will examine an argument potentially much more damaging to my conclusion because it rests on an analogously strong conception of need. Rather than concluding, as life-grounded materialist ethics does, that a social commitment to universal need-satisfaction is the foundation of individual freedom, Lawrence Hamilton contends that such a commitment cannot be realized without the coercive exercise of state power against individuals.

In *The Political Philosophy of Needs* Hamilton defends a conception of "true interest" relevantly similar to the life-grounded conception of shared life-interests, but concludes that, left to themselves, individuals will never reach political consensus about exactly what these true interests are. This lack of agreement does not entail that there is no true interest but only that an external coercive power is required to enforce it. This coercive power is the state. "The reality of the evaluation of needs and need-claims is a state of constant political conflict ... This is the case because the evaluation of true interests is ultimately an evaluation of extant felt needs and (possibly) cherished institutions and roles, all in the context of normative power differentials. The coercive authority of the state is a necessary condition for the evaluation and meeting of needs."[2] The individual's true interest coincides with his needs, but, since everyone

---

1 McMurtry, *The Cancer Stage of Capitalism*, 89.
2 Hamilton, *The Political Philosophy of Needs*, 144.

interprets his needs from his own standpoint, political agreement on the priority of satisfying those needs is impossible. The state must step in and impose an order on the needs. The effect of state power is socially good – needs are met – but contrary to at least some individuals' interpretation of their own good.

If it is the case, as Hamilton argues, that individuals' true interests coincide with their needs, then why should it be *necessary* that coercive state power be employed to satisfy those true interests? Coercion is only *necessary* if people's true interests, i.e., needs, differ. As I have argued, our real life-requirements do not differ, and the life-requirement criterion can be employed to distinguish in all cases between actual needs and subjective demands. Thus, the first response to Hamilton's conclusion – that serving the social good of life-requirement satisfaction depends on the coercive denial of individual interests – is that it fails to consider the possibility that the disagreements that he believes the state must resolve are not disagreements about true interests but about subjective demands which cannot all be satisfied because of relative resource scarcity. If the life-grounded materialist account of shared life-interest is true, then there are no grounds for disagreement about what is actually required.

Again, we can point to the history of struggles mentioned at numerous points in the earlier chapters to support this claim. To the extent that people become conscious of the life-ground of value, they begin to *demand* that political, economic, social, and cultural institutions satisfy life-requirements. To be sure, some people *will* disagree with these demands – those groups whose private money-interests will be compromised if the life-grounded demands are met. Nevertheless, in a democratic society, use of legitimate institutional power is not coercive since the society is actually democratic only to the extent that the common life-interest rules, as I argued in section 5.3.2. Where political power is used to institutionalize a life-grounded value system, the state *ceases* to be the servant of private interests and becomes a preserver and enabler of life-values. The power it exercises as a universal life-enabler is not coercive in any ethically meaningful sense of the term since state institutions would execute only those decisions manifestly in the shared life-interest and decided upon by duly constituted democratic bodies.

As McMurtry argues, "the organized provision of life-goods for all as they need and choose is, if we reflect upon it, an achievement that marks the evolution of human culture towards ever fuller realization of the life-code ... This underlying evolution of the civil commons goes beyond the imagined systems of justice that philosophers and theorists have conceived over millennia. It is a creation from the ground up of a consciously shared life-ground out of the killing fields of history, a slow and almost imperceptible construction of a form of social life that enables the health, expression, and thought of all citizens alike, which undergirds the lives of all citizens alike and not just those possessing or ingratiating themselves to rank or money-demand."[3] Thus, the extent to which coercion is necessary to ensure life-requirement satisfaction is determined not by some inevitable disagreement between people but by the degree to which life-blind private interest controls universally needed life-resources. Democratic control over those resources might appear coercive to those whose money-interests are compromised, but, since they can choose to become participants in that democratic society and limit their demands to what their lives require, it need not in fact be so.

Even if this argument against the necessity of coercion is sound, it leaves open a second objection, raised in the work of Christian Bay, that life-grounded materialism is naive if it expects that agreement on the content of shared life-interest entails agreement on priorities among the different elements that compose those life-interests. In *The Structure of Freedom* Bay argues that "the chief difficulty in this approach toward the maximization of freedom is the lack of consensus about the priorities between human rights – apart from a general acceptance, I believe, of the right to stay alive and not suffer physical violence ... There is no general agreement about which freedoms or rights are more important, among, for instance, the following: the right to work, the right to a living wage, the right to vote, the right to medical care, the freedom to travel, the right to plan parenthood, freedom of association, freedom of speech, ... and the right to leisure and privacy."[4] The challenge that Bay is posing to my argument is clear. If it is the case that people can agree on the content of the shared life-interest, they could still disagree on priorities. Those whose priorities lose out in the debate could then again feel that their own good is being sacrificed to the actual social good pursued, even if there is no principled disagreement about what the ideal social good is (comprehensive satisfaction of life-requirements for the sake of free expression and enjoyment of life-capacities).

My response to Bay's argument begins by agreeing with it insofar as it describes people's actual political behaviour in liberal-democratic capitalist society when funds are made available for life-valuable purposes. In actual social conditions in which most natural resources and social wealth are controlled by private powers, debates over how to best use what money is made available for life-requirement satisfaction invariably generate the sorts of disagreements that concern Bay. Take for example

3 McMurtry, *Unequal Freedoms*, 363.
4 Bay, *The Structure of Freedom*, 133.

the perennial Canadian debate about public funding for health care, education, and the arts. Each of these institutions and practices serves to satisfy a genuine life-requirement. Yet, in social conditions in which public funds are scarce, practitioners of each are forced to secure funds through a competitive process in which it becomes easy to target the other rather than the ruling value system that governs the ownership and control of resources and wealth. Once each is forced to please external funders as a condition of accessing resources, the argument will be conducted in terms of which of the alternatives is more instrumentally valuable to the money-economy. Once the debate is conducted in those terms, it becomes conceptually impossible to understand all three as members of a continuum of life-requirements which need not be opposed to each other.

It is true that no society will ever possess unlimited resources. If resources remain relatively scarce, then investment priorities will always have to be determined. Nevertheless, if the ruling value system prioritizes life-requirement satisfaction, and each group recognizes itself as lying along the continuum of life-requirements, then different groups could work together to determine appropriate distributions of funding given available social wealth. In this way life-valuable institutions need not struggle against each other for funding. Instead, all could co-operate in determining the level of funding sufficient for accomplishing the life-valuable missions of each institution within the known limitations imposed by overall social wealth.

Is this response still naive? It is certainly hopeful, but it looks to history for substantiating evidence. Wherever one finds solidarity in political struggle one finds a willingness to attenuate one's own demands for the sake of unity of purpose with others. Solidarity means the conscious binding and holding together of different elements by shared commitment to a common value. All major political struggles which succeed in releasing resources from the control of privately controlled money-value circuits depend as a matter of political necessity on successfully building solidarity. Solidarity is the life-ground in political action. The more solidarity, the broader the struggles; the broader the struggles, the wider and deeper the opening of each member beyond egocentric self-enclosure toward a renewed self-understanding as conscious and self-active members of the wider fields of life and life-support. The more that self-understanding is re-grounded in life-value, the less the question of priorities among the different sites of life-valuable activity arises. What counts is not whether one person's life-practice is more important than another's, but that the social field of life-support is organized such that the chosen paths of each lead back to contribution to improved quality of life for all. As McMurtry

argues, "as consciously human ... [we] know and abide by the rules [we]
live by as value bearing agents in a community. The mutually followed
rules are the collective subject."⁵ When these mutually followed rules are
life-grounded, i.e., when they are "conscious principles of more inclusively enabling life," then they can only have been developed from the
thought and action of individual human beings working *together* to make
them the ruling principles of their society.⁶

While it is true that the social good of life-requirement satisfaction can
appear coercive, this appearance is due to the fact that the ruling value
system is not consistently life-grounded. Thus, there is no *necessary* opposition between the social good and the individual good such that the
use of political power to ensure comprehensive life-requirement satisfaction is coercive. Having now examined the problem from the social side
of the equation, I turn to the individual side. It may be the case that the
use of political power to serve the common life-interest is not coercive.
That alone does not ensure that it is sound to claim, as life-grounded
materialist ethics does, that the individual good lies in fulfilling a duty
toward society. In order to make the case, I will begin not from the life-
ground of value but from Kant's conception of rational selves, and show
how the duty toward others which he affirms implies the life-ground of
value. By reconstructing these life-ground presuppositions step by step,
the meaning and the soundness of the life-grounded materialist claim
about individual good as duty toward society will become clear.

Kant argues that there is an individual duty to develop one's capacities.
To illustrate, he paints the following picture. A man in comfortable circumstances prefers not to develop a talent whose cultivation would render him "useful" to others.⁷ Kant next asks whether the maxim underlying
this choice (never develop useful talents when their development would
compromise one's comfort) could be willed as a universal law. He answers
as follows: "He cannot possibly will that this should become a universal
law of nature or that it should be implanted in us by a natural instinct.
For, as a rational being, he necessarily wills that all his faculties should be
developed, inasmuch as they are given to him for all sorts of purposes."⁸
The problem with this conclusion (aside from the empirical fact that faculties are not, strictly speaking, "given" to us; they have naturally evolved
and must be socially cultivated) is that it does not follow from the strict
picture of what it is to be a rational being from Kant's perspective.

5 McMurtry, "What is Good, What is Bad," 124.
6 Ibid.
7 Kant, *Foundations for the Metaphysics of Morals*, 46.
8 Ibid., 46–7.

To be useful to others, in a generic sense, is to contribute something of some value to others' lives through one's own labour and activity. The criterion of usefulness presupposes that human life requires input from outside itself. Yet in his account of rational being, examined in section 5.2, Kant argues explicitly that the wish of every rational being must be to free itself of the life-requirements through which it is connected to its own body and to other life (and, by implication, to the natural field of life-support and the social field of life-development). The passage is crucial, so I will repeat it: "The inclinations" Kant writes, "as the sources of needs ... are so lacking in worth that the universal wish of every rational being must be indeed to free himself completely from them."[9] I argued in section 5.2 that to "free" ourselves from our needs would be to free ourselves from the material conditions of exercising any capacity whatsoever. It would also mean "freeing" ourselves from having the need of anyone else's capacities. The entire basis of Kant's duty – others' need for our capacities – would collapse.

The realization of Kant's wish would amount to overcoming the material ties by which individual life is bound to individual life. However, these material ties are the real basis of the possibility of our being "useful" to others. Once the ties have been broken, the source of the duty to be actually useful to others in the development of our capacities has disappeared. In fact, the disappearance of material ties between individuals would undermine all duties: lying, treating others as exploitable means to our private ends, not developing one's talents, all are ethically wrong only for beings whose life can be better or worse, and *life* can be better or worse only if its well-being depends on certain life-requirements being met. If it is true, therefore, that the universal wish of *rational* beings is to be free of organic and social life-requirements, then it is also true by implication that the universal wish of rational beings is to be free of their material nature, and thus of the real bonds that tie life to life, and thus of the condition of the idea of duty even being meaningful.

It follows that the very possibility of ethical practice presupposes the material interdependence of individual human lives. Life-grounded self-consciousness is consciousness of self as dependent on the natural field of life-support and interdependent with others in the social field of life-development. Only insofar as one is conscious of one's individuality as an emergent reality out of these fields of life-support and development can the problem of duty arise, for only insofar as one recognizes oneself as dependent and interdependent can one care about the conditions, natural and social, that sustain and enable one's own life. If a rational being on

9 Ibid., 52–3.

Kant's terms has no needs, then it requires nothing of nature or society. If it requires nothing, it cannot be harmed by being deprived. What holds for one self holds for all selves. Thus, if no one requires anything and no one can be harmed by being deprived of anything, no one could owe anybody or the sustaining fields of life-support and development anything.

Of course, Kant recognizes the reality of life-requirements, but he sees them as sources of heteronomy rather than life-productive interdependence. At the same time, by arguing that we owe it to others to develop our "useful" capacities, Kant implicitly recognizes "life-productive interdependence". The problem, therefore, is that Kant's injunction against instrumental exploitation of others and his defence of the duty to improve their lives does not make sense from the rationalist-egocentric position from which Kant actually argues. Re-thinking Kant's conclusions on the basis of life-grounded materialist ethics resolves the contradiction by reinterpreting life-requirements as the source of the human interconnections. My drawing from those interconnections grounds the duty to repay. The meaning of duty is essentially bound up with the idea of debt, of owing an obligation. Embodied beings who draw resources out of the natural field of life-support and the social field of life-development owe it to others who also depend on those fields to develop their capacities in ways which are instrumentally life-valuable. This duty frames my purpose as a social self-conscious being. That purpose is to contribute to the worlds which sustain me by the life-activity those worlds enable. The forms of activity through which I contribute at the same time define me as this particular individual. To the extent that my consciousness is life-grounded, I recognize the higher value of my own life when it makes meaningful contributions to others' lives. The good for individuals was defined above as the highest form of activity of which humans are capable. The highest form of that activity is, in general, to enable others' lives through one's individual efforts. Hence, the good life for humans coincides with the duty to contribute in life-enabling ways to the natural and social fields of life-support and development on which all human beings depend.

Thus, to live a good life in the life-grounded materialist sense is to concern oneself not simply with the principles by which one lives (whether or not they can be justified according to some egocentric theory of ethics) but also with the environmental and social implications of acting on those principles. If good lives always involve reflection on the implications for others, then ethical reflection is always at the same time social and political reflection. When one judges whether an action is or is not good, one judges its contribution to the shared life-interest. The evaluation of whether or not one's life has been good thus involves considering whether one's modes of capacity realization and enjoyment have contributed to a good world and not just to one's being a good self, to paraphrase Brecht.[10]

However, the unity of the ethical and the political does not mean that the individual good is reducible to selfless devotion to the social whole or some party or faction which claims to speak on its behalf. It is, more deeply, the recognition in individual consciousness of the real underlying unity that life's shared conditions and requirements establish between individuals. The basis of this identification lies in the evolved and symbolically elaborated nature of human self-consciousness itself. As McMurtry argues, "human beings ... are uniquely capable of consciousness of who they are beyond immediate identity with their embodied present. They achieve across generations a cumulative understanding of the conditions that enable their possibility as a life-value base, shared platform of creative individuation, and steering knowledge for species advance of species-enabling conditions."[11] Judging maxims of action in this life-grounded way presupposes only that one is capable of asking to what sort of world does my action contribute. Is it helping to free social institutions from service to life-blind ruling value systems? While these questions make no sense for an ego treating itself as a rational being in abstraction from its embodiment or for a person treating his or her life as analytically and normatively separate from the shared life-interests of each and all, it does not elevate the shared life-interests to a world apart in relation to which the individual life-bearer is coercively subordinated as to an alien power.

The unity of the ethical and political which follows from our natural dependence and social interdependence thus entails that what is good for an individual must be good for the world in which the individual lives, and what is good for the world in which the individual lives must be good for the individual. In this sense, life-grounded materialist ethics is, as I put it in an earlier essay, "between egoism and altruism."[12] I mean that a life-grounded materialist understanding of one's self and one's good opens one's horizons beyond the confines of mere self-interest but does

10 The reference is to the dying words of Joan in *Saint Joan of the Stockyards*. Realizing that her personal ethical convictions have been exploited by the owners of a meat packing company and used to violently undermine a strike, Joan ruefully enjoins others to "take care that when you leave the world/you were not only good but are leaving/a good world." Brecht, *Saint Joan of the Stockyards*, 120.

11 McMurtry, "What is Good, What is Bad," 190.

12 Noonan, "Between Egoism and Altruism: Outline for a Materialist Conception of the Good."

not, for that reason, imply that good action is by definition self-sacrificing. One does not *compromise* one's own good by identifying it with the duty to contribute instrumental life-value to others' lives by improving in some way the natural field of life-support or the social field of life-development. On the contrary, one expresses and enjoys good activity *as an individual* and values oneself as a willing contributor to the health of the life-sustaining and life-enabling natural and social worlds. I conclude this section with concrete examples that further illustrate my meaning.

If a person thinks of himself as an atomic self-maximizing ego, then his decision to drive a gas-guzzling car is a matter of personal choice. Any interference with his choice would be perceived as oppressive and therefore unethical. At the same time, by driving a more rather than less polluting car, he is damaging the atmosphere on which everyone, including himself, depends. If that same person now begins to think of himself as an embodied being, he will realize that the atmosphere is shared with everyone, and that what he formerly took to be an act of private choice has, in reality, collective implications. Once one grounds one's sense of self in the collective natural and social reality, changes in what one takes to be one's own good become inevitable. A new layer of responsibility for the implications of one's actions emerges. By feeling responsible *as a self* for the natural and social implications of one's actions means that what formerly appeared as an oppressive external limitation is transformed into a willed internal self-limitation. The self then realizes that the ego-centric conception of the good was mistaken. Since the self no longer regards the world as external to it, but regards itself as a part of the world, it comes to see that any conception of the good which worsens rather than improves the world is ultimately self-undermining because materially irrational. The self thus changes its activities to avoid the contradiction involved in asserting as good for self something that destroys or worsens the natural and social worlds on which its life depends.

The identity of good for self and good for world can also be viewed from the side of the good of the world. The ultimate horizon of life-grounded development is the world as a whole, a position incompatible with arguments such as those of David Millar and Thomas Nagel who claim that the good of the world must be understood as the good of different national communities.[13] National communities are not ultimate

13 See Millar, *Principles of Social Justice,* 118–19, 263; Nagel, "The Problem of Global Justice." The global nature of the human good today raises important political problems of whether some nations are obliged to militarily interfere in other nations when those nations are serious human rights violators. I have dealt with this issue elsewhere so I will not repeat those arguments here. My main concern is with the structure of life-grounded

because they are composed of human beings with shared life-interests, and it is these life-interests *as humanly shared* that are the basis of the life-grounded materialist understanding of the good of the world.

Consider, for example, an individual in the developed world who reduces his or her spending on consumer goods and contributes the surplus to the alleviation of absolute poverty in the Global South. In order to develop this example, I adapt an argument of Peter Singer's. Singer defends as a moral necessity the principle that individuals contribute their surplus income to those in absolute poverty. In defence of this principle he draws an analogy between someone who, observing a child drowning in a pond, walks past and leaves the child to her fate, and someone living with surplus income who refuses to contribute anything to the alleviation of absolute poverty. Singer concludes, "the vast majority of us living in the developed world have disposable income that we spend on frivolities and luxuries ... if we do this while people are in danger of dying of starvation and when there are agencies which can, with reasonable efficiency, turn our modest donations of money into life-saving food and medicine, how can we consider ourselves any better than the person who sees the child fall in the pond and walks on?"[14] I am interested here not with whether a donation to a food agency is the best way to solve global poverty but with the life-grounded identity of good for world and good for self that Singer's argument implies. The very title of his book, *One World,* implies this identity. If we really do inhabit one world, and humanity forms, as he says, one community, then there must be *one good,* variously realized through different forms of individual action. What is at issue ethically when individuals attenuate their consumer demands so that they can donate surplus income to the benefit of the starving is the good of the world which they inhabit and not just their own good or the good of the particular other whom their donation helps. The complex mediations lying between donor and recipient mean that most donors will never see or know the people whom they assist, and thus most who contribute cannot intend the good of some assignable other. What motivates them is the life-grounded materialist principle that it is morally untenable to live in a world of vast resources in which hundreds of millions of people starve. That to which they contribute is the good of the world expressed as wider circles of life-requirement

---

materialist ethical thought, not particular questions of political strategy. Hence, it would disrupt the flow of argument to repeat here what I have argued elsewhere. See Noonan, "The Principle of Liberal Imperialism: Human Rights and Human Freedom in an Age of Evangelical Capitalism."

14 Singer, *One World,* 157.

satisfaction. These wider circles of satisfaction are only real, however, as the experience and enjoyment of the individuals whose lives are better as a consequence. In other words, though universal and shared, the good of the world is not a reified whole to which individuals can be sacrificed since it cannot be created or enjoyed apart from the willed actions of the individuals who create it or the increased life-capacity they enjoy as a result of it.

In order to be real, a meaningful and valuable life must be *realized* outside of the mind of the individual agent. Realized actions are always social actions because it is only as members of natural systems of life-support and social systems of life-development that we can act at all. If, therefore, the natural field of life-support and the social field of life-development are always the ground and target of realized action, it follows that only such actions as actually improve these fields and thus others' lives are objectively life-valuable, for the self, for others, and for the world. If actions are not objectively life-valuable then, for a *social-organic* being, they are not valuable at all since any particular valuation presupposes life and the life-capacities involved in making it, and actions which are not life-valuable do not develop, and often destroy, those capacities.

A self who treats an action that is in reality damaging for the fields of life-support and life-development as good for himself is necessarily alienated in consciousness and practice from the life-ground without which he could not act at all. People can of course be deceived into thinking that life-destructive action is in reality life-supportive action. A rich white person may deceive himself into thinking that paying an illegal immigrant less than minimum wage to work for him as a nanny is a good for the immigrant, i.e., better than the alternative of having no money. However, this sort of self-deception results from narrowing the range of alternatives contemplated, and it can be overcome, therefore, by considering those alternatives ruled out by the existing value system but not impossible for that reason.

Were the ruling value system itself life-grounded, such pathologies of alienation and self-deception would tend to disappear. If the ruling value system serves the shared life-interest by ensuring the satisfaction of all life-requirements, and individual action maintains the ruling value system through forms of realization which are expressed and enjoyed by the individual, then the unity of good for self and good for world is established in reality. In such a world the individual good is the expression and enjoyment of human capacities that contribute to the good of the world, and the good of the world is the real satisfaction of individuals' life-requirements such that everyone is capable of making and enjoying real contributions to the ongoing elaboration and deepening of life-value. In other words, the good of the world is the actual unity between the ruling value system and the life-ground of value, realized in life-valuable individual activity.

I have argued that the human good, construed individually, is life-valuable activity, and construed collectively – as a good world – is forms of organization which enable life-valuable activity. It is clear, therefore, that for life-grounded materialist ethics, a form of expressed capacity, even if enjoyed by the individual, is not necessarily good since some forms of capacity expression are not good for others or the world, and thus, by the logic of the argument of this section, not good for the self either. While there is no necessary contradiction involved in asserting limitations to the content of good lives, there does seem to be a contradiction in asserting that those limitations are not only compatible with freedom but in a sense definitive of freedom. Yet life-grounded materialist ethics claims that the good is free life-valuable capacity expression. In the next section I examine and resolve the potential contradiction involved in identifying free activity with life-valuable activity.

6.2 FREE CAPACITY REALIZATION AND THE GOOD FOR HUMAN BEINGS

I have identified the human good with the life-valuable realization of the capacities for feeling, thought, and creative action, and their life-valuable realization with freedom. It follows from this claim that not every form of capacity realization of which people are capable is actually a free mode of capacity realization. A serious contradiction might appear to be at work here. Freedom means self-determination. Self-determination seems incompatible with the sort of qualifying limitation on activity imposed by my claim that the activity must be life-valuable in order to be free. If people decide to express themselves in life-disvaluable ways, then, according to the conclusion of the previous section, their activity is not good. Why should it further follow from its not being good that it is not free? There seems to be a disconnection between freedom and goodness rather than an essential link, as I have claimed. If people are able to express their capacities as they choose, then it seems true by definition that they are free to realize them, which in turn means that it is a bald contradiction to say that if those capacities do not produce life-value for others, they are not undertaken freely. Although the consequences might be life-destructive and therefore wrong, nevertheless the agents who caused the consequences must have been free in so acting.

In order to resolve this contradiction I begin by reiterating certain general points that I made in part one concerning the organic basis of freedom. The argument can then proceed to examine general modes of expression of our sentient, cognitive-imaginative, and creative capacities in order to discover the difference between external and internal limitations on the content of expressed capacities. It will turn out that where the expressed content of life-capacities is life-destructive, the cause of this action is an external, life-blind ruling-value system. The self does not act freely in those cases but under the compulsion of this ruling value system. To act in life-serving ways, by contrast, is to internally limit one's activity, and thus to be the cause of that activity, or, in other words, to act as a free agent.

The difference between external and internal limitations on activity, crucial to the life-grounded materialist conception of freedom, follows from the foundations of freedom in organic life-activity first noted in part one. Non-living things are fixed in their functions *by* their material structure. Sentient life, by contrast, is capable of some degree of self-determined behaviour and activity *because* of its unique material structure. As Lewontin notes, "there is some principle of organization of living matter that is shared with no other assemblage of atoms. The question that biologists keep asking themselves is 'Why is this matter different from all other matter?'"[15] Whatever the ultimate answer to this question turns out to be, it is clear that the difference between living and non-living matter is that living matter is capable of changing itself in response to the environment and, at higher levels of emergent organization, changing the environment to suit its life-requirements. As Reid explains, "organismal wholes obey the fundamental rules of physics, chemistry, and biology, but their own novel emergent properties can override those of the lower hierarchical levels."[16] It is the connection that sentience establishes between the living thing and its world that distinguishes living sentience from machine sensors. While a machine sensor might have an engineered capacity to detect things that animal or human sense cannot (say, the atomic structure of chemical compounds), this engineered capacity establishes no felt bond of being between the machine sensor and the compounds that it has detected. Unlike an animal which will struggle against external impediments to reach a food source, the machine sensor puts up no struggle against the chemist who switches it off once the work has been accomplished. Sentience is thus the organic foundation of freedom in the sense that it is what supplies the information on the basis of which organisms *act*. The goal of organic activity in general is

MARXIST

15 Lewontin, *It Ain't Necessarily So: The Dream of the Human Genome and Other Illusions*, 114.
16 Reid, *Biological Emergences*, 83.

life-maintenance, and life-maintenance demands constant connection to the sustaining field of life-support. If any organism acts so as to break the connection with the field of life-support, it does not thereby increase the freedom of its activity but rather undermines the material possibility of any further activity at all. Freedom as organic activity not only origi-nates with life; it is also constrained by its nature to either serve life or cease to exist.

With sentient life we have not simply a chemical-evolutionary link be-tween life and life's requirements but a "felt bond of being" between the organism and its environment. All sentient life takes in and processes information from its environment and reacts, behaves, and (in the case of humans) acts on the basis of this information. Human beings share with other life forms this basic capacity to sense the external world and respond in a life-serving fashion to the information which the senses gather. However, sentience in humans is more complex because it is always bound up with feeling or emotional life in general. Human sen-sory capacities do not simply gather raw information but are always expressed in unity with feelings or emotions. As Anthony O'Hear ar-gues, "consciousness is not purely a matter of information processing ... in consciousness we also become aware of the pleasure and pains associ-ated with things and their appearance ... to take delight in the appear-ances themselves."[17] Together sentience and emotions constitute what McMurtry calls "the felt side of being."[18] A few basic examples will illus-trate this claim more clearly.

Human beings do not "see" light rays refracted through our retinas but a beautiful vista that arouses joy, or the brutalizing of a fellow human being or animal that arouses horror. Sensations arouse feelings and to-gether they produce the rich field of subjective felt relations to the exter-nal world which constitutes our emotional life. What Nussbaum says about the emotion of wonder might be applied to the felt side of being as a whole: "it responds to the pull of the object, and, one might say, that in it the subject is now really aware of the value of the object."[19] If we interpret this claim in life-grounded materialist terms, the value at issue is the life-value. Through the felt side of being, humans first become aware of the world *as a world of life-value.*

The felt side of being in general is the social-organic foundation of our caring and concerning ourselves with the natural field of life-support and the social field of life-development. However, our feelings are not

17 O'Hear, *Beyond Evolution,* 177.
18 McMurtry, "What is Good, What is Bad," 84.
19 Nussbaum, *Upheavals of Thought,* 54.

pure functions of our organism but are affected by the social context in which they develop. Thus, the content of expressed feelings is shaped by the ruling value system under which we live. It is thus possible to express certain feelings in regard to an object which the object itself in no way authorizes. Thus, in a racist society a sexual relationship between two people of different races may arouse disgust in someone who has internalized the racist value system even though there is nothing objectively disgusting about it. While this expression seems on the surface to be a free manifestation of feelings, it is, I will argue, imposed on the person from the outside, by the racist value system. It is thus not in essence a free expression of feelings, but a coerced distortion of feeling.

Where feelings that cut people off from affirmative connections with others are generated in people by a life-blind ruling value system, their inner, emotional life is impoverished. The ruling value system claims to be enriching that life but objectively does the opposite by erecting barriers to mutually enriching interactions. To impoverish one's emotional life while intending to enrich it is materially irrational in the dimension of the felt side of being. To act in such materially irrational ways is not to act freely, not only because the feelings on which one acts stem from a life-blind ruling value system, but equally because the consequences of one's actions perpetuate systems of rule that materially impede the richer development of sentience and feeling by restricting their scope to approved contents. Hence people are not freely determining the content of the felt side of being; they are acquiescing in the existing impoverished scope of socially approved feelings.

The point of life-grounded materialist ethics is not to decide what is and is not, in every particular case for each person, an enjoyed, life-valuable content of sensory experience, but to mark the general difference between free, life-valuable modes of realization of these capacities and unfree, life-destructive modes. The free, life-valuable form of expression of our sentient and emotional capacities is any whereby we act so as to expand the range of objects experienced as life-valuable. The freedom is expressed in the act of seeking out the expanded ranges of life-valuable experience. In unfree modes of expression, by contrast, we are *prevented* by the internalized ruling value system from extending the range of experienced life-value. Since the expansion of experience sometimes takes place through learning to recognize suffering where previously we were closed to it, not every such expansion of experience is joyful. This disquieting experience is itself life-valuable because being able to recognize suffering is the first step toward overcoming it. As McMurtry argues, "if people observe or know of the destruction or brutal reduction of vital life ranges where no compensating gain in or security of others' life can explain it, they rebel from within."[20] The key difference between free and unfree experience is thus not that the former is pleasurable and the latter painful but that in free experience we multiply the life-valuable connections between our felt side of being and the world we inhabit and in the unfree modes life-valuable connections are constricted by a life-blind ruling value system. Analogous arguments hold with regard to our cognitive and imaginative and creative capacities. I treat each in turn.

The felt side of human life cannot be divorced from our cognitive and imaginative capacities. Human beings are distinguished from other life forms by the much richer conceptual and imaginative constructions through which we theorize, explain, understand, analyse, criticize, plan, and build a social-symbolic world out of the natural world. It is also our cognitive and imaginative capacities that allow us to reflect on our individual and collective goals and to argue with each other, not only about the content of different plans of action but about their legitimacy in relation to ruling value systems and the legitimacy of those value systems themselves. Through our commitment to different principles of living, we prove that life for humans is a matter of meaning and value. Aristotle makes this point clearly: "the power of speech [sets] forth the expedient and the inexpedient, and therefore likewise the just and unjust. And it is characteristic of man that he alone has a sense of good and evil."[21] Just as we can feel that a course of action is life-valuable when in fact it is life-destructive, so too the capacity to think can be expressed in arguments that defend life-blind value systems. Thus some scientists can be paid to dispute global warming, not as an honest exercise of scientific criticism but in order to support existing economic interests. Philosophical reason likewise can be mobilized in endless skeptical refutations of the reality of life-requirements, again, not as a contribution to deeper understanding but as an impediment to mobilizing collective action for life-valuable social change. These modes of capacity realization are determined by the life-blind ruling value system. Thought is an emergent property of human neural and social organization. It thus finds its material grounds too in life-support systems, and contradicts its own conditions of existence and development when it is employed to legitimate life-destructive patterns of action. Its free exercise, by contrast, occurs when it breaks the chains of established opinion and creates more comprehensive structures of understanding the natural and social worlds and the real implications of their organization for the conduct of individual life.

20 McMurtry, *The Cancer Stage of Capitalism*, 214.
21 Aristotle, "Politics," in *The Basic Works of Aristotle*, 1129.

Human feeling, cognition, and imagination are objectively realized through the creative activity by which the human world is built from natural materials. Like feeling and thought, our creative activity is ultimately free only when it is exercised in life-valuable ways. If the value of our lives is ultimately a question of both the form and the content of our life-activity, then we cannot separate the question of human freedom from the question of the content of feeling, thought, and action. If freedom is indeed an emergent property of the natural history of life on earth, an opening of human capacities beyond their instinctual, programmed limitation, then the growth of freedom depends on the extent to which social organization satisfies the material conditions of this growth. Where societies are governed by ruling values systems which are wholly or in part life-blind, social organization, whose value is, first, to enable the possibility of truly human action and, second, to widen its scope, constricts and narrows it. If freedom is essentially freedom of creative activity, then any society which constricts and narrows rather than expands the scope of activity contradicts its own material purpose, and is thus materially irrational. Although it might appear externally unconstrained, human action which simply serves to replicate the life-blind elements of the ruling value system is more akin to instinctual than free action, insofar as it remains within a closed choice-space and cannot create anything not authorized by the narrow, life-blind ruling value system.

The more a ruling value system is life-grounded, the more each and all who live within it are able to express and enjoy their felt side of being as experiences of beauty and human solidarity; the more widely and deeply each and all are able to understand the natural universe and the social worlds we have built within it, the more each and all are able to act creatively in new life-serving ways. What McMurtry says of value thus applies equally to freedom. His general criterion of value states that "X is of value if and only if and to the extent that x consists in or enables a more coherently inclusive range of thought/experience/action"[22] In the life-grounded understanding of freedom, we could say that x is a free act if and only if x consists in or enables a more coherently inclusive range of thought/experience/action. This life-grounded qualification is not, like life-blind ruling value systems, an external constraint which narrows the space of feeling, thought, imagination, or activity, but an internal constraint which rules out *only what confines feeling/thought/action* to established life-blind value systems intent on their own replication and not on the good of those who live under them. Expressions of feelings or thoughts or actions which cannot prove their "consistency ... with

22 Ibid., 72.

life-support systems" are thus ruled out as unfree because in ultimate contradiction with the natural and social conditions of activity in general.[23]

Thus, life-grounded, internal self-limitation does not destroy freedom but ensures that its natural and social conditions are preserved and improved. This claim distinguishes the life-grounded materialist conception of freedom from classical liberal conceptions of negative liberty. The life-grounded materialist conception of freedom distinguishes *action* from *consumer behaviour* in commodity markets. Despite the ubiquitous appearance of the word freedom in classical and neo-classical economic literature, all the equations describing micro-economic behaviour are deterministic. In other words, the scientific study of market "freedom" assumes the truth of classical mechanics and simply transfers its equations to the social realm, assuming that people are programmed functions of their "desires." Jevons's hope to rebuild economics as the "mechanics of utility and self-interest" lives on today in the master assumption of orthodox micro-economics, namely, that "each consumer *will* pursue his or her opportunities until the marginal cost of a transaction exceeds the benefit of it." Were this assumption true, Jevons's science would have long since succeeded.[24] As the unpredictability of the 2008 economic crisis proved, the entire edifice of neo-classical economics as built on these determinist assumptions is shaky at best. The important point for present purposes, however, is to see how the science of "the free market" assumes that human behaviour is as determined as the behaviour of the elements that Laplace's demon can know with absolute accuracy.

Human action is not predictable in this way and thus human enjoyment, which always follows from action, cannot be reduced to a utility function. *Human* enjoyment is feeling affirmed as an active individual contributor to the good of the world by virtue of the expression and enjoyment of capacities for the sake of the life-value of the nature and society of which one is a moment. Kasser once again usefully illustrates the psychological reality of this position. Commenting on a series of studies concerning what he calls "intrinsic motivation," Kasser concludes, "in the midst of such experiences people often report a strong sense of connection and oneness with whatever they are doing ... During these experiences people feel most themselves, as though their behaviour stems from their authentic interests and needs. They feel free and fully behind what they are doing."[25]

23 McMurtry, "Rationality and Scientific Method," 82.
24 Jevons, quoted in Nicolas Georgescu-Roegen, *The Entropy Law and the Economic Process*, 40.
25 Kasser, *The High Price of Materialism*, 77.

In life-grounded materialist terms, these experiences are intrinsically life-valuable. Intrinsic life-value is the precise opposite of programmed consumer behaviour, which is always determined by an end external to the action itself.

The life-grounded materialist conception of freedom is also distinct from some elements of Marx's conception. In particular, it reveals Marx's error in counterposing nature as a realm of necessity to a future society as the realm of freedom.[26] What Marx calls "necessity" and opposes to freedom is in life-grounded terms dependence on the natural field of life-support. This dependence is freedom-enabling rather than freedom-negating since nature is the ultimate basis of human social interdependence, and human social interdependence the instituted basis from which grows our power of individuating activity. Freedom, for life-grounded materialism, does not open up beyond the realm of necessity, but necessarily within it.

People must grasp the necessity of understanding the life-ground of their action if they are to act freely. In contrast to people whose consciousness has been programmed to decide what is good or bad on the basis of what serves or contradicts a life-blind ruling value system, the person whose consciousness is life-grounded recognizes that "life-support systems and means of life-provision [are] the base line of value judgements."[27] By thus limiting ourselves to choices that ensure the health of life-support and life-development systems, we ensure the present and future conditions for more life-valuable action. As Marcuse argues, "the Form of freedom is not merely self-determination and self-realization, but rather the determination and realization of goals that protect, enhance, and unite life on earth."[28] In building these higher unities of life, we expand rather than constrict the overall space for human sentience and feeling, thought and action. The more our societies comprehensively satisfy the life-requirements of everyone, the wider the field of choices in relation to which we as individuals can decide to act.

Where the natural and social enabling conditions of action are met, and the political situation is such that external coercive forces have been reduced to a minimum, individual life-enjoyment would only be experienced as a result of life-valuable action. This claim draws its main support from millennia of human struggles to bring about life-coherence in ruling value systems. In striving to bring about coherence between the ruling value system and natural and social support for free activity, people show

26 Marx, *Capital*, 3: 818–20.
27 McMurtry, "What is Good, What is Bad," 156.
28 Marcuse, *An Essay on Liberation*, 46.

that what ultimately moves them when their action stems from their own life-requirements is an inner drive to make a life-valuable contribution to the world. No one enjoys a life reduced to machine functioning; living life as a machine function causes the displacement of enjoyment outside the realm of human activity proper into the realm of passive consumption of commodities and canned experiences. Once thinking has become life-grounded, people demand to be valuable, not just in their own minds but as agents who make a positive difference to others' lives. But this is freedom in its highest form – acting as a social self-conscious agent to expand instrumental and intrinsic life-value and not as a programmed function of the money-value system.

Free action is life-valuable action and life-valuable action makes a demonstrable contribution to the maintenance and improvement of the natural field of life-support and the social field of life-development. Thus, it always has instrumental life-value for others as well as intrinsic life-value for the self who acts. I argue that this essential link between the goodness of free activity and making demonstrable contributions to the natural and social worlds on which individuals depend most clearly distinguishes life-grounded materialist ethics from the "capabilities approach" to social justice developed in different ways by Sen and Nussbaum.

6.3 LIFE-VALUE AND THE CAPABILITIES APPROACH TO SOCIAL JUSTICE

The "capabilities approach" to social justice has been developed in distinct ways by Amartya Sen and Martha Nussbaum. While these differences are not unimportant, they are not so strong as to make it inaccurate to talk in general terms of *the* capabilities approach to social justice. In what follows I discuss the differences between Sen and Nussbaum only insofar as they are relevant to understanding the more important difference between the capabilities approach and life-grounded materialist ethics. I do not insist on these differences simply for the sake of making life-grounded materialist ethics a distinctive product in the philosophical marketplace. Rather, I emphasize the difference because I believe, and attempt to demonstrate in this section, that the life-valuable practical goal of the capabilities approach – expanding the substantive freedom of individuals – is more coherently served by life-grounded materialist ethics. I begin the argument by noting the concerns shared by the capabilities approach and life-grounded materialist ethics. Once the shared concerns are clear, the differences, and the reasons to insist on those differences, can be better appreciated.

There are three key ideas shared by the capabilities approach and life-grounded materialist ethics. First, human freedom is not simply absence of constraint but rather the active expression of human capacities. Second, there are general material conditions that must be met if people are to express their capacities. Nussbaum develops this point more fully than Sen. Finally, the good life for human beings involves the full flourishing of their potentialities. Again, Nussbaum develops the more robust conception of what flourishing involves.

The capabilities approach to social justice emerged from Sen's critique of neo-classical economic measures of economic health like Gross Domestic Product and Rawls's conception of justice. Sen was concerned that the dominant measures of economic growth and Rawls's conception of justice as rooted in equality of primary goods failed to account for the most important element of human life – the ability to convert resources into "functionings." "Capability is primarily a reflection of the ability to achieve valuable functionings. It concentrates directly on freedom rather than on the means to achieve freedom, and it identifies the real alternatives we have."[29] Sen is making the crucial point that human well-being cannot be measured by abstractions like income per capita or mechanically egalitarian principles like Rawlsian primary goods because neither focuses on what people are materially able to achieve at a given income level or with a given share of primary goods. What is important in life is what we are able to achieve over a life-time. Thus, the guiding value of the capabilities approach to social justice is the free expression of human capacities. "In analyzing social justice," Sen writes, "there is a strong case to be made for judging individual advantage in terms of the capabilities that a person has, that is, the substantive freedoms he or she enjoys to lead the kind of life he or she has reason to value."[30] This shift of focus from abstract metrics of income and equality to concrete expression of substantive human freedoms laid the foundation on which Nussbaum has built her interpretation of the capabilities approach.

By his own admission, Sen was less interested in constructing a theory of the material conditions of freedom than he was in refocusing attention from the means of freedom to the expressed content of freedom. Perhaps the greatest difference between Nussbaum's version and Sen's is that Nussbaum tries to theorize the means without which freedom or human flourishing is impossible. As she says, she "uses the idea [of capabilities] in a more exigent way, as a foundation for basic political

29 Sen, *Inequality Reexamined*, 49.
30 Sen, *Development as Freedom*, 87.

principles that should underwrite constitutional guarantees."[31] Those political principles are founded on the needs of human beings. Like life-grounded materialist ethics, Nussbaum asserts a connection (implied but never explicated in Sen) between needs and capabilities. Her version of the capabilities approach "begins with the intuitive idea of a creature which is both capable and needy."[32] Like life-grounded materialist ethics, she sees the development of capacities (capabilities in her terms) as intrinsically valuable and the satisfaction of needs as instrumentally valuable conditions of that realization. "Human capabilities," she argues, "exert a moral claim that they should be developed. Human beings are creatures that, provided with the right educational and material support, can become capable of the major human functionings."[33] Given the fact that all human beings have the same general potential to realize their capacities in a life-valuable fashion if those life-requirements are satisfied, all have an equally legitimate claim on the material conditions without which that potential cannot be realized: "social support for basic life-functions ... is what we owe people's humanity and dignity."[34]

While the principle that the goodness of human life depends crucially on the satisfaction of material needs is clearly implied in Sen and explicitly developed in Nussbaum, neither provides an explicit distinction between needs encoded in our organic-social nature and consumer desires that we may subjectively feel. The closest the capabilities approach comes to making a systematic distinction between objective conditions of the good life for human beings and subjective demands people can be socialized to make is Nussbaum's famous and controversial "capabilities list."[35] The problem with this list, as its name implies, is that it is just a *list*. There is no principle or criterion stated and defended which justifies the implicit claim that any item on the list is an objective life-requirement and not a mere consumer demand. Given the absence of such a criterion, the contents of the list appear ad hoc and confused. The "capabilities" on her list include, without distinction, both instrumental and intrinsic values, both life-requirements and forms of life-capacity

31 Nussbaum, *Women and Human Development*, 70.
32 Nussbaum, "Human Capabilities, Female Human Beings," 75.
33 Nussbaum, *Sex and Social Justice*, 43.
34 Ibid., 20.
35 Most of the controversy centres around the question of whether her list is ethnocentric. In my reading of the list it is not, for the same reasons that I argued life-grounded materialism's understanding of life-requirements is not. Hence I will not examine that controversy here. See Hurley, "Martha Nussbaum: Non-Relative Virtues," 270–6; Fabre and Miller, "Justice and Culture: Rawls, Nussbaum, Sen, and O'Neil," 4–17; and Gould, *Globalizing Democracy and Human Rights*, 52–60.

expression. To give but one glaring example, the list asserts both the need for "adequate nourishment and shelter," a key physical-organic life-requirement according to life-grounded materialism, and the life-capacity of "being able to live with and toward others, to recognize and show concern for other people." The latter is not a life-requirement but a life-capacity for non-instrumental, mutually affirming relations, which, as I argued in chapter 2, develops if our life-requirement for care and love is satisfied. Thus she conflates the crucial difference between instrumental and intrinsic life-values and fails to spell out in any rigorous way just what the life-requirements are to which all human beings *must* have access if they are to fully express their potentialities.

Despite the conceptual confusion generated by the absence of a clear definition of needs as life-requirements and the absence of a distinction between life-requirements and the life-capacities they enable, Nussbaum's capabilities approach nevertheless shares with life-grounded materialist ethics the principle that unless the material conditions of life are satisfied, the vaunted "choices" celebrated in the classical liberal tradition are without ethical value. "The various liberties of choice," Nussbaum claims, "have material conditions in whose absence there is merely a simulacrum of choice."[36] Yet, she does not explain (and in this she follows Sen) what the *content* of choices *worth* making must be. Thus, while there is again abstract agreement in principle between the capabilities approach and life-grounded materialist ethics that the good life involves flourishing, or realization and enjoyment of life-capacities, the capabilities approach fails to distinguish *life-valuable* from potentially *life-destructive* modes of capacity realization.

Nussbaum and Sen fail to make this crucial distinction because they fear being accused of paternalism. This problem is most pronounced in Sen. While the connection that he established between social justice and substantive freedom is implicitly life-grounded, his failure to explicitly determine the *materially rational limits* of capability realization leaves his argument open to the charge that it is ethically incoherent because it can rule nothing out. "A person's capability," he writes, "can be characterized as well-being freedom (reflecting the freedom to advance one's own well-being) and agency freedom (concerned with the freedom to advance whatever goals and values a person has reason to advance)."[37] As is evident, neither other people within the social field of life-development nor the natural life-support system plays any role in determining or defining the meaning of freedom in Sen's account. If freedom is only concerned

36 Nussbaum, *Women and Human Development*, 53.
37 Sen, *The Idea of Justice*, 288–9.

with the values and goals that one as an abstract individual has reason to advance, then other people can just as well be the victims as the beneficiaries of freedom. Racists have reasons to advance racist values, sexists sexist values, and so on. There is simply no explicit conceptual foundation in Sen's understanding of well-being that rules out these life-destructive goals. Yet, as I have argued in 6.1 and 6.2, life-destructive goals are not freely determined goods for socially self-conscious agents. Because social self-conscious agents act in full understanding of the natural and social conditions of free action, they do not call "good" actions which, though personally pleasurable, damage or destroy the social and natural conditions of life. They understand that there is a difference between materially rational values and goals and materially irrational values and goals, and they understand that since freedom presupposes nature and society, to act as an individual so as to damage nature and society is not free and cannot contribute to one's well-being, precisely because it undermines the material conditions of both.

In Nussbaum this problem takes the form of a reversion back to the abstract oppositions between self and society, "economic needs" and "political liberties," typical of classical liberalism but incompatible, for reasons already explicated above, with life-grounded philosophy and thus with the capabilities approach insofar as it is life-grounded. While her capabilities approach criticizes governments for failure to ensure the satisfaction of needs, Nussbaum at the same time argues that "economic needs should not be met by denying liberty."[38] This liberal platitude is completely inconsistent with her argument that liberties of choice are irrelevant if the material conditions of choice are not met. She falls into this contradiction because she never completely frees her argument from a classical liberal understanding of people as separate atoms. "Liberalism," she stresses, "holds that the flourishing of human beings taken one by one is both analytically and normatively prior to the flourishing of the state or nation ... because the recognition of that separateness is taken to be a fundamental fact for ethics, which should recognize each separate entity as an end and not a means to the ends of others."[39] In fact, the separateness of persons is precisely the doctrine that classical liberalism appeals to in its denunciation of claims, absolutely central to Nussbaum's argument, that society *owes* people the material conditions of their dignity, as tyrannical and confiscatory. If one rigidly separates individuals from each other and the instituted collective whole in this way, then the *social* support for life-functions that Nussbaum insists is necessary does not

38 Nussbaum, *Women and Human Development*, 12.
39 Nussbaum, *Sex and Social Justice*, 62.

follow. Where governments act so as to provide social support for basic life-functions by redistributing income, they will be attacked for violating the liberty of the rich. Nussbaum would surely disagree politically with these conclusions, but her insistence on the separateness of individuals leaves her with no coherent basis for that disagreement.

Life-grounded materialist ethics avoids these contradictions by demonstrating that individuals are not separate atoms but socially self-conscious *members* of natural and social fields of life-support and life-development. The charge of paternalism which so concerns Sen and Nussbaum is a concern only if the debate is allowed to be conducted within the conceptual parameters of classical liberalism. As soon as the conceptual parameters are expanded beyond the abstractions of the desiring ego to the fields of life-support and life-development on which the ego depends but liberalism ignores, it becomes clear that life-grounded materialism is the opposite of paternalism. Paternalism claims to know what the good for others in a particular sense is. Life-grounded materialism, by contrast, exposes the *universal* conditions for any individual life to experience and enjoy the good of free capacity realization *in concrete forms which follow from life-individual grounded choices.*

The highest good for human beings is therefore to freely contribute to the health of the natural field of life-support and the social field of life-development. By enjoying as an individual the contributions that one's actions make to the common natural and social wealth, one elevates one's self above the narrow and life-blind egoism that would reduce freedom to merely unconstrained action. To be free is to be self-determining, and to be self-determining means to be able decide for oneself how one will contribute to the betterment of one's world.

There is no reified good imposed on individuals; the good of the world is the realized good of the individuals. This good cannot be achieved, the social support for life-functions not ensured, if social policy, democratically determined, is prevented from interfering with the life-blind choices of individuals acting as programmed functions of the ruling value system. The target of intervention is not the individual chooser in the abstract but system dynamics and value systems which permit and justify life-destructive forms of activity as good. I conclude with a general explanation of the institutional implications of a life-grounded materialist ruling value system and the nature of life-valuable forms of political struggle required to bring about fundamental social change.

Institutional and Political Implications

IN CHAPTER 6, I argued that life-grounded materialist ethics is concerned with both the principles which must be obeyed in a good individual life and the principles that define a good world. In contrast to modern, egocentric traditions of ethical thought which are concerned solely with abstract rules of individual conduct, life-grounded materialist ethics, like the ethical philosophy of classical Greece, is concerned with the principles and institutions that structure collective life. Insofar as life-grounded materialist ethics necessarily concerns itself not only with criticism of existing social dynamics and institutions and the ruling money-value system that legitimates them but equally with the positive conditions of the good life for all human beings, it is obliged to articulate the fundamental principles that define a life-valuable society.

In meeting this obligation, life-grounded materialist ethics must avoid substituting itself for the creative intelligence of human beings acting politically in the face of concrete problems. While life-grounded materialism maintains that the *form* that fundamental political problems take is the same – they are all conflicts between money-value and life-value determination of the control and use of natural resources, social wealth, and the goals served by major social institutions – the content can vary significantly depending on the specificities of local histories. There is no life-grounded materialist *formula* for social change or *blueprint* for institutional design; there are philosophical *principles* that follow from the conception of life-requirements and the good life for human beings that I have defined and defended. The extent to which the contradictions that exist between money-value and life-value can be overcome within existing liberal-democratic institutions or require new institutions is an open question that only the actual contours of collective political struggle can answer. What is most important for life-grounded materialist politics is not the name of the institution but the principles it serves. If existing parliamentary systems, for example, can be freed from their current captivity to political parties all of whom serve the money-value system and reoriented to the service of a life-value system, then those institutions can remain the basic political institutions of a democratic life-value society. If they cannot, then new institutions will be required.

However, while it is possible to further democratize existing political institutions along life-valuable lines, a democratic life-valuable society cannot coexist with the structure of private ownership of the universal means of life-maintenance on which capitalism depends. In this sense, a democratic life-value society must be a socialist society. By "socialist society" I do not mean a) a society in which the "state" owns and controls the means of production or b) a society ruled by the "dictatorship of the proletariat" or c) a society governed by a vanguard party claiming to rule in the name of the proletariat. Socialism too must answer to the higher court of life-value. The basic life-value justification of the need for socialism is that unless democratic (*not* state) control is established over universally required life-resources (*not* personal property for life-valuable use), the structure of dependence on money-value examined in chapter 5 remains intact. That is, people cannot live freely but only as instruments of the money-value system. The life-value derives from this principle of democratic control over the universal means of life-support and life-development. Six criteria which follow from this basic principle must be met by a life-valuable democratic socialist society.

A life-valuable socialist society must 1) develop an economic system which comprehensively satisfies all human beings' life-requirements, 2) for the sake of the free expression and enjoyment of all members' sentient, cognitive, imaginative, and creative capacities, 3) in constellations of concrete expression which do not depend on the exploitation or degradation or oppression or impediment of others' capacities, but rather positively enable others' lives, 4) through an economic system which is environmentally sustainable over an open-ended future, 5) is consistent with all other societies on earth also realizing 1 to 4, and 6) be achieved through means of struggle which are democratic and not militarized. In conclusion, I comment briefly on each criterion.

As I have demonstrated in chapters 4 and 5, capitalism and the colonialist projects it has generated do not recognize the objective reality of life-requirements but only effective market demand. Anything one can pay for will be provided even if it is not a life-requirement; anything that is required will not be provided in the absence of effective demand. Capitalism thus generates life-crises because it does not use the productive wealth it creates to satisfy human life-requirements. A life-valuable socialism's first goal is to use natural resources and social wealth to ensure the comprehensive satisfaction of all three classes of human life-requirement. Achieving this goal presupposes the democratic control over life-resources discussed above, democratic transformations of existing economic institutions (business firms, etc.), and the subordination of money-value to life-value. Money will still circulate as means of exchange but the reified, undemocratic, life-blind power it exercises in capitalism will be overcome. Economic decisions will not be made on the basis of which of any set of alternatives is most money valuable; money will be invested in the alternative determined by democratic planning bodies to be most life-valuable.

The second criterion answers the objection that the so-called "democratic life-economy" is really just a euphemism for statist oppression. The fundamental life-value is not life-requirement satisfaction but free capacity expression. The production and distribution and use of natural and social wealth, as well as the political and economic institutions through which these processes unfold have no intrinsic but only instrumental life-value. Intrinsic life-value lies in the enjoyed expression of life-valuable capacities, and the enjoyed expression of life-valuable capacities is freedom. The democratic planning of economic life vastly increases the scope of individual freedom by enabling collectivities to do what they currently cannot do: democratically decide how the resources and wealth of their communities can be used to best satisfy the life-requirements that link them together as human beings.

"Human being" is not a generic abstraction but a real organic-social nature which encodes objective life-requirements. If those life-requirements are comprehensively met, then cultural and individual differences develop. These differences are not a threat to the universality of life-values but rather one form of the concrete expression of life-value. In order to ensure that all groups and individuals are able to freely realize and enjoy life-value in their actual lives, more than workers' control of production is necessary. There are three reasons for this. First, productive activity has effects outside the plant gates or office door, which means that all groups who are so affected (by noise, effluents, etc.) must be involved in the democratic decisions through which the local economy is planned. Second, the working class itself has been shaped by racist, sexist, hetero-normative, and ableist histories of oppression and exploitation. Unless historically oppressed groups are specifically represented in firm-level and society-wide planning bodies, there is no guarantee that those histories will not be carried forward into the socialist society. Finally, economic life in a specific locality must be coordinated with economic activity in the region, nation, and world. The coherent planning of economic life as a whole thus depends on workers' control of production as

the organic basis out of which evolve higher-level democratic planning
bodies which would have the power to make changes in local economies
(closing inefficient plants, for example) even against the narrow and
short-term interests of specific groups of workers.

One of the largest sources of conflict between local and higher-level
planning bodies would almost certainly concern the environmental im-
pacts of certain productive activities. As the institutionalized form of a
ruling life-value system, the democratic life-economy would have to be
committed in the first instance and consistently to ending the materially
irrational rate of natural resources consumption on which capitalism depends. That means closing inefficient and polluting plants, ending environmentally destructive projects like the oil sands, and, most importantly,
gradually reducing the energy demands that human beings make on the
planet, for our own well-being but also for the well-being of other species
which have their own intrinsic life-value. These changes will most certainly affect the short-term interests of workers who are employed in
these industries. However, if these changes are planned, if losses are
compensated, if the structure of work life is transformed, if productivity
gains can be used to re-divide labour time, enabling more people to contribute to socially necessary labour, the changes that a sustainable economy would require can be achieved in ways that expand the life-value of
the workers whose lives will initially be disrupted. The alternative is un-
planned response to environmental catastrophe in which lives will be
sacrificed without compensation or life-gain elsewhere.

Since human life-value is rooted in our shared organic-social nature, it
follows that the particular histories of different human groups in no way
entitle them to more or less of what is life-valuable. All have the same
life-grounded claim on sufficient resources for the comprehensive satisfaction of the three classes of life-requirement for the sake of the fullest
possible expression and enjoyment of their life-capacities (subject to criteria 1 to 4 above). Life-valuable socialism is an internationalist project
which is committed by its life-value base to overcoming the gross inequities in access to life-requirement satisfiers and realized quality of life.
The first step toward overcoming these global inequities is not charitable
redistribution from wealthy to poor countries but securing democratic
control over natural resources and social wealth within the countries of
the Global South combined with planned reductions in the consumption of resources and energy in the global North. Were these twin changes progressively realized even the poorest countries at present could free
themselves from poverty.

Normative criteria are all well and good as means of determining how
far a given society is from a stated ideal. They are useless as guides to

realizing that ideal if they cannot be made politically effective. In closing, I offer an explanation of what life-grounded politics is and why understanding the nature of life-grounded politics makes the realization of these criteria less utopian than it initially sounds.

For much of its history, socialist politics was infected with the disease of vanguardism. Political practice, on this view, is the art of converting socialist theory into reality through heroic acts of political negation (tearing down the existing institutions) and construction (building the new institutions on the new model provided by the theory). Members of the party considered themselves to be experts in reading the blueprints and putting up new institutions. Socialist politics was thus abstracted from everyday politics, the politics that most people, including workers, are willing to be involved with. For the vanguard, socialist politics is radically distinct from existing politics. The experts take sides in the global opposition between the existing world and the world to come but not in the day-to-day battles that define existing political reality. The problems can be solved only by overthrowing capitalism and building the world anew. Ironically, in practice vanguard politics becomes, on a day-to-day basis, apolitical, uninvolved in actual fights over how resources will be used. Because it sits out the real fights, vanguard politics does not effectively mobilize people. Since the sort of total transformation it envisages will require total transformations of peoples' motivations and activities, and since it cannot provide the motivation for people to become subjects of their own transformation, it ends by treating people exactly as they are treated by the existing system – as instruments, as tools, as objects to be worked on in the service of ends which the people themselves feel are alien.

Life-valuable politics rejects the abstraction of radical demands from the impurities of day-to-day politics. While the ultimate trajectory of its principles leads to a different society, its concrete demands are rooted in the existing and contradictory institutional structures of money-value rule. It does not confront those contradictions with a blueprint for a new society in which the contradictions have been theoretically solved. Instead, it situates itself in the midst of existing contradictions and political struggles and seeks in each case to bring out the opposition between a life-valuable alternative and a money-value alternative. By translating the language of existing contradictions and struggles against them into life-value terms, the real opposition between the interests of private money-value agents and those of planetary and human life becomes clear.

The demands that life-valuable politics makes are not inferred from what is theoretically necessary but from what is concretely possible given the alternatives around which people are actually mobilizing. In any case of political conflict, life-valuable politics identifies the alternative with the most life-value potential. Thus, if the choice is between privatizing more of the health care system or maintaining the existing degree of public funding, life-valuable politics builds support for the public option, *not* because the public option coheres with abstract philosophical premises but because public health care demonstrably does a better job meeting health care requirements. The social institution of health care is held to its testable life-function of maintaining and restoring physical and mental health so that people's lives are richer in capacity expression and enjoyment. Opponents are confronted not with theoretical promissory notes that everything will be better in the new dawn that is about to shine but with evidence and concretely realizable projects which build their own support because they work.

At the same time, life-valuable politics seeks to unify struggles around a global alternative to the rule of capitalist money-value. The political process of building this alternative may be called "organic" to emphasize the way in which the struggle to build a new society is rooted in the life-valuable side of existing social institutions. The organic grounding of life-valuable politics in the life-function of existing institutions – what McMurtry calls the civil commons – enables it to determine concrete demands by identifying the real alternative with maximum life-value potential.[1] Single victories that successfully realize the life-value potential cannot, on their own, solve the structural problems of life-crisis endemic to the capitalist money-value system. Life-value politics is thus not identical to piecemeal reformist demands; it treats each successful realization of life-value potential as but a moment in an open-ended, long-term, but eventually complete transformation of the ruling money-value system into a conscious and coherent steering of all social institutions by life-valuable laws, policies, and regulations. Single victories are both victories and plateaus for the next round of struggle. The unifying thread of struggle is in all cases the principle of life-coherence and the principle of material rationality – democratic determination of public policy that satisfies everyone's real life-requirements at levels that are sustainable over an open-ended future.

Instead of treating the majority of people as *instruments* of political theory, life-valuable politics must *involve people as agents of change*. It must involve people as agents of change because it is subject to the same principle of life-coherence to which it holds social institutions. The justifying value of critical politics over millennia has been the coherent inclusion of the voices and ideas of oppressed and exploited groups. From ancient slave revolts to the battle over gay marriage, those who have not been

---

1 McMurtry, *Value Wars*, 117.

allowed to speak their own ideas have demanded the space to express themselves and participate in the creation of the laws they are expected to obey. Voices and ideas of excluded groups can be *coherently included* organically in life-valuable politics only if the people who compose the groups are allowed to actually and fully and freely speak and act. Hence a critical politics which involves people as silent foot soldiers doing the bidding of the theoreticians reading the blueprint is life-incoherent. The whole point of critical politics is to create institutional space in which the excluded and silent can speak and participate as socially self-conscious *agents*.

Bibliography

Abrams, Richard D. "The U.S. Military and Higher Education: A Brief History." *Annals of the American Academy of Political Science* 502 (1989): 15–28

Adorno, Theodor. *Minima Moralia*. London: Continuum 2002

– *Negative Dialectics*. London: Continuum 2003

Ali, Tariq. *Mr. Bush Goes to Baghdad*. London: Verso 2005

Archer, Margaret. *Being Human: The Problem of Agency*. Cambridge: Cambridge University Press 2000

Arendt, Hannah. *Lectures on Kant's Political Philosophy*. Chicago: University of Chicago Press 1992

Aristotle. *The Basic Works of Aristotle*. Edited by Richard McKeon. New York: Random House 1966

Armstrong, Pat, Hugh Armstrong, Ivy Lynn Bourgeault, Jacqueline Choiniere, Joel Lexchin, Eric Mykhalovsky, Suzanne Peters, and Jerry P. White. "Market Principle, Business Practices, and Health Care: Comparing the U.S. and Canadian Experiences." *International Journal of Canadian Studies* 28 (Fall 2004): 13–38

Aronowitz, Stanley, and Jonathan Cutler, eds. *Post-Work*. New York: Routledge 1998

Assiter, Alison, and Jeff Noonan. "Needs: A Realist Perspective." *Journal of Critical Realism* 6, no. 2 (2007): 173–98

Badiou, Alain. *Being and Event*. London: Continuum 2005

– *Ethics: An Essay on the Understanding of Evil*. London: Verso 2001

– *Logics of Worlds*. London: Continuum 2008

Barlow, Maude. *Profit Is Not the Cure*. Toronto: McClelland and Stewart 2002

Barrett, Michele, and Mary McIntosh. *The Anti-Social Family*. London: Verso 1982

Baudrillard, Jean. *For a Critique of the Political Economy of the Sign*. St. Louis: Telos Press 1981

Bay, Christian. *The Structure of Freedom*. Stanford: Stanford University Press 1958

Beetham, David. *Democracy and Human Rights.* Cambridge: Polity 2003

Benedict, Ruth. *Patterns of Culture.* Boston: Houghton Mifflin 1934

Biello, David. "Bush Administration Pushes Climate Change Action into the
    Future." *Scientific American,* 28 September 2007, http://www.sciam.com/
    article.cfm?/id=bush-administration-pushesclimate-change-plans-into-the-
    future, accessed 8 October 2008

Bin Laden, Osama. *Fatwa of August, 1996.* Originally published in *Al Quds al
    Arabi,* August 1996, http:// www.pbs.org/newshour/terrorism/international/
    fatwa_1996.html, accessed 16 November 2008

Braverman, Harry. *Labour and Monopoly Capital: The Degradation of Work in the
    Twentieth Century.* New York: Monthly Review Press 1998

Braybrooke, David. *Meeting Needs.* Princeton: Princeton University Press 1987

"Breathing is for Closers." *Harper's.* June 2008, 28

Brecht, Bertolt. *Saint Joan of the Stockyards.* Bloomington: Indiana University
    Press 1969

– *The Three Penny Opera.* London: Eyre Methuen 1973

Brenner, Robert. "Agrarian Class Structure and Economic Development in
    Pre-Industrial Europe." In *The Brenner Debates: Agrarian Class Structure and
    Economic Development ion Pre-Industrial Europe,* edited by T.H. Ashton and
    C.H.E. Philpin, 10–63. Cambridge: Cambridge University Press 1988

– "The Agrarian Roots of European Capitalism." In Ashton and Philpin, *The
    Brenner Debates,* 213–328

Brown, Peter G. *The Commonwealth of Life: Economics for a Flourishing Earth.*
    Montreal: Black Rose Books 2008

Brown, Peter G., and Geoffrey Garver. *Right Relationship: Building a Whole Earth
    Economy.* San Francisco: Berrett-Koehler 2009

Bruno, Giordano. *Cause, Principle, Unity.* Castle Hedington, Essex: Daimon
    Publishing 1967

Bryant, Levi, Nick Srnicek, and Graham Harman. "Towards a Speculative
    Philosophy." In *The Speculative Turn: Continental Materialism and Realism,* edit-
    ed by Levi Bryant, Nick Srnicek, and Graham Harman, 1–18. Melbourne:
    re.press 2011

Casebeer, William D. *Natural Ethical Facts: Evolution, Connectionism, and Moral
    Cognition.* Cambridge: MIT Press 2003

Callinicos, Alex. *Equality.* Cambridge: Polity Press 2000

– *The New Mandarins of American Power: The Bush Administration's Plans for the
    World.* Cambridge: Polity Press 2003

– *Resources of Critique.* Cambridge: Polity Press 2006

Camus, Albert. *The Myth of Sisyphus.* New York: Vintage Books 1955

Césaire, Aimé. *Discours sur le colonialism.* Paris: Présence Africaine 1955

Chirot, Daniel, and Clarke McCauley. *Why Not Kill Them All? The Logic and
    Prevention of Mass Political Murder.* Princeton: Princeton University Press 2006

Clinton, Hillary. "Speech on the Human Rights Agenda for the Twenty-first Century." 14 December 2009, http://www.americanrhetoric.com/speeches/hillaryclintonhumanrightsagenda.htm, accessed 22 March 2011

Cohen, Stanley. *States of Denial: Knowing about Atrocities and Suffering.* Cambridge: Polity Press 2006

Collier, Andrew. *Being and Worth (Critical Realism, Interventions).* London: Routledge 1999

Cooke, Maeve. *Re-Presenting the Good Society.* Cambridge: MIT Press 2006

Darwin, Charles. *The Origin of Species.* New York: Gramercy 1979

Deacon, Terence W. *The Symbolic Species.* New York: W.W. Norton 1997

DeLanda, Manuel. *Deleuze: History and Science.* New York: Atropos Press 2010

Dennett, Daniel. *Freedom Evolves.* New York: Viking 2003

De Tocqueville, Alexis. *Democracy in America.* New York: Mentor Books 1956

D'Holbach, Baron. *System of Nature.* J.P. Merton: Boston 1886

– *Système Sociale,* Vol. 1. Hildeshiem: Georg Olms Verlag 1969

Diamond, Jared. *Collapse: How Societies Choose to Succeed or Fail.* New York: Penguin 2005

Dostoyevsky, Fyodor. *The Possessed.* NewYork: Dell 1961

Doyal, Ian, and Len Gough. *A Theory of Human Needs.* New York: Guilford 1991

Drummond, Don. "The Cost of Bill C–288 to Canadian Families and Business." Ottawa: Ministry of the Environment 2007

Economic Policy Institute. "Annual Median Hours Worked for Middle Income Husbands and Wives with Children, 1975–2002." (2007), http://www.epi.org, accessed 14 September 2007

Engels, Friedrich. *The Condition of the Working Class in England.* Frogmore, St Albans: Granada Publishing 1976

Environmental Defence. *Canada's Toxic Tar Sands: The Most Destructive Project on Earth,* February 2008, http://www.environmentaldefence.ca., accessed 28 March 2008

Fabre, Cécile, and David Miller. "Justice and Culture: Rawls, Nussbaum, Sen, and O'Neil." *Political Studies Review* 1, no.1 (2003): 4–17

Fairfield, Paul. *Why Democracy?* Albany: State University of New York Press 2008

Falk, Richard. *The Declining World Order: America's Imperial Geopolitics.* New York: Routledge 2004

Florida, Richard. *The Rise of the Creative Class: And How It's Transforming Work, Leisure, Community, and Everyday Life.* New York: Basic Books 2002

Foresight. *The Future of Food and Farming.* London: Government Office for Science 2011

Foster, John Bellamy. *Marx's Ecology: Materialism and Nature.* New York: Monthly Review Press 2000

Fraser, Ian. *Hegel and Marx: The Concept of Need.* Edinburgh: University of Edinburgh Press 1998

Fraser, Nancy. *Unruly Practices: Power, Discourse and Gender in Contemporary Social Theory.* Minneapolis: University of Minnesota Press 1989
– "What's Critical about Critical Theory: The Case of Habermas and Gender." *New German Critique* 35 (Spring–Summer 1985): 97–131
Fromm, Erich. *Escape from Freedom.* New York: Henry Holt 1969
Furedi, Frank. "Is There No Room Left for Reflection?" *Canadian Association of University Teachers/Association canadienne des professeures et professeurs d'université Bulletin* 55, no. 1 (2008): 2
Geertz, Clifford. "Anti-anti-Relativism." *The American Anthropologist* 86, no. 2 (June 1984): 263–78
Georgescu-Roegen, Nicolas. *The Entropy Law and the Economic Process.* Cambridge: Harvard University Press 1971
Geras, Norman. *Solidarity in the Conversation of Humankind: The Ungroundable Liberalism of Richard Rorty.* London: Verso 1995
Gewirth, Alan. *The Community of Rights.* Chicago: University of Chicago Press 1996
Gilbert, Alan. "An Ambiguity in Marx and Engel's Account of Justice and Equality." *American Political Science Review* 76, no.2 (June 1982): 328–46
– "Historical Theory and the Structure of Moral Argument in Marx." *Political Theory* 9, no. 2. (May 1981): 173–205
– "Moral Realism, Individuality, and Justice in War." *Political Theory* 14, no.1 (February 1986): 105–35
Global Policy Forum. "Iraq's Humanitarian Crisis." (2009) http://www.global policyforum.org/security/isuues/iraq/attack/crisisindex.htm, accessed 9 January 2009
Goldman, Lucien. *Immanuel Kant.* London: New Left Books 1971
Goodin, Robert E., James Mahmud Rice, Antti Parpo, and Lina Eriksson. *Discretionary Time: A New Measure of Freedom.* Cambridge: Cambridge University Press 2008
Goody, Jack. *Capitalism and Modernity: The Great Debate.* Cambridge: Polity Press 2004
Gould, Carol C. *Globalizing Democracy and Human Rights.* Cambridge: Cambridge University Press 2004
Graham, Keith. *Practical Reasoning in a Social World: How We Act Together.* Cambridge: Cambridge University Press 2002
Habermas, Jurgen. *Between Facts and Norms.* Cambridge: MIT Press 1995
– *The Postnational Constellation.* Cambridge: MIT Press 2001
– *Theory of Communicative Action.* Vol. 2. Boston: Beacon Press 1987
– "What Does Socialism Mean Today?" In *After the Fall: The Failure of Communism and the Future of Socialism,* edited by Robin Blackburn, 25–46. London: Verso 1991
Hamilton, Lawrence. *The Political Philosophy of Needs.* Cambridge: Cambridge University Press 2006

Harding, Sandra, ed. *Feminism and Methodology: Social Science Issues.* Bloomington: University of Indiana Press 1987

Harris, Marvin. *Cows, Pigs, Wars and Witches: The Riddles of Culture.* New York: Random House 1974

Hartmann, Heidi I. "The Family as the Locus of Class, Gender, and Political Struggle: The Case of Housework." In Harding, *Feminism and Methodology,* 109–34

Hartsock, Nancy M. "The Feminist Standpoint: Developing a Ground for a Specifically Feminist Historical Materialism." In Harding, *Feminism and Methodology,* 157–80

Harvey, David. *The New Imperialism.* Oxford: Oxford University Press 2003

Haselow, Nancy, Musa Obadiah, and Julie Akame. "The Integration of Vitamin A Supplement into Community-Directed Treatment with Ivermectin: A Practical Guide for Africa. Helen Keller International, 2005, http://hki.org/research/pdf_zip_docs/integ_vita_oncho_eng.pdf, accessed 15 October 2007

Heckman, James A. "The Economics, Technology, and Neuroscience of Human Capability Formation." *Proceedings of the National Academy of Science* 104, no. 33 (August 2007): 13250–55

Hegel, G.W.F. *The Phenomenology of Spirit.* Oxford: Oxford University Press 1977

Held, David. *Global Covenant: The Social Democratic Alternative to the Washington Consensus.* Cambridge: Polity 2004

Heller, Agnes. *The Theory of Need in Marx.* New York: St. Martin's Press 1976

Hirst, Paul. "Can Associationalism Come Back?" In *Associative Democracy: The Real Third Way,* edited by Paul Hirst and Veit Bader, 15–30. London: Frank Cass 2001

Hobbes, Thomas. *Leviathan.* Peterborough: Broadview Press 2002

Holland, John H. *Emergence: From Chaos to Order.* Oxford: Oxford University Press 1998

Horkheimer, Max. "Materialism and Morality." *Telos* 69 (1986): 85–121

Horkheimer, Max, and Theodor Adorno. *Dialectic of Enlightenment.* London: Verso 1997

Hume, David. *A Treatise of Human Nature.* Oxford: Oxford University Press 1987

Hurley, Susan. "Martha Nussbaum: Non-Relative Virtues: An Aristotelian Approach." In Nussbaum and Sen, *The Quality of Life,* 270–6

Huws, Ursula. "The Making of a Cybertariat? Virtual Work in the Real World." In *Socialist Register 2001,* edited by Leo Panitch and Colin Leys, 1–25. London: Merlin Press 2001

Ignatieff, Michael. *The Lesser Evil: Political Ethics in a Time of Terror.* Toronto: Penguin 2004

Inwood, Brad, and L.P. Gerson, eds. *Hellenistic Philosophy: Introductory Readings.* Indianapolis: Hackett 1988

Johnson, Chalmers. "Going Bankrupt: Why the Debt Crisis is now the Greatest Threat to the American Republic." *Antiwar* (2008), http://www.antiwar.com., accessed 14 February 2008

Joyce, Richard. *The Evolution of Morality.* Cambridge: MIT Press 2006

Kant, Immanuel. *Foundations of the Metaphysics of Morals.* Indianapolis: Bobbs-Merrill 1969

Karatani, Kojin. *Transcritique: On Kant and Marx.* Cambridge: MIT Press 2003

Kasser, Tim. *The High Price of Materialism.* Cambridge: MIT Press 2002

Kelman, James. *Translated Accounts.* New York: Vintage Books 2002

Kesterton, Michael. "Kindercramming." *Globe and Mail* (Toronto), 30 November 2007, L8

Kheel, Marni. "From Heroic to Wholistic Ethics: The Ecofeminist Challenge." In *Earth Ethics*, edited by James Sturba, 221–34. Engelwood Cliffs: Prentice Hall 1995

Korn, Robert W. "The Emergence Principle in Biological Hierarchies." *Biology and Philosophy* 20 (2005): 137–51

Kovel, Joel. *The Enemy of Nature: The End of Capitalism or the End of the World?* London: Zed Books 2007

Kussi, Peter. *Toward the Radical Center: A Karel Čapek Reader.* North Haven, CT: Catbird Press 1990

Labonte, Robert, and Ted Schresker. "Globalization and the Social Determinants of Health: Promoting Health Equity in Global Governance." *Globalization and Health* 3, no. 7 (2007): 1–46

Lange, Frederick. *The History of Materialism and Criticism of Its present Importance.* New York: Humanities Press 1950

Lean, Geoffrey. "Multinationals Make Billions in Profit out of Growing Global Food Crisis." *The Independent on Sunday*, 4 May 2008, 4

Lebowitz, Michael. *Build it Now.* New York: Monthly Review Press 2006

– *The Socialist Alternative: Real Human Development.* New York: Monthly Review Press 2010

Lewontin, Richard. *It Ain't Necessarily So: The Dream of the Human Genome and Other Illusions.* New York: New York Review of Books 2001

– *The Triple Helix.* Cambridge: Harvard University Press 2000

Lucretius. *On the Nature of the Universe.* Harmondsworth: Penguin 1994

Lukacs, Georg. *History and Class Consciousness: Studies in Marxist Dialectics.* Cambridge: MIT Press 1971

Lukes, Steven. *Power: A Radical View.* London: MacMillan 1975

MacLaine, Craig, and Michael Baxendale. *This Land is Our Land: The Mohawk Revolt at Oka.* Optimum Publishing: Montreal and Toronto 1990

Malthus, Thomas. *An Essay on the Principle of Population.* Amherst: Prometheus 1998

"Many Rights, Some Wrong." *The Economist*, 24 March 2007, 67–8

Marcuse, Herbert. "The Concept of Essence." In *Negations*, 43–87. Boston: Beacon Press 1968
– *Eros and Civilization: A Philosophical Inquiry into Freud*. Boston: Beacon Press 1966
– *An Essay on Liberation*. Boston: Beacon Press 1969
– *One-Dimensional Man: Studies in the Ideology of Advanced Industrial Society*. Boston: Beacon Press 1964
Marshall, T.H. *Sociology at the Crossroads and Other Essays*. London: Heinemann 1964
Marx, Karl. *Capital*, Vols 1 and 3. Moscow: Progress Publishers 1986
– *On Colonialism*. New York: International Publishers 1972
– *Contribution to the Critique of Political Economy*. Moscow: Progress Publishers 1970
– "Critique of the Gotha Program." In *The Marx-Engels Reader*. 2nd ed. Edited by Robert C. Tucker, 525–42. New York: W.W. Norton, 1977
– "Economic and Philosophical Manuscripts of 1844." In *Karl Marx and Friedrich Engels, Collected Works* 3: 229–348. New York: International Publishers 1975
– "The Eighteenth Brumaire of Louis Bonaparte." In *Karl Marx and Friedrich Engels: Selected Works* 1: 394–497. Moscow: Progress Publishers 1969
– *The German Ideology*. Moscow: Progress Publishers 1975
– *The Holy Family*. Moscow: Progress Publishers 1980
– *Outline of a Critique of Political Economy (Grundrisse)*. In *Karl Marx and Friedrich Engels, Collected Works* 28: 49–540. New York: International Publishers 1986
– *The Poverty of Philosophy*. Moscow: Progress Publishers 1978
Marx, Karl, and Friedrich Engels. *The Communist Manifesto*. Moscow: Progress Publishers 1986
McDougall, William. *Modern Materialism and Emergent Evolution*. London: Methuen 1934
McMurtry, John. *The Cancer Stage of Capitalism*. London: Pluto 1999
– "Human Rights Versus Corporate Rights: Understanding Life-Value, the Civil Commons, and Social Justice." *Studies in Social Justice* 5, no.1 (Summer 2011): 11-61
– "Rationality and Scientific Method: Paradigm Shift in an Age of Collapse." *Interchange* 40, no. 1 (2009): 69–91
– *Unequal Freedoms: The Global Market as an Ethical System*. Toronto: Garamond 1998
– *Value Wars: The Global Market versus the Life Economy*. London: Pluto 2002
– "What is Good, What is Bad: The Value of All Values Across Times, Places, and Theories." In *Encyclopaedia of Life Support Systems*. Oxford: EOLSS Publishers 2010, http://www.eolss.net
McNally, David. *Another World is Possible*. Winnipeg: Arbeiter Ring Press 2002

– *Bodies of Meaning: Studies on Language, Labor, and Liberation.* Albany: State
    University of New York Press 2001
– "Mubarak's Folly: The Rising of Egypt's Workers." 11 February 2011, http://
    www.davidmcnally.org, accessed 12 March 2011
– *Political Economy and the Rise of Capitalism.* Berkeley: University of California
    Press 1988
Mepham, John, and David Hillel Rubin, eds. *Issues in Marxist Philosophy.* Vol-
    ume 2, *Materialism.* Atlantic Highlands: Humanities Press 1979
Mill, John Stuart. *On Liberty.* New York: W.W. Norton 1975
Millar, David. *Principles of Social Justice.* Cambridge: Harvard University Press
    1999
Moody, Harry R. "Who's Afraid of Life-Extension?" In *Death and Anti-Death,*
    edited by Charles Tandy, 1: 229–40. Palo Alto: Ria University Press 2003
Mooney, Pat Roy. "The ETC Century: Concentration in Corporate Power."
    Development Dialogue 1–2 (1999): 74–114
Moore, G.E. *Principia Ethica.* Buffalo: Prometheus Books 1988
Moores, Colin. *The Making of Bourgeois Europe.* London: Verso 1991
Moser, Paul K., and J.D.Trout, eds. *Contemporary Materialism: A Reader.* New York:
    Routledge 1995
Nagel, Thomas. "The Problem of Global Justice." *Philosophy and Public Affairs*
    33, no. 2 (2005): 113–47
"National Security Strategy of the United States." White House Document,
    September 2002 (NSS 2002), http://www.whitehouse.gov
Nietzsche, Friedrich. *Beyond Good and Evil.* Amherst: Prometheus Books 1989
Noddings, Nel. *Caring: A Feminine Approach to Ethics and Moral Education,* 2nd
    ed. Berkeley: University of California Press 2003
Noonan, Jeff. "Between Egoism and Altruism: Outline for a Materialist
    Conception of the Good." In Seglow, *The Ethics of Altruism,* 68–86
– *Democratic Society and Human Needs.* Montreal: McGill-Queen's University
    Press 2006
– "Marcuse, Human Nature, and the Foundation of Ethical Norms." *Philosophy
    and Social Criticism* 34, no. 3 (March 2008): 267–86
– "Need-Satisfaction and Group Conflict: Beyond a Rights-Grounded
    Approach." *Social Theory and Practice* 30, no. 4 (April 2004): 175–92
– "The Principle of Liberal Imperialism: Human Rights and Human Freedom
    in an Age of Evangelical Capitalism." *Socialist Studies* 2, no. 1 (Spring 2006):
    5–22
Novack, George. *The Origins of Materialism.* New York: Merit Publishers 1965
Nussbaum, Martha. "Duties of Justice, Duties of Material Aid." *Journal of Political
    Philosophy* 8, no. 2. (2000): 176–206
– *Frontiers of Justice: Disability, Nationality, Species Membership.* Cambridge:
    Harvard University Press 2006

- "Human Capabilities, Female Human Beings." In *Women, Culture, and Development*, edited by Martha Nussbaum and Jonathon Glover, 61–104. Oxford: Oxford University Press 1995
- "Non-Relative Virtues: An Aristotelian Approach." In Nussbaum and Sen, *The Quality of Life*, 242–69
- *Not for Profit: Why Democracy Needs the Humanities.* Princeton: Princeton University Press 2010
- *Sex and Social Justice.* Oxford: Oxford University Press 1999
- *Upheavals of Thought: The Intelligence of Emotions.* Cambridge: Cambridge University Press 2001
- *Women and Human Development: The Capabilities Approach.* Cambridge: Cambridge University Press 2000

Nussbaum, Martha, and Amartya Sen, eds., *The Quality of Life.* Oxford: Oxford University Press 1993

O'Hear, Anthony. *Beyond Evolution: Human Nature and the Limits of Evolutionary Explanation.* Oxford: Oxford University Press 1997

Overall, Christine. *Aging, Death, and Human Longevity: A Philosophical Inquiry.* Berkeley: University of California Press 2003

Pagels, Heinz R. *The Cosmic Code: Quantum Physics as the Language of Nature.* New York: Bantam Books 1982

Panitch, Leo, and Sam Ginden. "Capitalist Crisis and the Crisis This Time." In *The Crisis This Time: Socialist Register 2011*, edited by Leo Panitch, Greg Albo, and Vivek Chibber, 1–20. London: Merlin Press 2011

Pearson, Carole. "The Future of Food." *Our Times* 25, no. 4. (August–September 2006): 21–9

Plato. *The Collected Dialogues of Plato.* Edited by Edith Hamilton and Huntington Cairns. Princeton: Princeton University Press 1989

Pogge, Thomas, ed. *Global Justice.* Oxford: Basil Blackwell 2001

Polaris Institute. "Controversial Oil Substitutes Increase Emissions, Devour Landscapes," 2008, http://www.polarisinstitute.org/controversial_oil_substitutes_sharply_increase_emissions_devour_landscapes, accessed 4 November 2008

Pollin, Robert, and Heidi Garrett-Peltier. *The U.S. Employment Effects of Military and Domestic Spending Priorities.* Washington: Institute for Policy Studies 2007

Popham, Peter. "The Price of Food Is at the Heart of This Wave of Revolutions," *The Independent*, 27 February 2011, http://www.independent.co.uk/news/world/africa/the-price-of-food-is-at-the-heart-of-this-wave-of-revolutions-2226869.html, accessed 3 March 2011

Postone, Moshe. *Time. Labour, and Social Domination: A Reinterpretation of Marx's Critical Theory.* Cambridge: Cambridge University Press 1993

Project for a New American Century. *Statement of Principles*, 1996, http://www.newamericancentury.org/statementofprinciples.htm

Public Citizen, "Democratic vs. Corporate Control of Water: A Fight for Survival." *Public Citizen*, 2007, http:// www.citizen.org/cmap/water/activist/ articles.cfm?ID=9589, accessed 4 September 2008

Radhakrishnan, Sarvepalli. *Indian Philosophy*. London: Unwin and Hyman 1989

Radhakrishnan Sarvepalli and Charles A. Moore. *A Source Book in Indian Philosophy*. Princeton: Princeton University Press 1957

Radice, Hugo. "Cutting Government Budgets: Economic Science or Class War." In *Saving Global Capitalism*, edited by Carlo Fanelli, Chris Hurl, Priscilla Lefebvre, and Gulden Ozcan, 87–102. Ottawa: Red Quill Books 2010

Rawls, John. *A Theory of Justice*, rev. ed. Cambridge: Harvard University Press 1999

Reid, Robert G.B. *Biological Emergences: Evolution by Natural Experiment*. Cambridge: MIT Press 2006

Rifkin, Jeremy. *The End of Work: The Decline of the Global Labor Force and the Dawn of the Post-Market Era*. New York: Penguin 2004

Roberts, Paul. *The End of Food*. (Boston: Houghton Mifflin 2008

Rorty, Richard. *Contingency, Irony, and Solidarity*. Cambridge: Cambridge University Press 1989

Ruse, Michael, and Jane Maienschein, eds. *Biology and the Foundation of Ethics*. Cambridge: Cambridge University Press 1999

Ryerson, Stanley B. *The Founding of Canada ̈Beginnings to 1815*. Toronto: Progress Books 1974

Samarasekera, Indira. "Partnerships Are the Order of the Day." *Globe and Mail*, 21 January 2008, A15

Sartre, Jean Paul. *No Exit and Three Other Plays*. New York: Vintage Books 1989

Sayers, Sean. "Labour in Modern Industrial Society." In *Karl Marx and Contemporary Philosophy*, edited by Andrew Chitty and Martin McIvor, 143–58. London: Palgrave MacMillan 2009

Schultz, Jim. "Bolivia's War over Water." *The Democracy Centre*, 2000 http://www. democracyctr.org/bolivia/investigations/water/the_water_war.htm, accessed 4 February 2000

Searle, John. *The Rediscovery of the Mind*. Cambridge: MIT Press 1994

Seglow, Jonathon, ed. *The Ethics of Altruism*. London: Frank Cass 2004

Sembene, Ousmane. *God's Bits of Wood*. Anchor Books: New York 1970

Sen, Amartya. *Development as Freedom*. New York: Knopf 1999

– *The Idea of Justice*. Cambridge: Harvard University Press 2009

– *Inequality Reexamined*. Cambridge: Harvard University Press 1992

Shaker, Erica, and Bernie Froese-Germaine. "Beyond the Bake-Sale: Exposing Schoolhouse Commercialism." *Our Schools, Ourselves* 15, no. 4 (Summer 2006): 73–94

Shiva, Vandana. *Biopiracy: The Plunder of Nature and Knowledge*. Cambridge: South End Press 1997

Silverstein, Michael, and John McGeever. "The Search for Ontological
Emergence." *The Philosophical Quarterly* 49, no.195 (April 1999): 182–200

Singer, Peter. *One World: The Ethics of Globalization.* New Haven: Yale University
Press 2002

Slaughter, Sheila, and Gary Rhoades. *Academic Capitalism and the New Economy:
Markets, State, and Higher Education.* Baltimore: Johns Hopkins University
Press 2004

Smith, Adam. *The Theory of Moral Sentiments.* Indianapolis: Liberty Classics
1976

– *The Wealth of Nations.* London: Penguin 1979

Soper, Kate "Marxism, Materialism, and Biology." In Mepham and Rubin, *Issues
in Marxist Philosophy* 2: 61-100

Stiglitz, Joseph. "Stagflation Waiting in the Wings." *Toronto Star,* 8 January 2008,
AA6

Sumner, Jennifer. "Serving Social Justice: The Role of the Commons in
Sustainable Food Systems." *Studies in Social Justice* 5, no 1, 63–75

Teixera, Roy. *Public Opinion Snapshot: Americans' Budget Priorities.* Washington:
Center for American Progress, 27 July 2007, http:www.americanprogress.
org/issues/2007/07/snapshot_budget.html/print.html

Timpanaro, Sebastiano. *On Materialism.* London: Verso 1980

Trotsky, Leon. *The Permanent Revolution and Results and Prospects.* New York:
Pathfinder Press 1974

Turcotte, Martin. "Time Spent with Family during a Typical Workday, 1986–
2005." *Canadian Social Trends* 82 (February 2007): 2–9

United Nations. "The Millennium Development Goals Report." New York:
United Nations, 2007, http://www.un.org.

Van der Linden, Harry. *Kantian Ethics and Socialism.* Indianapolis: Hackett
1988

Van der Poel, Hugo. "Leisure and the Modularisation of Daily Life." *Time and
Society* 6, nos 2–3 (1997): 171–94

Victor, Peter A. *Managing without Growth: Slower by Design, Not Disaster.*
Cheltenham: Edward Elgar 2008

Von Hayek, Friedrich. *Law, Legislation, and Liberty.* Volume 2, *The Mirage of Social
Justice.* Chicago: University of Chicago Press 1976

Warren, James. *Epicurus and Democritean Ethics.* Cambridge: Cambridge
University Press 2002

Wilpert, Gregory. *Changing Venezuela by Taking Power: The History and Policies of
the Chavez Government.* London: Verso 2007

Wilson, E.O. *Consilience: The Unity of Knowledge.* New York: Random House 1998

Wolf, Martin. *Why Globalization Works.* New Haven: Yale University Press 2005

Wood, Ellen Meiksins. *Democracy against Capitalism: Renewing Historical
Materialism.* Cambridge: Cambridge University Press 1995

– *The Origins of Capitalism.* London: Verso 2002
Young, Iris Marion. "Communication and the Other: Beyond Deliberative
   Democracy." In *Democracy and Difference*, edited by Seyla Benhabib, 120–36.
   Princeton: Princeton University Press 1996

Index